Why Psychology Needs Theology

Why Psychology Needs Theology

A Radical-Reformation Perspective

Edited by

Alvin Dueck *&* Cameron Lee

William B. Eerdmans Publishing Company
Grand Rapids, Michigan / Cambridge, U.K.

Wm. B. Eerdmans Publishing Co.
255 Jefferson Ave. S.E., Grand Rapids, Michigan 49503 /
P.O. Box 163, Cambridge CB3 9PU U.K.

Printed in the United States of America

10 09 08 07 06 05   7 6 5 4 3 2 1

Library of Congress Cataloging-in-Publication Data

Why psychology needs theology: a Radical-Reformation perspective /
  edited by Alvin Dueck & Cameron Lee.
      p.   cm.
  Includes bibliographical references.
  ISBN 0-8028-2907-4 (pbk.: alk. paper)
    1. Christianity — Psychology. 2. Anabaptists — Doctrines. 3. Psychology
and religion.   I. Dueck, Alvin C., 1943–   II. Lee, Cameron.

  BR110.W49   2005
  261.5′15 — dc22

                                    2005041732

www.eerdmans.com

Contents

Contents

Contributors

Mari L. Clements earned her Ph.D. in child clinical psychology at the University of Denver, and is Assistant Professor of Psychology in the School of Psychology at Fuller Theological Seminary. Clements has written extensively on the effect of marital conflict on family members, paying careful attention to the effects on parent-child relationships and children's peer relationships. She has also examined couples' perceptions of their own constructive and destructive strategies for managing conflict.

Alvin Dueck completed his Ph.D. at Stanford University in psychology and education. He holds the Frank and Evelyn Freed Chair of Integration at Fuller's School of Psychology. In his book *Between Jerusalem and Athens,* he has explored the implications of theological themes such as the reign of God, the church, and discipleship for psychotherapeutic practice. Dueck has also been actively involved in developing integrative, cross-cultural programs for mental health services in Guatemala and China.

Cynthia Neal Kimball has a Ph.D. in psychology from the University of New Mexico. She is an Associate Professor of Psychology at Wheaton College in Wheaton, Illinois, and past chair of the Department of Psychology. Her research focus is on high-risk families, attachment theory as a means for understanding one's relationship to God, and the area of women and "voice." She is also active in an inner-city organization that serves minority teenage mothers and their babies.

Cameron Lee obtained his Ph.D. in theology and marriage and family ministries from Fuller Theological Seminary. He is now Professor of

Family Studies at Fuller and a Certified Family Life Educator. His most recent book, *Unexpected Blessing,* explores how the Beatitudes of the Sermon on the Mount can help Christians understand the counter-cultural nature of God's reign.

J. Derek McNeil has a Ph.D. in counseling psychology from Northwestern University in Chicago, and is an Associate Professor of Psychology at Wheaton College in Wheaton, Illinois. McNeil maintains that culture and ethnic identity are subjects that have generally been absent in the integrative dialogue between psychology and Christian faith. His research areas include the impact of globalization on families, marriages and identity, peacemaking, trauma, grief, and loss.

Alexandra E. Mitchell received her master's degree in clinical psychology from Pepperdine University. She is currently working on her doctorate in clinical psychology at Texas A&M University. Her research focuses on emotional intimacy in couple relationships and observational coding of intimate behaviors.

Nancey Murphy received her Ph.D. in philosophy of science from the University of California, Berkeley, and her Th.D. in theology from the Graduate Theological Union in Berkeley. Murphy is Professor of Christian Philosophy at Fuller Theological Seminary. She is best known for her writing and speaking on the relationship between theology and science. Her book, with Warren Brown and Newton Malony, *Whatever Happened to the Soul?* was awarded the 1999 Templeton Prize for Outstanding Books in Theology and the Natural Sciences.

Kevin Reimer has a Ph.D. in family studies from Fuller Theological Seminary, School of Psychology. He is Associate Professor of Psychology at Azusa Pacific University. Reimer was selected to be a participant in the John Templeton Scholar program at Oxford University. His research focus is on the structure of moral character, and he has conducted research on moral exemplars and caregivers in the L'Arche communities for the disabled.

Frank C. Richardson received his Ph.D. from Colorado State University in counseling psychology. He is currently Professor of Psychology in the Department of Educational Psychology at the University of Texas at Austin. He is past president of the Division of Theoretical and Philosophical Psychology (Division 24) of the American Psychological Association. He is the co-author, with Blaine J. Fowers and Charles B. Guignon, of *Re-Envisioning Psychology*. His research includes philosophical and value issues in psychotherapy theory and practice and in philosophy of social sciences.

Brent D. Slife has a Ph.D. in clinical psychology from Purdue University. He is Professor of Psychology at Brigham Young University and chair of the doctoral program in Theoretical and Philosophical Psychology. Slife is past president of Division 24 of the American Psychological Association. His most recent books include *Critical Issues in Psychotherapy: Translating New Ideas into Practice* and *Psychotherapists as Crypto-Missionaries: Managing Values in the "Post" Modern Era* (forthcoming).

Introduction

For more than three decades, Fuller Theological Seminary has sponsored an annual lectureship and conference whose express purpose is to encourage creative conversation between our theological convictions and our work as mental-health professionals. This conversation is generally referred to as the "integration" of psychology and theology or the Christian faith. The invited lecturers (see the list on p. xviii), all well-known scholars in their own right, have ranged broadly over the terrain of possible integration topics, from psychological studies of religious experience to the clinical treatment of emotional stressors from a Christian viewpoint. In 2003 our lecturer was Dr. Nancey Murphy, Professor of Christian Philosophy at Fuller. Her lectureship was entitled "A Radical Proposal for Integration: Psychology in Dialogue with the Anabaptist Tradition." Selected for both her awareness of psychological issues and her theological acumen, Nancey presented three lectures, to which a panel of scholars from other institutions wrote responses.[1]

The story of her personal and professional journey provides a meaningful context for her lectures. Nancey was born in Alliance, Nebraska, and for some eighteen years lived on her family's cattle ranch. (She has said that if someone had only two weeks to live, they should be spent in Nebraska. It would seem like a lifetime.) Not the anticipated son, she nonetheless rode fences, wrestled calves, worked in the hay field, and even broke a few horses (nonviolently, we trust). In terms of religion,

1. We are grateful to the Coalition of Christian Colleges and Universities for its grant and to Evelyn and Frank Freed for their endowment to Fuller Seminary's Graduate School of Psychology. These funds made the 2003 Integration Symposium possible.

hers was a pre-Vatican II Catholic world of sensory worship (choirs, bells, incense, and candles), Franciscan devotional practices, and veneration of the saints. But in the end, she turned out to be neither a nun nor a horse rancher, but a philosopher and a theologian.

Nancey attended Creighton University as a President's Scholar and graduated with a major in psychology and philosophy. She began college wanting to be a therapist. An internship at the Nebraska Psychiatric Institute, which utilized primarily behavior modification, disillusioned her with positivist behaviorism.

After driving her Toyota across the continental and cultural divides between Nebraska and Berkeley, she found herself feeling like the last Christian on earth in the philosophy department of the University of California. She joined a charismatic prayer group in the local Catholic parish. This is how she describes her experience:

> I spent most of my week among those who took religious believers to be (at best) naive, and several nights a week participating in a form of Christian worship that even in the eyes of many fellow Christians required a high degree of gullibility. What I found striking about the life of the "charismatic," as opposed to more typical forms of Christian life, was the availability of a wide array of rather dramatic experiences that seemed to confirm the teachings. So here were two worlds, not merely different but apparently irreconcilable.[2]

Such an experience, one might imagine, would be good background for lecturing on integration.

It was upon her undergraduate reading of Paul Feyerabend's article "Against Method" that she decided to pursue doctoral studies in the philosophy of science at Berkeley with Feyerabend himself. He must have made quite an impression on her, for she has stated in print that having seen him in intense debate with his opponents, she now projects his manner onto Jesus when she reads the Gospel accounts of Jesus' debates with the Pharisees. His openness to a variety of methods also intrigued her. She wrote her dissertation, entitled "Progress and Proliferation in Psychiatry," under his exacting scrutiny. There she claimed that

2. Nancey Murphy, "At the Intersection of Several Possible Worlds," in *The Philosophical I: Personal Reflections on Life in Philosophy,* ed. George Yancy (Lanham, Md.: Rowman & Littlefield, 2002), pp. 219-35.

the proliferation of competing theories produced a better understanding of mental illness than would have been the case if weaker theories had been eliminated.

After obtaining her Ph.D. in philosophy of science, she went on to complete another doctorate in theology at the Graduate Theological Union (GTU), also at Berkeley. Her second dissertation was entitled "Theology in an Age of Probable Reasoning," which introduced her proposal for using the work of mathematical philosopher Imre Lakatos as a model for theological research programs.

Having grown up in a Catholic home and attended a Jesuit college, she had wrestled with America's involvement in Vietnam in the sixties. She entered the GTU holding a "just war" position. But a turning point came for her in a seminar with theologian and ethicist James McClendon about the Anabaptist tradition. She writes,

> Reading about the widespread torture and killing of Anabaptists had a profound impact on my life. It was clear to me that if Jesus had to choose between the ones being killed and the ones doing the killing, both Catholic and Protestant, he would be on the side of those who were dying. I felt a claim on my life at that time to join a church in which nonviolence was not an optional extra.[3]

She did just that. At present, she is a member of the Pasadena Church of the Brethren and is ordained to the teaching ministry. We might add that there are actually two consequences of Nancey's attending that seminar: not only did she become a convinced Anabaptist, but the instructor eventually became her husband.

Since 1989 she has been a faculty member in Fuller's School of Theology. The author of six books and numerous articles, Dr. Murphy earned a Templeton award, honoring books that integrate theology and the natural sciences, for her book *Theology in the Age of Scientific Reasoning*. She also received an award for the book *Whatever Happened to the Soul?* which she co-edited with Drs. Warren Brown and Newton Malony. She is currently completing another manuscript with Brown entitled "Did My Neurons Make Me Do It? Philosophical and Neurobiological Perspectives on Moral Responsibility and Free Will."

3. Murphy, "At the Intersection of Several Possible Worlds."

The present book is organized into three parts. The first part comprises three essays by Murphy that are based on the original symposium lectures. They are an extension of her earlier work with George Ellis in a volume entitled *On the Moral Nature of the Universe,* in which they considered together the relationship between theology, ethics, and the social sciences.[4] One part of their argument is reprised here in Chapter 1, as Murphy explores the applicability of Imre Lakatos's notion of "scientific research programmes" and Arthur Peacocke's hierarchical model of the sciences to the task of integrating theology and scientific psychology. The importance of the former is that Lakatos provides a possible model for understanding how the pursuits of theological and psychological study share a similar rational structure. The importance of the latter is that locating psychology within a hierarchy of scientific disciplines suggests its incompleteness. All psychological theories have theological assumptions embedded within them — that is, assumptions about the nature of human flourishing — that require the resources of ethics and theology.

A further contribution of Murphy and Ellis's work is presented and extended in Chapter 2. Having explored potential philosophical contributions to the integration project in Chapter 1, Murphy turns to theological resources. Because Christian traditions differ in their understanding of what constitutes human flourishing, Murphy focuses on one particular tradition to illustrate the idea of a theological research program: the Anabaptist or Radical-Reformation tradition, with its emphasis on self-renunciation. Using the theology of John Howard Yoder as a basis, Murphy summarizes the "hard core" (a term borrowed from Lakatos) of the Anabaptist perspective: "The moral character of God is revealed in Jesus' vulnerable enemy love and renunciation of dominion. Imitation of Jesus in this regard constitutes a social ethic."[5] Put more simply, the core of Murphy's ethical theory is that "self-renunciation for the sake of the other is humankind's highest good."[6] She draws upon the work of Simone Weil to specify the practical consequences of this kenotic ethic of renunciation in greater detail, and poses a challenge to psychology: what would a psychology that took seriously self-renunciation as a moral good

---

4. Murphy and Ellis, *On the Moral Nature of the Universe: Theology, Cosmology, and Ethics* (Minneapolis: Fortress Press, 1996).

5. See Chapter 2, section 4, this volume.

6. See Chapter 2, section 5, this volume; see also Murphy and Ellis, *On the Moral Nature of the Universe,* p. 118.

look like? And of what importance is the study of noncoercive personal relationships?

Chapter 3 attempts a preliminary answer to these questions. Here Murphy sketches the outlines of a Radical-Reformation research program in psychology that has a kenotic ethic at its core. Drawing upon the work of Alasdair MacIntyre, Murphy asks three questions: (1) "What is the character of untutored/ungraced human nature?"; (2) "What is the character of ideal human existence?"; and (3) "What are the means by which the transition from (1) to (2) can be made?"[7] The answers to the first two questions are assumed in a theory's hard core, together with the assumption that a transition such as that described in (3) can in fact be made. For Murphy's Radical-Reformation program, the answer to the second question is self-renunciation and noncoercion. She holds up existing psychological research on altruism and forgiveness as empirical examples of a program compatible with Radical-Reformation assumptions, and ends by posing similar directions for future research and development.

In Part Two, four essays extend — and in some places challenge — Murphy's model. Mari Clements and Alexandra Mitchell lead off in Chapter 4 with an essay that extends Murphy's reflections on the possibility of a psychological research program based on Radical-Reformation principles. Clements and Mitchell review the psychological literature on family interaction, showing how existing research already demonstrates the relational benefits of noncoercive interaction. They observe that while some parental coercion is necessary for the socialization and protection of children, it is the respectful use of power that "provides the foundation from which coercion and violence may be eschewed and sacrifice may be chosen" by children as they mature.[8] This is confirmed by research on parental warmth and control, parenting practices and child aggression, and abusive violence in families. Further, the research on interpersonal sacrifice suggests that when children see their parents sacrificing for them and for each other, they learn how to relate in prosocial and noncoercive ways themselves.

Cynthia Neal Kimball follows in Chapter 5 by applying Radical-Reformation perspectives to issues of gender justice. Young women and men are subjected to restrictive cultural expectations. Girls learn they

7. See Chapter 3, section 2, this volume.
8. See Chapter 4, section 2, this volume.

must be "perfect" or risk being rejected in relationships, experiencing what Kimball and others refer to as a "loss of voice." Boys, too, learn that they must prove their masculinity in ways that disconnect them from their emotions and hence their very selves. Even the church contributes to this silencing of the self. What, then, does self-renunciation mean, when one may have no self to renounce? Kimball asserts that a proper understanding of kenosis views such gender oppression as a form of violence against the self. Self-renunciation as a moral principle must therefore presume participation in a caring servant community.

In chapter 6, Kevin Reimer raises a similar point. "Murphy's criteria for self-renunciation," he writes, "unfairly burden mere humans in the absence of grace."[9] His concern is that holding up kenosis as a moral good may lead to inappropriate expectations of ideal Christ-likeness in ordinary people engaged in altruistic pursuits. To that end, he presents his own study of volunteers in L'Arche communities who have dedicated their lives to the care of the developmentally disabled. Their matchless altruism exacts a heavy emotional toll, resulting in compensatory behaviors such as alcohol abuse. Reimer argues that self-renunciation can function as the core of a psychological research program only if it is understood realistically, in ways that help us to appreciate the ambivalence of such caregivers. Methodologically, he also suggests that such psychological realism requires a narrative understanding of character that may be better suited to semantic analysis.

J. Derek McNeil, in Chapter 7, observes a different limitation in Murphy's model. While he appreciates the potential of the Anabaptist tradition, the very particularism that leads her to make this theological choice raises the question of culture. In his view, Murphy's project presumes a type of psychology that is grounded in a modern Western scientific ideology which values the creation of universal principles and the treatment of culture as an individual variable. If such assumptions provide the basis for our integrative discussion, he wonders, how relevant will the results be to a global Christendom whose center is shifting away from the Western world? In service of a more biblically inclusive understanding of culture, McNeil proffers interpretations of the stories of Babel and Pentecost in which transcendent universality does not eclipse the particular distinctives of human culture.

9. See Chapter 6, section 1, this volume.

Thus, the four chapters in Part Two generally support the Radical-Reformation ideas of Part One, but raise progressively more serious doubts about aspects of the model, particularly Lakatos's logic of science. The latter concern is the primary focus of Part Three, where two scholars take fundamental issue with Murphy's proposed methodology, advocating a hermeneuticist perspective over against what they perceive as the philosophical limitations of modern Western science.

Brent Slife presents an argument in Chapter 8 that focuses more specifically on methodological issues. Psychology has long emulated the natural sciences in its research methods, thus importing assumptions of objectivism, materialism, and reductionism. The question, however, is whether such assumptions are compatible with theism. Slife believes that there are internal inconsistencies in Murphy's model, such that she rejects the possibility of value-neutrality while failing to address the values implicit in the reductive naturalism of quantitative psychological methods. Her rejection of "objectivism, materialism, and reductionism in her theology," in other words, is not matched by the actual logic of research that she employs in her argument. For this reason, Slife is skeptical about the value of the model for integration.

Frank Richardson's concern in Chapter 9 is also with the objectivism that appears to be inherent in Murphy's model.[10] Is the Lakatosian model of research programs, borrowed from the logic of the natural sciences, a good basis for understanding the theological or psychological task, or even the integration of the two? Modern social science and psychology are imbued with a tacit liberal ethic that views human action in instrumental and individualist terms. They do not supply value-neutral descriptions of the phenomena they study, but force our thinking into "black or white choices," such as that between the confirmation or disconfirmation of a hypothesis.[11] This in turn colors how we approach theology, bringing an instrumentalist orientation to the project of integration. Richardson proposes that the hermeneuticist metaphor of full dialogue is more adequate to understanding what it means to bring psychological perspectives into contact with the authority of religious traditions in human life.

Obviously, not all of the scholars here speak with the same voice.

10. See, however, Murphy's response in Chapter 1, note 8.
11. See Chapter 9, section 4, this volume.

That is as it should be. As several of the authors here recognize, the integration of theology with psychology and social science must deal with the plain fact of the plurality of perspectives within both disciplines. Progress will not be made on a single front alone; it requires an active conversation between representatives of different fields and areas of expertise. We appreciate the contributions of each author and their willingness to expose their work to mutual critique. In the end, we hope that the present volume stands on its own merit as a valuable interchange in the ongoing dialogue we call integration.

Speakers at the Integration Symposiums, 1971-2003

Fuller Theological Seminary
School of Psychology

2003   Nancey Murphy. "A Radical Proposal for Integration: Psychology in Dialogue with the Anabaptist Tradition."

2002   Nancy Boyd-Franklin and Archie Smith. "Spirituality in the Treatment of African American Families."

2001   Stephen Post. "Agape, Dementia, and the Family."

2000   Everett Worthington. "The Virus of Forgiveness."

1999   David G. Myers. "The Pursuit of Personal and Social Well-Being."

1998   James Fowler. "Faith Development, Practical Theology, and Clinical Practice."

1997   David Larson. "The Forgotten Factor in Mental and Physical Health: What Does the Research Show?"

1996   H. Newton Malony. "Brainwashing and Religion."

1995   Malcolm A. Jeeves. "Psychology and Christianity: Partners in Understanding Human Nature."

1994   Sidney Callahan. "Christ and the Unconscious."

1993   Nicholas Wolterstorff. "Living with Grief."

1992   Don S. Browning. "Love in America: Practical Theology and Family Decline."

1991   L. Rebecca Propst. "Christian Contributions to the Treatment of Clinical Depression."

1990   Paul Vitz. "The Importance of Narratives for Christian Psychology."

1989   Lucy Bregman. "Death in the Midst of Life."

1988   C. Stephen Evans. "Psychology as a Human Science and the Prospects for Christian Psychology."

1987   Donald M. MacKay (presented by Warren S. Brown after Dr. MacKay's death). "The Pastor and the Brain Scientist."

1986   Alvin C. Dueck. "Ethical Contexts of Healing."

1985   Morton Kelsey. "Christianity as Psychology: Philosophy, Psychology, and Christian Faith."

1984   Vernon C. Grounds. "Unselfing the Self: A Pivotal Problem in Psychology and Theology."

1983   David O. Moberg. "Wholistic Christianity: Sociological Interpretations."

1982   Mary Stewart Van Leeuwen. "The Sorcerer's Apprentice: A Christian Looks at the Changing Face of Psychology."

1981   J. Harold Ellens. "God's Grace and Human Health."

1980   John G. Finch. "Can Psychology Be Christian?"

1979   David G. Myers. "Our Human Condition."

1978   Gary Collins. "Psychology and Theology: Prospects for Integration."

1977   Orlo Strunk. "Personal Religious Values: A Psycho-Theological Understanding."

1976   Stanley R. Hopper. "Psyche, Logos, and the Human Spirit."

1975   William P. Wilson. "Christian Nurture, Life Adjustment, and Mental Disease."

1974   Orville S. Walters. "Christian Psychotherapy and the Legacy of Freud."

1973   Richard L. Gorsuch. "The Nature of Man: A Social Psychological Perspective."

1972   Thomas C. Oden. "The Human Potential and the Evangelical Hope."

1971   Walter H. Clark. "Religious Experience: Its Nature and Function in the Human Psyche."

ONE   **Integration from a
Radical-Reformation Perspective**

In the Ravensbruck concentration camp, where an
estimated 92,000 men, women and children were
exterminated by the Nazis, a piece of wrapping paper
was found near the body of a dead child. On the paper
was written this prayer:

> *Oh Lord, remember not only the men and women of
> good will but also those of ill will. But do not only
> remember the suffering that they inflicted on us;
> remember the fruits we bore, thanks to the suffering:
> our comradeship, our loyalty, our humility, the
> courage, the generosity, the greatness of heart which
> has grown out of all this. And when they come to
> judgment, let all the fruits that we have borne be
> their forgiveness.*

Richard J. Foster, *Finding the Heart's True Home*

Chapter 1

*Philosophical Resources
for Integration*

NANCEY MURPHY

1. Introduction

Prior to the question of how theology and psychology are to be integrated is the oft-debated issue of what psychology is itself. In an era that places high value on science, there has been a strong motive to show that psychology is scientific. Thomas Kuhn's justly famous book *The Structure of Scientific Revolutions* played an important role in such discussions, raising the question, for instance, of whether psychology is an "immature" science because there is no overarching paradigm governing its research.[1]

In these essays, I shall assume the scientific character of psychology. I believe, however, that while the philosophy of Thomas Kuhn has received much attention by psychologists, a more useful account of the nature and evaluation of scientific theories is found in the writings of Imre Lakatos, a Hungarian-born philosopher of mathematics. Lakatos's contributions to philosophy of science incorporated responses to Karl Popper's falsificationism and to the (perceived) relativism of Kuhn's account of paradigm change. My interest in Lakatos's work increased considerably when I perceived that his account of "progressive" and "degenerative" research programs could be adapted for purposes of describing and reforming theological methodology.

In this chapter I first summarize Lakatos's account of research programs in science. Second, I show how his methodology can be applied to

1. Thomas Kuhn, *The Structure of Scientific Revolutions,* 2d ed. (Chicago: University of Chicago Press, 1970).

3

theology. The purpose of this second move is to show that theology is sufficiently akin to science so that it makes sense to attempt to integrate its claims into a psychological research program. Third, I turn to a model intended to help conceive of the proper relationship between the disciplines of theology and psychology. This is the model of the hierarchy of the sciences, which extends from physics at the bottom, through chemistry and biology, to psychology and the social sciences. I follow Arthur Peacocke in arguing that theology is best understood as the science at the top of the hierarchy, in that it studies the most encompassing and complex system of all — the relation of God to all that is. If this is the case, then theology relates to psychology in the same manner as any higher-level science does to those below it.

I end this chapter with a preliminary consideration of how the content of theology might best be employed in formulating a Christian research program in psychology. Lakatos's account of the structure of a research program is as follows. The program takes its identity from a central theory, often of an abstract metaphysical nature, which describes the basic character of the program's subject matter — for example, atomism in early modern physics, or the thesis that all behavior is a product of conditioning for the Skinnerian program. This "hard core" is surrounded by additional theoretical statements, called auxiliary hypotheses, that spell out the content of the core theory in such a way as to make it empirically testable. The "name of the game" in science is to adjust and expand the belt of auxiliary hypothesis in a way that avoids falsification of the hard core and at the same time increases the program's empirical content.

My proposal for theology-psychology integration depends on Lakatos's concept of a metaphysical hard core. I suggest that theological accounts of human nature and of the goal or *telos* of human life entail ethical theses about what constitutes human flourishing. Such an account of human flourishing should be used to formulate hard cores of psychological research programs. Since there is no "generic" Christian theory of human nature, I shall present in my second chapter a particular Christian subtradition, my own Radical-Reformation tradition, and consider its consequences for ethics. In my third chapter, I shall suggest some concrete implications of this theological and ethical position, particularly the central place it gives to self-renunciation and nonviolence, for rethinking assumptions in psychology.

2. Imre Lakatos's Scientific Methodology

I want to begin by placing Lakatos's work in a historical perspective that I believe will be familiar to psychologists. Philosophy of science of the twentieth century has had a tremendous impact on the field of experimental psychology. In fact, it was my perception of these connections that led me to change my career plans from psychology to philosophy — in particular, to the philosophy of science.

When philosophers of science speak of scientific methodology, they intend to speak not of the concrete experimental or observational methods used in particular sciences but rather of the "logic" of science — of the relation between theories and evidence, of the criteria for judging one theory to be rationally superior to its rivals. It was neopositivist philosopher Carl Hempel who most clearly formulated the *basic* logical structure of research. It is neither inductive nor deductive, but rather "hypothetico-deductive": begin with observations, formulate a hypothesis to explain them, then deduce predictions from the hypothesis that can be confirmed or disconfirmed by empirical investigation.[2] Around the same time, Percy Bridgman emphasized the necessity of operational definitions as a means of connecting abstract concepts to empirical research.[3]

Karl Popper was the most prominent member of the neopositivist school — those mid-twentieth-century philosophers who revised and moderated the goals of the earlier logical positivists. Popper's emphasis was on falsification. Recognizing that great quantities of evidence can be produced in favor of almost any theory (assuming adequate ingenuity on the part of the scientist), he argued that the essence of scientific method consists in proposing hypotheses and specifying in advance what observations would count as falsifying the theory. Science progresses by elimination of all hypotheses that do not stand up to such testing.[4]

Popper is known to psychologists, first, because he used psychoanal-

2. Carl G. Hempel, *Aspects of Scientific Explanation* (New York: Free Press, 1965).

3. Percy W. Bridgman, *The Nature of Some of Our Physical Concepts* (New York: Philosophical Library, 1952).

4. Karl Popper, *The Logic of Scientific Discovery* (New York: Harper, 1965); translation of *Logik der Forschung* (Vienna, 1935) by Karl Popper with Julius Freed and Lan Freed.

ysis as one of his prime examples of pseudoscience. He claimed that psychoanalytic theory was so flexible that *any* instance of human behavior could be explained in its terms, and hence it was not a falsifiable theory.

A second and much more important contribution was Popper's work on probability theory, which has been incorporated into the statistical methodologies so important to the behavioral sciences. His motivation was to solve the problem of how to falsify a hypothesis that is presented in probabilistic terms rather than as a universal statement. That is, we know that one white raven falsifies the claim that *all* ravens are black, but how can one falsify the claim that 25 percent of all swans are black, short of catching and examining them all?[5]

Popper is also important for the purpose of introducing Lakatos. Kuhn's famous work on paradigm shifts in science was largely a reaction against Popper's tidy account of scientific rationality,[6] and Lakatos's work was a development of Popper's (although Popper was distinctly unappreciative) which was intended to counter the perceived irrationalism of Kuhn's reaction. I speak of the *perceived* irrationality of Kuhn's position; I believe his work is better seen as a statement to the effect that the actual history of science does not support the neopositivist view of scientific rationality, given the assumption that science as practiced *is*, in the main, rational. Kuhn's major innovation was to show that theory choice in science depends upon factors other than observation and logic. He described the history of science as a succession of paradigms (standard examples of problem solutions in a field) that carry with them laws, theories, applications, and instrumentation. Those who share the view of science associated with a particular paradigm share the same rules and standards for scientific practice, but when paradigms change, so do these standards. Kuhn's contribution to the understanding of theory confirmation was to show that it is the paradigm as a whole — that is, exemplar along with associated theories, standards, and so forth (later termed a "disciplinary matrix") — that is accepted by scientists, and that the acceptance of a paradigm involves at the same time acceptance of a certain domain of data that are interpreted in terms of the paradigm's view of the world. Thus, there is no pool of independent data that allows scientists to arbitrate between competing paradigms.

5. Popper, *The Logic of Scientific Discovery*, chap. 8.
6. Kuhn, *The Structure of Scientific Revolutions*.

This lack of a common pool of data is easily illustrated in psychology: compare the notes of a psychoanalytic therapist and the records of response rates of rats in a Skinner box.

Once a paradigm is accepted, its basic laws and theories are not subjected to testing, as Popper and Hempel claimed, but rather they are *assumed* and used for solving the many problems that a paradigm encounters. Thus, a comprehensive view of the subject matter is accepted all at once and is maintained "dogmatically" until its problem-solving ability is seen to be outweighed by anomalies *and* a new paradigm appears to take its place.

Lakatos's most influential piece in philosophy of science is titled "Falsification and the Methodology of Scientific Research Programmes."[7] Here he made it plain that he intended to continue in the positive (rather than critical) tradition of Popper, while taking account of criticisms of Popper's work by historicist philosophers of science. On Lakatos's view, scientific rationality requires the specification of a criterion for choice between competing "research programs." A research program consists of a set of theories and a body of data. One theory, the "hard core," is central to the research program. Conjoined to the core is a set of auxiliary hypotheses that together add enough information to allow the data to be related to the theory. Auxiliary hypotheses include statements of initial conditions, lower-level theories that apply the core theory in different kinds of cases, and also theories of observation or of instrumentation that justify the research methods appropriate to that program and its subject matter.[8] The auxiliary hypotheses form a "protective belt" around the hard core since they are to be modified when potentially fal-

7. Imre Lakatos, "Falsification and the Methodology of Scientific Research Programmes," in *The Methodology of Scientific Research Programmes: Philosophical Papers*, vol. 1, ed. John Worrall and Gregory Currie (Cambridge: Cambridge University Press, 1978), pp. 8-101.

8. So, contra Slife and Richardson (Chapters 8 and 9 respectively, this volume), there is nothing in Lakatos's methodology that would require "objectivist" methods in psychology. Insofar as one's core theory of human nature sees humans as essentially constituted by interpersonal relationships, as essentially engaged in "strong evaluation" (see section 5 below), as understandable only in narrative terms, as a product of "thick" cultural contexts (cf. McNeil, Chapter 7, this volume), then Lakatos's methodology not only permits but *requires* that the methods devised for studying humans take these features into account. This would include but not be limited to the use of qualitative data and hermeneutic methods.

sifying data are found. A research program, then, is a series of networks of theories whose core remains the same while auxiliary hypotheses are successively modified, replaced, or amplified in order to account for problematic observations.

Lakatos claimed that the history of science is best understood not in terms of *successive* paradigms, as Kuhn proposed, but rather in terms of *competing* research programs. Some of these programs Lakatos described as "progressive" and others as "degenerating." A degenerating research program is one whose core theory is saved by ad hoc modifications of the protective belt — mere face-saving devices, or linguistic tricks, as Lakatos called them.

Rather than spell out Lakatos's criteria for progress in technical detail, I quote a clever story he invented to illustrate his point:

> The story is about an imaginary case of planetary misbehavior. A physicist of the pre-Einstein era takes Newton's mechanics and his law of gravitation, *(N)*, the accepted initial conditions, *I*, and calculates, with their help, the path of a newly discovered small planet, *p*. But the planet deviates from the calculated path. Does our Newtonian physicist consider that the deviation was forbidden by Newton's theory and therefore that, once established, it refutes the theory *N*? No. He suggests that there must be a hitherto unknown planet *p'* which perturbs the path of *p*. He calculates the mass orbit, etc., of this hypothetical planet and then asks an experimental astronomer to test his hypothesis. The planet *p'* is so small that even the biggest available telescopes cannot possibly observe it: the experimental astronomer applies for a research grant to build yet a bigger one. In three years' time the new telescope is ready. Were the unknown planet *p'* to be discovered, it would be hailed as a new victory of Newtonian science. But it is not. Does our scientist abandon Newton's theory and his idea of the perturbing planet? No. He suggests that a cloud of cosmic dust hides the planet from us. He calculates the location and properties of this cloud and asks for a research grant to send up a satellite to test his calculations. Were the satellite's instruments (possibly new ones, based on a little-tested theory) to record the existence of the conjectural cloud, the result would be hailed as an outstanding victory for Newtonian science. But the cloud is not found. Does our scientist abandon Newton's theory, together with the idea of the perturbing

planet and the idea of the cloud which hides it? No. He suggests that. . . .'[9]

Lakatos's point is to highlight the difference it would make to our evaluation of this story if one of these additional hypotheses were actually confirmed. He claims that it is just such surprising facts — he calls them novel facts — that distinguish a progressive program from one that is just making up excuses for itself.

Lakatos distinguished, as Kuhn did, between mature and immature science. Kuhn claimed that mature sciences can be recognized by the fact that they operate under the guidance of a single set of assumptions. As noted above, one of the discussions in psychology has been whether psychology is in this sense a mature science, since there are competing theoretical standpoints. Richard Gorsuch argues persuasively that there is an accepted paradigm in experimental psychology.[10] Lakatos, however, frees psychologists from having to worry about this debate, since he sees progress in even the most exalted sciences as driven by the *competition* among different research programs. His account of maturity instead focuses on the concept of a *positive heuristic*.

In mature science, according to Lakatos, a research program includes both a negative and a positive heuristic, which are plans for future development of the program. The negative heuristic is simply the plan (or methodological rule) to avoid falsification of the hard core — to direct potentially falsifying data against the auxiliary hypotheses and make suitable modifications there. This aspect of the heuristic takes account of the fact, emphasized by both Paul Feyerabend[11] and Kuhn, that comprehensive theories need time to develop before they can be judged; progress in science requires a certain amount of "dogmatism." Both mature and immature programs are characterized by a negative heuristic — without the decision to pursue and defend some central theory, there is no program at all.

Mature science differs from immature science in that the development of the auxiliary hypotheses in the former proceeds according to a preconceived plan: the positive heuristic. This is "a partially articulated

9. Lakatos, "Falsification and the Methodology of Scientific Research Programmes," pp. 16-17.

10. This argument was made by Richard Gorsuch in personal communication with me.

11. Paul K. Feyerabend, *Against Method* (London: New Left Books, 1975).

set of suggestions or hints on how to change, develop the 'refutable variants' of the research-programme, how to modify, sophisticate, the 'refutable' protective belt."[12] In other words, the positive heuristic sets out a program for a chain of ever more complicated *models* simulating reality. In immature science, on the other hand, there may be progressive modifications, but they are random and unplanned. They may be motivated more by external events such as the need to take account of competing programs' new discoveries.

Lakatos's work is less widely known than Kuhn's outside of philosophy of science, but I hope that the reader will be convinced by the end of these three chapters that he provides an extremely valuable tool for understanding the structure, development, and testing of the various theoretical points of view in psychology. My more ambitious proposal is to show his usefulness for understanding both theology itself and its relations to psychology.

3. Research Programs in Theology

I began my doctoral studies in theology with an apologetic intent: I wanted to show the secular academy that theology is in fact a respectable body of knowledge. If scientific reasoning is the gold standard, then is it possible to show that theology meets that standard?

A number of important authors precede me in applying the canons of scientific reasoning to theology. Popper's falsificationism stirred lively debate among philosophers of religion. In the fifties, Antony Flew rewrote John Wisdom's parable of the gardener in such a way as to raise the question of whether believers do not so qualify their statements about God as to make them entirely unfalsifiable.[13] Flew, unlike Popper, took falsifiability as a criterion of meaning and intended, therefore, to call into question the meaningfulness of the claim that God exists.[14]

12. Lakatos, "Falsification and the Methodology of Scientific Research Programmes," p. 50.

13. The original parable is in John Wisdom, "Gods," *Proceedings of the Aristotelian Society* 45 (1944-45): 185-206.

14. *New Essays in Philosophical Theology*, ed. Antony Flew and Alasdair MacIntyre (London: SCM Press, 1955), pp. 96-130. Flew mentioned (in private conversation) that his essay was not influenced by Popper.

Compare Flew's parable to Lakatos's story (above) of planetary misbehavior:

> Once upon a time two explorers came upon a clearing in the jungle. In the clearing were growing many flowers and many weeds. One explorer says, "Some gardener must tend this plot." The other disagrees, "There is no gardener." So they pitch their tents and set a watch. No gardener is ever seen. "But perhaps he is an invisible gardener." So they set up a barbed-wire fence. They electrify it. They patrol with bloodhounds. (For they remember how H. G. Wells's *The Invisible Man* could be both smelt and touched though he could not be seen.) But no shrieks ever suggest that some intruder has received a shock. No movements of the wire ever betray an invisible climber. The bloodhounds never give cry. Yet still the Believer is not convinced. "But there is a gardener, invisible, intangible, insensible to electric shocks, a gardener who has no scent and makes no sound, a gardener who comes secretly to look after the garden which he loves." At last the Sceptic despairs, "But what remains of your original assertion? Just how does what you call an invisible, intangible, eternally elusive gardener differ from an imaginary gardener or even from no gardener at all?"[15]

Thomas Kuhn's work has attracted a fair amount of attention among theologians and philosophers of religion. Basil Mitchell has compared the argument for a theistic interpretation of experience to that for a new paradigm in science.[16] Ian Barbour made use of Kuhn's work in *Myths, Models, and Paradigms,* where he argued that the Christian *religion* is a paradigm much like those Kuhn described in science.[17] Barbour's book has been discussed and emulated by others such as Sallie McFague in *Metaphorical Theology*[18] and Gary Gutting in *Religious Belief and Religious Skepticism.*[19] Hans Küng has used Kuhn's theory of

15. Flew and MacIntyre, eds., *New Essays in Philosophical Theology,* p. 96.

16. Basil Mitchell, *The Justification of Religious Belief* (London: Macmillan, 1973).

17. Ian G. Barbour, *Myths, Models, and Paradigms* (New York: Harper & Row, 1974).

18. Sallie McFague, *Metaphorical Theology: Models of God in Religious Language* (Philadelphia: Fortress Press, 1982).

19. Gary Gutting, *Religious Belief and Religious Skepticism* (Notre Dame: University of Notre Dame Press, 1982).

paradigm change as a tool for reconstructing the history of theology, suggesting that the works of Augustine, Aquinas, Luther, and Calvin initiated new paradigms in Christian theology.[20] Nicholas Wolterstorff's *Reason within the Bounds of Religion* makes use of a feature of science described by Kuhn, Lakatos, and others.[21] Arguing from the thesis that scientific theories are *underdetermined* by data, Wolterstorff urges the development of Christian scholarship wherein scientists choose from among the class of empirically adequate theories those that are most consistent with Christian convictions.[22]

As far as I knew when I was writing my dissertation, no one had attempted to apply Lakatos's methodology to theology. I later learned that Philip Clayton, an M.Div. graduate of Fuller Seminary, was writing a dissertation at the same time on explanation in the sciences and theology, and making significant use of Lakatos's work.[23]

Let us see, then, whether schools of theological thought can fairly be described as theological *research programs*. Recall that the hard core of a scientific research program is a theory so central to the entire project that to give it up is to give up the entire program. It makes a claim about the general character of the aspect of reality under investigation; in so doing it ties together all of the more specialized theories within the program. Lakatos says that the hard core of a scientific research program is often so abstract as to count as metaphysical. A good example here is Galileo's atomic theory of matter, which served as the hard core for early modern physics.

The hard core of a research program in systematic or doctrinal theology, therefore, will most likely be one's non-negotiable and most general understanding of God and of God's relation to the created order.

---

20. Hans Küng, "Paradigm Change in Theology: A Proposal for Discussion," in *Paradigm Change in Theology,* ed. Hans Küng and David Tracy (New York: Crossroad, 1991), pp. 3-33.

21. Nicholas Wolterstorff, *Reason within the Bounds of Religion,* 2d ed. (Grand Rapids: Eerdmans, 1984).

22. For a more detailed account of this history, see my *Theology in the Age of Scientific Reasoning* (Ithaca, N.Y.: Cornell University Press, 1990), pp. 79-85. This work presents an extended argument for the applicability of Lakatos's methodology to theology.

23. Philip Clayton, *Explanation from Physics to Theology: An Essay in Rationality and Religion* (New Haven: Yale University Press, 1989).

The doctrine of the Trinity functions nicely as a core theory for classical orthodoxy, since all of the rest of the Christian doctrines can be unified by means of their direct or indirect relation to one of the persons of the Trinity.

There are, of course, other starting points for systematic theology. The statement "The God of Jesus Christ is the All-Determining Reality" functions as the core of Wolfhart Pannenberg's program. "God is the God of the oppressed" might be seen as the core of Latin-American liberation theology. *Sola gratia* must figure into the organizing principle of Martin Luther's vision of Christianity; and likewise the sovereignty of God is a unifying theme for the Reformed tradition.

Recall, also, that the rest of the theories in a scientific research program are called auxiliary hypotheses, and they bear most of the explicit theoretical content of the program. The auxiliary hypotheses in systematic theology, then, will be the remainder of the Christian doctrines: theories of the church, of the person and work of Christ, and so on. These doctrines are elaborated differently in different programs. The differences will be due, in large part, to differences in the hard cores of the programs. Consider two versions of the doctrine of the work of Christ: substitutionary atonement depends on the doctrine of the divinity of Christ, which is contained implicitly in a Triune conception of the nature of God; the liberationists' very different account of the work of Christ is equally dependent on their core assumption about the character and purposes of God — namely, liberation of the oppressed.

The objection that critics are most likely to raise to the project of likening theology to science is to argue that there is no parallel to scientific data. Theologians might reply that the Scriptures are treated as data by most theologians, and that there are additional data from history and religious experience, and perhaps other sources as well. So the problem is not the absence of anything that *functions* for theologians as data do for scientists; it is instead that scriptural texts and religious experiences seem *defective* when compared to scientific data. Religious experience is too subjective; and how do we know that Scripture tells us anything reliable *about* God rather than merely about Jews' and Christians' *ideas* of God?

To meet these objections, we need to return to philosophy of science for further resources. An important component of scientific research programs is what philosophers call theories of instrumentation. To illustrate, consider the relation between experimental measurement of temperature and theories of heat. There are a variety of means by which temperature can be measured: the familiar mercury and alcohol thermometers, procedures based on the thermo-electric effect, changes in electrical resistance of material such as platinum, and others. The confidence we can place in any of these measuring techniques is based in part on the consistency of results obtained by the various methods. But, more importantly for my purposes here, the operation of some of these instruments is explained by, and thus validated in part by, the same scientific theory that they are used to establish. The kinetic theory of heat, according to which heat is defined in terms of motion of particles of matter (as average molecular kinetic energy), also partially explains the expansion of liquids when heated, and so stands behind the use of ordinary thermometers.

Thus, an entire network of theory, laws, research methods, and experimental results is accepted as a whole because of its consistency and its explanatory power. There is always a degree of circular reasoning involved, but it might be called virtuous rather than vicious circularity because it is part of what is involved in showing the consistency of the entire network.

Now, what about using Scripture as a source of data for theology? Just as the kinetic theory provides justification for taking thermometer readings to be a genuine source of knowledge about certain physical processes, so we have in theology a theory (or doctrine) of revelation that serves as a theoretical justification for taking the Scriptures to be a reliable source of knowledge about God. So in theology, in place of theories of instrumentation, we incorporate theories of *interpretation*. In particular, we have theories about the nature of the texts that tell us how to make proper use of them in our science of God. Note that different theological programs with different understandings of the *nature* of revelation will employ the texts differently. If "revelation" means divine dictation, we take our "Scripture readings" differently than we do if revelation is understood to take place through salvation history, or through personal encounter with the Word. As David Kelsey has noted, the manner in which Scripture functions to authorize theological proposals is dependent upon a prior judgment about the manner in which God is present to the community — "a single, synoptic, imaginative judgment" in which the theologian attempts to "catch up what Christianity is basically all about."[24]

A great deal more needs to be said about the use of Scripture as a source of data for theology — all of the questions about interpretation, historical accuracy, and so forth. However, I shall not pursue these issues here. If we are looking for parallels between theology and science, the more interesting possibility for theological data is religious experience, since we tend to equate confirmation of theories with empirical or experiential confirmation.

Now, what about religious experience? We surely do not want to count all so-called religious experiences as data for theology. But we do not want to count all sensory experiences as data for science either. If we did so, we would have to explain, for instance, how oars bend when we put them in water and straighten immediately as we take them out.

I suggest that the relevant parallel in theology to a theory of instrumentation in science is a "theory of discernment." In the Christian tradition there is a rich treasury of answers to the question of how it is possible to distinguish religious experiences that represent encounters with God or impulses of the Spirit from those that do not. There are some variations from one denomination to another, and some individual variation from one author to another, but quite a bit of agreement. So we have here a theory, the theory of discernment, which states that it is possible to recognize the activity of God in human life by means of signs or criteria, some of which are public and relatively objective. My claim is that the theory of discernment functions in Christian theology in exactly the same way as theories of instrumentation do in science.

The criteria for discernment can be grouped conveniently under two headings: consistency and fruits. "Consistency" for Protestants means consistency with Scripture. For Catholics it also includes consistency with church teaching. The use of the consistency criterion, of course, raises all of the problems of interpretation that go along with use of the Bible for any purpose. I shall not go into such problems here, except to note the following: A wooden application of this criterion would mean that no religious experience could ever challenge traditional teaching, since such an experience would automatically be judged inauthentic.

24. David Kelsey, *The Uses of Scripture in Recent Theology* (Philadelphia: Fortress Press, 1975), p. 159.

However, if this criterion is used in conjunction with others, there will be cases where an experience, attested on the grounds of other signs, conflicts with a traditional *interpretation* of Scripture, and the experience, together with critical reflection on the received interpretation, may result in that interpretation being overturned. So there is room for a dynamic interplay among texts, interpretations, and religious experiences.[25]

If this is the case, there is a clear parallel with science, where an observation or experimental result that conflicts with accepted theory will be regarded with suspicion. The decision either to ignore the datum or to revise the theory can go either way, and will be made only after reevaluating the theory and performing additional experiments.

The criterion of "fruits" refers to various effects in the life of the recipient and her community. The term is appropriate in that Jesus declared that false prophets could be known by their fruits (Matt. 7:16). Paul listed the fruits of the Holy Spirit as love, joy, peace, patience, kindness, generosity, faithfulness, gentleness, and self-control (Gal. 5:22-23, NRSV). Many other spiritual writers would add humility and contrition for sin.

The one significant difference in views of discernment from one branch of the Christian tradition to another has to do with *who* does the discerning. In both the Catholic and the Reformed traditions, the assumption is that discernment is exercised by the one receiving the experience, or at most by that person and his pastor or confessor. In a third major tradition — the Anabaptist or Radical-Reformation tradition — discernment is a function exercised by the gathered community. That is, it is the job of the whole church to decide who are the true and false prophets.

The communal nature of discernment among Mennonites, Brethren, Quakers, and other groups from this radical tradition allows for another kind of fruit to be added to the list — the agreement and unity of the church congregation. This means in the first instance that all members need to agree that the other criteria are met — consistency with Scripture and production of love and virtue. But, in addition, the experience being judged must contribute to the building up of the body of believers

---

25. I give an example of such interaction in "What Has Theology to Learn from Scientific Methodology?" in *Science and Theology: Questions at the Interface,* ed. Murray Rae et al. (Edinburgh: T&T Clark, 1994), pp. 101-26.

— not to discord and dissension. It is important to note that this criterion presupposes a church community in which evidence of conversion is required for membership since, as Jesus himself noted, the presence and activity of God produces conflict between true believers and the world. Yet, even among "true believers" dissension is so common that the church's being brought to unity of mind and heart can well be taken as a sign of the activity of God in their midst.

In the case of science, theories of instrumentation are confirmed by the conjunction of two factors. One is the experienced reliability of the instrument — it produces similar or identical readings again and again under similar circumstances — and these results correlate with results produced by other measuring devices. The other is that the theory of instrumentation follows from theoretical beliefs that we have no good reason to call into question. In other words, the truth of the theory of instrumentation is supported by its consistency with a network of other statements, some rather directly from experience, others of a theoretical nature.

I claim that the Christian theory of discernment is likewise supported by its connections to a variety of other statements, some from experience, others of a theoretical (or theological) nature. For example, Jonathan Edwards presents a simple theoretical account of why the fruits of the Spirit should provide valid signs of God at work in a human life. The fruits of the Spirit jointly constitute a particular kind of character — what Edwards calls the "lamb-like, dove-like character" of Christ. In light of Christian theology, this is exactly what is to be expected. The fruits are signs that the Holy Spirit is at work in a person's life; the Holy Spirit is otherwise known as the Spirit of Christ; Christ's spirit should manifest itself in a Christ-like character.[26]

The second kind of support for the theory of discernment needs to be experiential — does it work *reliably*, and is it connected in a consistent way with other experiences? As we saw above, the process of discernment is exactly the test of whether the inner experience, putatively of God, is correlated with the other sorts of experiences that our theories lead us to expect. Reliability means, simply, that a measurement or

---

26. Jonathan Edwards, *A Treatise Concerning Religious Affections* (1746), reprinted in *The Works of Jonathan Edwards*, vol. 4, ed. C. C. Goen (New Haven: Yale University Press, 1972), pp. 344-45.

process results in roughly or exactly the same results under similar circumstances. Reliability is always a matter of degree; different degrees are required depending upon the complexity of the matter under study. Measurement with a ruler is highly reliable; measurement with an I.Q. test is only moderately reliable.

We have anecdotal data on the reliability of believers' judgments regarding the presence or absence of God's agency in certain events. However, it would seem to be possible to design research to measure the reliability of these practices.[27] I anticipate that the development of an adequate methodology would be difficult but not impossible. Were such a study to be done, positive results of this second-order investigation would provide valuable tools for the validation of theological knowledge. Just as scientific instruments are tested before being used in a laboratory or in field research, this "instrument" for detecting the presence and activity of the Spirit of God might be validated for future first-order research in theology.[28]

This is all I shall say about the structure of a theological research program for now. In the following chapter I shall put some exemplary meat on these theoretical bones.

4. Psychology and Theology in the Hierarchy of the Sciences

In this section I offer not a model for understanding the internal structure of theology or science, but rather a way of conceiving of the proper *relations* among the sciences and between the sciences and theology. One of the most influential ideas carried forward from the work of the logical positivists in the 1920s was a plan for the unification of the sciences by showing that all science could be organized hierarchically according to the complexity of the entities studied. Thus, physics would be at the bottom, then chemistry, biology, psychology, and sociology. In addition, they hoped to show that the laws of each science could be re-

27. This suggestion was made to me by Richard Gorsuch in private conversation.
28. This discussion of religious experience as data for theology is adapted from "The Role of Discernment in Seeking Spiritual Knowledge," in *Spiritual Information,* ed. Charles L. Harper Jr. (Philadelphia: Templeton Foundation Press, 2004).

duced to (i.e., be shown to be special cases of) the laws of the next lower discipline, and thus the behavior of all of the entities in the universe could ultimately be shown to be a consequence of the laws of physics.

Arthur Peacocke has written extensively on this view of the relations among the sciences, accepting the hierarchical model but qualifying it in several crucial respects.[29] First, while he accepts one form of reductionism — the view that entities at higher levels of the created order are composed of entities from lower levels — he rejects the view that the behavior of entities at higher levels is strictly determined by the lower-level entities or laws. There is also "top-down causation" to be taken into account — the effect of the environment or the larger whole on its constituents. Second, in sharp contrast to the predominant atheism of the logical positivists, Peacocke adds theology to the hierarchy of the sciences, placing it at the top, since the interaction between God and the whole of created reality must be the most complex level of reality.[30]

Peacocke's work, I believe, provides an essential starting point for reconceiving the relations between theology and science. His position provides a critique of both liberal and fundamentalist views while recognizing what is true in each. It recognizes, with the liberals, that theology represents a different level of analysis than science: it has its own peculiar language and concepts and point of view. It also recognizes, with the conservatives, that theology and science cannot be isolated from one another. Peacocke's model suggests that theology will relate to a given science in much the same way that any two sciences relate to one another.

It is important to note that the hierarchy of the sciences is a model or idealization and does not provide a flawless account of all of the sciences and their interrelations. It has no place for the historical sciences, and it fails to represent disciplines that cut across levels, such as genetics. Most important, it is ambiguous as to whether higher levels pertain to more *encompassing* wholes (such as ecology as the scientific study of organisms in relation to one another within their natural environment) or to more *complex* systems. These two criteria tend to overlap in the

29. Arthur R. Peacocke, *Theology for a Scientific Age: Being and Becoming — Natural, Divine, and Human,* 2d ed. (Minneapolis: Fortress Press, 1993).

30. Whenever I present this model in a lecture, some scientist always complains that it makes theology the queen of the sciences, but this is to forget that it is an adaptation of the logical positivists' model, which began with the assumption that physics, at the bottom, is the most basic science.

basic sciences. At higher levels, though, if the hierarchy is taken to be based on more encompassing wholes, then cosmology, the study of the origin and evolution of the entire universe, is the highest possible science in the hierarchy (apart from theology). However, if the hierarchy is based on increasing complexity of the systems studied, then we have to ask whether a social system or the human nervous system is not more complex than the abstract account of the cosmos provided by cosmologists. There seems to be no good way to answer this question; therefore, it is helpful to represent the relations among the sciences by means of a branching hierarchy, with the human sciences forming one branch and the natural sciences above biology forming the other.[31]

I mentioned earlier the positivists' assumption that for any two neighboring disciplines in the hierarchy, the higher could be reduced to the lower in the sense that the behavior of the higher-level entity could be explained in terms of the behavior of its parts. So there are many questions that arise at, say, level two that can only be answered by means of knowledge of level one.

However, I also mentioned the phenomenon that is referred to as top-down causation. That is, we also sometimes need to move to level three or higher to answer questions at level two. Evolutionary biology is rife with examples of both bottom-up and top-down explanation. Mutations are explained primarily via physics, while survival of an altered life form is largely explained environmentally — that is, in terms of factors germane to the science of ecology. Let us call questions that arise at a particular level of the hierarchy but can only be answered from a higher-level perspective *boundary questions*.

The wisdom of counting theology as the top-most science in the hierarchy can be seen when we consider some of the boundary questions that arise in the natural sciences. For example: What happened before the Big Bang? It is not clear whether science can address this issue at all, Stephen Hawking notwithstanding.[32] If cosmologists do produce a scientific account of the cause of the Big Bang, then the boundary question is simply pushed back a step.

---

31. For an argument for this branching model, see Nancey Murphy and George F. R. Ellis, *On the Moral Nature of the Universe: Theology, Cosmology, and Ethics* (Minneapolis: Fortress Press, 1996).

32. Stephen Hawking, *A Brief History of Time: From the Big Bang to Black Holes* (New York: Bantam, 1988).

Another example: Why are the cosmological constants apparently "fine-tuned" for life? That is, why do the particular laws of nature that we find in operation in the universe, among all of the uncountably many other possibilities, happen to be among the very narrow range of those resulting in a life-supporting universe? For that matter, why are there any laws at all? What is their ontological status? What gives them their force?

While none of these questions strictly requires a theological answer, it is clear enough to Christians that our traditional conception of God and of God's purposes answers them all rather easily. God is the ultimate cause of the universe, whatever that first event may have been. The laws are fine-tuned because God designed the universe with creatures like us in mind. The laws of nature reflect the will of God for ordering the cosmos.

So my proposal regarding the relations between psychology and theology begins with the recognition that psychology fits into one branch of the hierarchy of the sciences, above biology and below the social sciences. Furthermore, psychology and the other human sciences raise their own sorts of boundary questions, which ultimately require theological answers. I shall argue that the connections between psychology and theology are primarily ethical.

5. Ethics in the Hierarchy of the Sciences

George Ellis and I have argued that the most significant boundary questions that arise in the human sciences are best understood as ethical questions. Our focus was on the social sciences; in these chapters I hope to extend our argument to consider the boundary questions that arise in psychology.

There has been a long-standing debate as to whether the social sciences are value-free. The debate goes back to the very beginning in that Auguste Comte, who coined the term "sociology," understood the discipline to be the science of the improvement of society. Thus, a concept of what is good for society was an essential aspect of the new science.[33]

33. See "Plan des travaux scientifiques necessaires par organiser la societé," in *Opuscules de philosophie sociale 1819-1828* (Paris, 1883).

Max Weber argued, in contrast, that blurring the distinction between fact and value led to prejudice.[34] Weber's view predominated through much of the history of the social sciences in the English-speaking world.

However, I believe that Charles Taylor has dealt a mortal blow to the concept of value-neutrality. In brief, Taylor argues that the human sciences study humans; a distinctive aspect of human selves is that they engage in what he calls "strong evaluation." That is, they make judgments about right and wrong, better and worse, higher and lower, which are not rendered valid by their own desires or choices but are intended to stand independent of these desires and choices and offer standards by which they can be judged.[35] Consequently, the attempt at value-free description of human affairs is bound to fail; a self who can be understood only against the background of distinctions of worth cannot be captured by a scientific language that essentially aspires to neutrality.[36]

To illustrate the involvement of moral evaluations in the social sciences, Ellis and I developed several examples.[37] The one most germane to my work here concerns the role of violence in sociology and political theory. The assumption that violent coercion is necessary to maintain society goes back at least to Thomas Hobbes's claim that the state of nature, prior to the social contract, is the war of each against all. Here is a handy summary of Hobbes's account written by James O'Toole:

> In nature, man "finds no stop in doing what he has the will, desire or inclination to do."
>
> To Hobbes the "Natural Right" of every individual in this Edenic state is "the liberty each man has to use his own power for the preservation of his own nature, that is to say his own life . . . and consequently of doing anything which in his own judgment and reason he shall conceive to be the aptest means thereunto." . . . Unhappily, he says, in this free and natural state the condition of life is "solitary,

34. Peter Winch, "Max Weber," in *Encyclopedia of Philosophy,* ed. Paul Edwards (New York: Macmillan, 1967), 8:280.

35. Charles Taylor, *Sources of the Self: The Making of the Modern Identity* (Cambridge, Mass.: Harvard University Press, 1989), p. 4.

36. Charles Taylor, *Philosophy and the Human Sciences: Philosophical Papers,* vol. 2 (Cambridge: Cambridge University Press, 1985).

37. See Murphy and Ellis, *On the Moral Nature of the Universe,* chap. 5.

poor, nasty, brutish and short" because there is a perpetual "war . . . of every man against every man." Hence, to procure security, and the progress of civilization, humans reluctantly surrender the liberty of nature, entering into a "social contact to live under the rule of law."[38]

It is revealing that O'Toole uses the phrase "Edenic state" to describe the state of nature, for what we have in social contract theory is a new myth of origins at variance with the account in Genesis. In fact, Hobbes's myth is the antithesis of the biblical story, at least as we receive it through Augustine's interpretation. Life for the original inhabitants in the biblical Eden is cooperative, not combative; bountiful, not poor; idyllic, not nasty; angelic, not brutish; and everlasting. It represents an aberration, a fall, when the earth-creatures assert their will (against God, not one another) to take that for which they have a desire and an inclination. These two myths of origin reveal antithetical theories of the nature of the person — two antithetical theologies.

A variety of social theorists since Hobbes have followed him in claiming that coercion is necessary to maintain society, and that violence is merely the ultimate form of coercion. As Peter Berger says, "Violence is the ultimate foundation of any political order."[39]

Now, in what sense is this an ethical assumption? Is it not, rather, simply a statement of empirical fact, a law of human behavior? Reinhold Niebuhr, known primarily as a Christian ethicist, has influenced a generation of policy-makers in the United States. He concurs with the majority on the impossibility of noncoercive, nonviolent social structures. We can see that his view is dependent upon a prior ethical judgment, a judgment regarding the highest good for humankind. This view of the human good is in turn the consequence of a particular theological doctrine. Niebuhr writes,

Justice rather than unselfishness [is society's] highest moral ideal. . . . This realistic social ethic needs to be contrasted with the ethics of religious idealism. . . . Society must strive for justice even if it is forced to use means, such as self-assertion, resistance, coercion and perhaps re-

38. James O'Toole, *The Executive's Compass: Business and the Good Society* (New York: Oxford University Press, 1993), pp. 35-36.

39. Peter Berger, *Invitation to Sociology: A Humanistic Perspective* (New York: Doubleday, 1963), p. 69.

sentment, which cannot gain the moral sanction of the most sensitive moral spirit.[40]

Niebuhr's judgment that justice is the highest good that can reasonably be expected to be attained in human history is in turn based upon his eschatology — his theological vision for the end of history. Salvation, the kingdom of God, the eschaton, are essentially *beyond* history. The reason Niebuhr takes this stand on eschatology, in contrast to a view of the kingdom as realizable within history, is that he has set up the question in terms of the problem of the temporal and the eternal. Since it is not possible to conceive of the eternal being realized in the temporal, he concludes that the kingdom of God is beyond history, and this, in turn, means that guilt and moral ambiguity must be permanent features of the interim.

So, contrary to claims for the value-free character of the social sciences, it takes but a little scratching to find ethical judgments under the surface. These judgments may be taken for granted within the mainstream of the intellectual world: for instance, who could doubt that justice is the highest good at which governments aim? But these assumptions *are* questionable. When called into question, they all raise ethical questions, which cannot be answered by any scientific means. The social sciences are suited for studying the relations between means and ends (e.g., if your goal is to avoid surpluses and shortages, the best economic system is the free market), but they are not suited for determining the ultimate ends or goals of human life. This is, instead, the proper subject matter of ethics.

Yet, at the end of the modern era we recognize that ethicists have not been able to provide answers to moral questions to which all rational people can assent. I follow Alasdair MacIntyre in taking moral reasoning to be essentially dependent upon some concept of the ultimate purpose of human life. Such concepts, he points out, are usually provided by religious traditions, although some philosophical traditions provide such answers as well.[41] Thus, while ethics is needed to answer boundary questions that arise from the human sciences, ethics itself

40. Reinhold Niebuhr, *Moral Man and Immoral Society* (New York: Charles Scribner's Sons, 1932), pp. 257-58.

41. Alasdair MacIntyre, *After Virtue,* 2d ed. (Notre Dame: University of Notre Dame Press, 1984).

raises a central question — What is the purpose of human life? — that can be answered only by theology or some substitute for theology.

It would be useful if we could insert a "science" of ethics into the hierarchy between the social sciences and theology. This would be the science whose job it is to compare and evaluate systematic theories of the good for humankind and assist in spelling out the consequences when such theories are embodied in social practices.[42]

6. Theological Resources for Research Programs in Psychology

I am at long last in position to put forward a formal proposal for the integration of theology and psychology. I claim that Christian theology is properly the source of concepts of *human flourishing* that should inform the hard core of any Christian research program in psychology.

Allow me first to review the resources I have mustered in the previous sections of this chapter; then I shall state my argument for this claim. First, I described Lakatos's account of the structure of a scientific research program, including his claim that research programs are formed by elaborating a core thesis about the ultimate nature of the subject matter under investigation. I assumed without argument that psychological schools will fit Lakatos's model; thus, each psychological research program will comprise a network of theories and data that spells out some core thesis about the ultimate nature of human beings.

I next argued that theology, too, can be "rationally reconstructed" to fit Lakatos's model of science, and suggested that theological research programs will have their own hard cores — non-negotiable ideas that account for the "system" in "systematic theology."

I then offered Peacocke's model for the relations between theology and the sciences: theology is the topmost science in the hierarchy. I mod-

---

42. The notion that ethics could be scientific, of course, cuts against the whole of modern meta-ethics. For a justification of this move, see Murphy and Ellis, *On the Moral Nature of the Universe,* chap. 5; and also Owen Flanagan, *The Problem of the Soul* (New York: Basic Books, 2002), chap. 7, which is titled "Ethics as Human Ecology." It is no accident that Flanagan and I have reached similar conclusions in that we have both been deeply influenced by MacIntyre. See his *After Virtue* and *Dependent Rational Animals: Why Humans Need the Virtues* (Chicago: Open Court, 1999).

ified his account by arguing that something like a science of ethics needs to be added between theology and the social sciences. My argument was that human phenomena cannot be understood or even described without the employment of morally evaluative language. When we examine the ethical assumptions in the social sciences, we are essentially in the territory of ethics. So the social sciences raise boundary questions that only ethics can answer. Yet ethics itself requires us to choose among competing accounts of the ultimate purpose of human life, a question that calls for a theological answer.

What I propose to you now is this: Psychology no more than the social sciences can be value-free. Any well-developed account of what is normal or abnormal, healthy or unhealthy, functional or dysfunctional is posited against the backdrop of assumptions about the highest good that humankind can reasonably strive to attain. A vision of the highest good for humankind is, of course, an ethical vision. MacIntyre has argued forcefully that such moral visions are necessarily indebted to some concept of ultimate reality, whether theistic or nontheistic.

So I am making two claims, one descriptive and one normative. I am claiming that comprehensive psychological theories of human nature are bound to incorporate some assumptions about ultimate reality, if nothing more than the naturalist assumption that the physical universe itself is the ultimate reality. These theological or a-theological assumptions delimit one's vision of the human good. One's vision of the ultimate human good has implications for what one judges to be normal versus abnormal, healthy versus unhealthy; for what one perceives as progress, development, maturation; and for what one counts as the greatest threats to human flourishing. This is the descriptive thesis, a hypothesis about the indebtedness of psychological theories of all sorts to an ethical and theological vision.

My normative claim is this: If it is the case that all psychological research programs are in fact "theology laden," then Christian psychologists are not only entitled but *obligated* to attempt to work out the consequences of their theologies for psychology. Thus, the normative claim depends in large measure on the descriptive claim. But is the descriptive claim true?

My hypothesis about the actual nature of psychology needs to be tested. Such a test would involve the examination of the major personality theories in psychology to see whether they do in fact assume ethicotheological accounts of the nature of ultimate reality and of human flourishing. I hope that some of my respondents will take up this challenge.[43]

Another way to lend credence to my normative claim regarding the relation between theology and psychology would begin with a theology (or a-theology), tracing first its implications for a vision of the ultimate goal of human life, and then the implications for judgments regarding what is normal, what counts as human flourishing, growth, and disease. Consider the different accounts of what human life can ever possibly amount to that follow from evolutionary naturalism, on the one hand, and from Eastern Orthodox anthropology, on the other hand, which describes the goal of human life as "theosis" — that is, becoming divine as Christ became human. We need not go to such extremes, however, to find different accounts of human possibilities. There are different visions of human perfectibility represented within Protestanism, from the Holiness tradition's emphasis on sanctification to the Lutheran account of Christian life as inevitably sinful while nonetheless justified.

Because there is no single Christian account of the good life for humans, I shall turn in the next two chapters to a particular account of theology, that of my (adopted) Anabaptist tradition, and attempt to show how theology implies ethics, and ethics in turn requires an account of mental health and illness far different from that of naturalistic psychologies.

---

43. Editors' note: An example may already be found in the work of Don Browning, *Religious Thought and the Modern Psychologies* (Philadelphia: Fortress Press, 1987).

Chapter 2

*Theological Resources
for Integration*

Nancey Murphy

1. Introduction

The previous chapter set forth an abstract (or formal) model for understanding the proper relation between theology and psychology. Adapting
Arthur Peacocke's hierarchical model, I claimed that theology ought to
relate to psychology in the same manner as any higher-level science does
to those below it. Specifically, theology answers boundary questions that
arise within psychology but cannot be answered by psychology alone.
Psychology raises questions such as "What is the ultimate goal of human
life?" and "What constitutes human flourishing?" These questions are
generally thought of as the province of ethics, yet ethicists have failed to
provide any single answer. The reason they have not is that their answers
must presuppose some account of the nature of ultimate reality — this
last being the province of theology or of some nontheistic substitute for
theology.

At the end of Chapter 1 I suggested that Christian theologians do
not all speak with one voice on the matter of human nature. In fact, I
claim, we need to resist the desire to find a generic Christian answer to
questions of human flourishing. Different subtraditions organize their
theological systems around different core theories, and these cores,
along with the doctrinal elaboration that concretizes them, lead to strik-
ingly different accounts of human nature and the human good.

In this chapter I first illustrate some of the ways in which different
doctrinal formulations within Christian subtraditions result in different accounts of the possibilities and limitations of human life. I examine the roles of theories of creation and fall, salvation and atonement,

and eschatology (that is, doctrines about the end of history). This divergence will show why it is necessary to seek integration in a particularistic manner rather than to try to speak in general terms of a Christian psychology. Therefore, in this chapter I present one particular theological position in order to try to think concretely in the next chapter about its implications for integration. I choose the Anabaptist or Radical-Reformation tradition not only because I think it represents the most authentic development of original Christian thought and practice, but also because, being at variance with culture Christianity, it may be useful for provoking consideration of the ways in which Christian psychologists have to call cultural assumptions about human nature into question.

Following a brief history of the Anabaptist tradition, I shall summarize work done by myself and George Ellis, a Quaker activist and cosmologist in South Africa. In our book titled *On the Moral Nature of the Universe,* we attempted to formulate an Anabaptist theological research program and then show how it relates to contemporary sciences.[1]

We formulated the hard core of Anabaptist theology as follows: "The moral character of God is revealed in Jesus' vulnerable enemy love and renunciation of dominion. Imitation of Jesus in this regard constitutes a *social* ethic." An important component of a research program is what Lakatos called the positive heuristic — that is, a plan for development of the auxiliary hypotheses in ways that anticipate potential falsifying data. The positive heuristic of a theological research program, then, would be a plan to address all of the major Christian doctrines in a way consistent with the hard core of the program. We found that Mennonite theologian John Howard Yoder had already addressed most of these issues and had provided alternative readings of biblical texts that might otherwise have been taken as contrary evidence.

Our means of relating our theological research program to science was through ethics. We claimed that our program entails a "kenotic" ethic of self-renunciation, which includes detachment from material possessions, renunciation of one's rights to rewards and to retaliation, nonviolence, acceptance of suffering, and submission to God. We argued that, because this mode of life is so much at variance with basic presup-

---

1. Nancey Murphy and George F. R. Ellis, *On the Moral Nature of the Universe: Theology, Cosmology, and Ethics* (Minneapolis: Fortress Press, 1996).

positions of social science, there is a need for alternative social-scientific research programs that take this ethic seriously and pursue empirical research in its light. For example, mainstream economics assumes that the market runs on enlightened self-interest, but in fact a large part of economic behavior is based on sharing. Many legal systems are based on a concept of retributive justice, but some evidence shows that restorative justice works better. We argued that these alternatives need to be studied, and that such investigation could lead to better, more moral social arrangements.

The purpose of this chapter will be to lay the theological (and ethical) groundwork so that in the next chapter it will be possible to begin to think out the consequences of this view of the human good for some of the many facets of psychology. I shall end this chapter with a very abbreviated consideration of some alternative points of view.

2. The Difference Doctrine Makes

I suggested in the previous chapter that the doctrinal differences that divide Christian subtraditions make for different accounts of the possibilities and limitations of human flourishing in this life. I mentioned differing accounts of the extent to which Christians can be expected to transcend sin, from the Lutheran account of *simul justus et peccator,* to the Holiness movement's account of a second blessing that brings entire sanctification, to the Eastern Orthodox understanding of *theosis* or divinization as the goal of the Christian life. There are a variety of other ways in which Christians differ with regard to human potentialities. I suggest that we can understand most such disagreements by looking at differences in doctrine at three points: (1) creation and fall, (2) atonement/salvation, and (3) eschatology.[2]

There were already important differences in understandings of creation and fall in the early centuries of the church. For example, Irenaeus and Augustine offered different accounts of the original state of God's human creatures. Augustine attributed to them a state of original perfection that included immunity from disease, fear, desire, sadness, and even fa-

---

2. In light of the chapters by Kimball and Reimer (Chapters 5 and 6 respectively, this volume), I should also add Christology and Incarnation.

tigue.[3] In contrast, Irenaeus had written earlier of humans as originally immature beings upon whom God could not yet profitably bestow his highest gifts.[4] These two views led to different accounts of the depth of sin: Augustine's Adam and Eve had much farther to fall than Irenaeus's did.

We also find in the tradition different accounts of the extent of the corruption of human nature due to the fall. According to Augustine, all parts of the soul (will, intellect, and appetites) are disordered. Thomas Aquinas, in contrast, believed that the intellect was largely preserved from the consequences of the fall. This difference led to different accounts of the extent to which it is possible, apart from grace, to resist sin.

In the past century or so, even more radical differences have appeared in conceptions of human nature. There are those who accept the basic storyline of original perfection followed by catastrophic fall, and others influenced by paleontology, archaeology, and evolutionary biology who reject the concept of original perfection. For the latter, "original sin" refers not to the effect on the whole human race of a first sin (although logically there had to have been *some* first sin) but rather to conditions that predispose all of us to sin.[5] Some theologians emphasize the social contagion of sin; others consider the extent to which the genetic endowment that led to survival in the evolutionary process now predisposes us to act in ways contrary to the will of God.

There is a nest of controversies regarding the closely related doctrines of atonement and salvation, and the equally closely related doctrines of salvation and last things. In fact, there are too many issues to sort out here, so I shall simply list some of the questions. What is involved in atonement? Is it Christ's paying the penalty for sin, or the repair of fallen human nature, or the conquest of evil powers that hold humans in bondage? Is atonement limited to the elect or did Christ's life, death, and resurrection make a difference to all of humankind? Does salvation refer primarily to God's definitive act in the past, or to current transformation of human lives, or does it primarily regard the individual's fate at the final judgment?

3. See John Hick, *Evil and the God of Love,* rev. ed. (New York: Harper & Row, 1997), p. 65.

4. Hick, *Evil and the God of Love,* p. 212.

5. For an excellent discussion of all of the essential issues in light of an evolutionary account of human origins, see Keith Ward, *Religion and Human Nature* (Oxford: Clarendon Press, 1998).

Related to the question of the prevalence of God's salvific work in this life is another question, germane to eschatology: Is the kingdom of God partially realized in this aeon, or only to appear in the next? Answers to this question have a bearing on issues such as the role of the church in society and the ultimate value of life in *this* world. An equally important question is whether Christian hope for eternal life resides in expectation of one's immortal soul surviving death or in the resurrection of the body. This question, of course, grows out of sharply contrasting views of what a human being, most basically, *is:* a unity of body and soul (or body, soul, and spirit) or a purely organic being. All of these questions have a bearing on one's assumptions regarding the highest good to which humans can reasonably aspire in this life.

I hope that this sketchy overview is enough, first, to provoke readers to consider their own theological accounts of human nature, and second, to show that there is no possibility of a generic account of the implications of Christian theology for integration. So I now turn to one particular account, that of the Radical-Reformation churches. But even here I shall need to pass over differences within that subtradition.

3. Radical-Reformation Distinctives

The history of the Radical Reformation is still being pieced together. For four centuries the "Anabaptists" were associated almost exclusively with dreaded sects such as the Münsterites, and thus dismissed from mainline church histories. Exactly how and when the movement started is still in dispute. Although the Radical movement was diverse,[6] an important event in the consolidation and definition of this form of Christian life was a meeting of leaders of the Swiss Brethren at Schleitheim, on the Swiss-German border, in 1527.

The Schleitheim Confession presented the Anabaptist distinctives — those points on which the Radicals differed from other Protestants. These seven distinctives were as follows: first, baptism was to be reserved for believers; second, unrepentant sinners were to be admonished and, if necessary, banned from the congregation; third, the "breaking of

---

6. George Hunston Williams, *The Radical Reformation* (Philadelphia: Westminster Press, 1962).

bread" was to be reserved for those who were baptized and at peace with one another; fourth, the church was to be separated from the world; fifth, shepherds (pastors) were to be chosen from among the congregation; sixth, "concerning the sword," Christians should not use any punishments other than the ban to enforce church discipline, and should not engage in any civic duties that involve violence; and seventh, (consequently) Christians should not swear loyalty oaths to the government.[7]

A document concerning congregational order was written by the same hand and apparently circulated with these seven articles. It urged frequent meetings for study and the Lord's Supper, admonishing of sinners, simple living — no frivolity or gluttony — and communal provision for members in need.[8]

Summing up the character of an entire Christian subtradition is impossible here. I shall therefore mention four *practices* that (with some exceptions) have characterized the Radicals through much of their history. These four practices are (1) voluntary church membership (entailed by belief in the separation of church and state), (2) nonviolence, (3) revolutionary subordination, and (4) simple living. All four of these practices can be seen as strategies for living in such a way as to curb the *will to power*. Nonviolence is the refusal to use physical force against another. Revolutionary subordination is a strategy for righting injustices without the use of any power other than that of the imagination. The separation of church and state (and more thorough de-Constantinization) is the rejection of institutional longing for alliance with the power of the state. Finally, learning to live with less reduces the need for power to defend one's economic privilege.

4. A Research Program in Radical-Reformation Theology

I mentioned earlier that I intend the present chapters to be an extension of work done in the past with Quaker activist and cosmologist George Ellis. Ellis and I first met at a conference on scientific cosmology and di-

7. *The Legacy of Michael Sattler*, ed. John Howard Yoder (Scottdale, Pa.: Herald Press, 1973), pp. 27-43.
8. Yoder, ed., *The Legacy of Michael Sattler*, pp. 44-54.

vine action sponsored by the Vatican Observatory. Afterward we asked ourselves whether this abstruse intellectual pursuit had any implications for the "real world," which meant at that time the anti-apartheid movement in South Africa, and in the United States the buildup to the Gulf War. All of the other participants in the conference were Catholics or liberal, mainline Protestants, and the theological discussions were all carried on in those terms. Our questions were, first, whether our theological allegiance to the Radical-Reformation tradition makes any difference to the way one approaches the relations between theology and science; and second, whether a marriage of Radical-Reformation theology and science has any implications for pressing social issues. We decided to try to make the case that it does.

First we had to clear away some philosophical underbrush. In the evangelical half of the Protestant Christian world (and in much of Catholicism as well), the status of theology as a *body of knowledge* can be taken for granted. Not so in the liberal Protestant world. Other participants in the theology-and-science dialogue had made a case (contrary to their liberal tendencies) for the cognitive status of theology, but we did not find these arguments persuasive.[9] Hence our first move was to provide our own argument for theology's right to have a voice in describing the nature of reality. This is the point of my extended argument in chapter 1 for the scientific status of theology — an argument that may make us appear to evangelical readers to be, in the terms of an old Russian saying, beating our way through an open door!

So Imre Lakatos gave us the *structure* for understanding theology, and, as already described, we adapted Arthur Peacocke's model of the hierarchy of the sciences for our own purposes. The *content* of the theological level of the hierarchy was to come from the Radical-Reformation tradition. Fortunately for our purposes, Mennonite theologian John Howard Yoder had already produced an account of theology in line with the thinking and practices of the early Anabaptists.

Yoder disclaimed being a systematic theologian, since he believed

9. Ian Barbour, a liberal theologian much influenced by process thought, has led the way in arguing for a "critical realist" understanding of the epistemological status of both theology and science. I take the entire realist–anti-realist debate to be confused. See Nancey Murphy, "Scientific Realism and Postmodern Philosophy," in *Anglo-American Postmodernity: Philosophical Perspectives on Science, Religion, and Ethics* (Boulder, Colo.: Westview Press, 1997), pp. 39-48.

that theology should serve the church by addressing issues as they arise rather than being driven by philosophical or systematic motivations. However, this perspective does not prevent others from perceiving the coherence of his writings as a whole.[10] We claim that over the course of his lifetime Yoder provided a fairly complete, systematic account of Christian theology in which nonviolence is shown to be not an optional extra for heroic Christians but the very substance of Christian faithfulness.

In an attempt to sum up what is central to and distinctive of Yoder's theology, we proposed the following statement as the hard core of his program:

> *The moral character of God is revealed in Jesus' vulnerable enemy love and renunciation of dominion. Imitation of Jesus in this regard constitutes a social ethic.*

That is, Yoder claims that what Christianity is basically all about is political, not doctrinal or mystical or metaphysical. This starting point yields a theological system (in our terms, a network of doctrinal auxiliary hypotheses) very different from those of mainline churches.

Yoder's Christology and his doctrine of the Trinity are close to the historic orthodoxy of the ancient creeds. His account differs from the standard account in his justification of these doctrines. Doctrinal affirmations are in general justified because they explain why the ethic of Jesus is morally binding. That is, Jesus *must* have the "metaphysical" status attributed to him by the early creeds in order for the church to worship *and obey* him as absolute Lord.[11] Yoder writes:

> When later, more "theological" New Testament writings formulated the claim to preexistence and cosmic pre-eminence for the divine Son or Word (John 1:1-4; Col. 1:15ff.; Heb. 1:2ff.) the intent of this language was not to consecrate beside Jesus some other way of perceiving the eternal Word, through reason or history or nature, but rather to af-

---

10. In contrast, see Chris K. Huebner, "Globalization, Theory, and Dialogical Vulnerability: John Howard Yoder and the Possibility of a Pacifist Epistemology," *Mennonite Quarterly Review* 76 (January 2002): 49-62.

11. He must also be *fully* human in order to serve as a model for human faithfulness (cf. Reimer, Chapter 6, this volume).

firm the exclusivity of the revelation claim they were making for Jesus. The same must be said of the later development of the classic
ideas of the Trinity and the Incarnation. . . . "Trinity" did not originally mean, as it does for some later, that there are three kinds of revelation, the Father speaking through creation and the Spirit through
experience, by which the words and example of the Son must be cor-
rected; it meant rather that language must be found and definitions
created so that Christians, who believe in only one God, can affirm
that that God is most adequately and bindingly known in Jesus.[12]

For Yoder, then, the doctrines of Christ's divinity and of the Son's unity
with the Father guarantee that no other claims are more binding on humankind than those of Jesus. No other redeemer figure takes precedence
over Jesus the Messiah; no other source of divine revelation can contra-
dict Jesus' moral teaching.

The doctrines of atonement and justification, Christian anthropology and sin are points where Yoder most clearly diverges from the standard account of Christian doctrine, by which I mean especially the Reformation and post-Reformation forms of Christian doctrine that owe
much to Augustine. The standard account includes a doctrine of the fall
as a key to understanding human nature, an emphasis on substitutionary atonement, and a doctrine of justification as imputed righteousness.

Since the publication of Gustaf Aulén's *Christus Victor,* it has been
common to speak of three types of atonement theories: the Anselmian or
substitutionary theories; the Abelardian or moral influence theories; and
the "classical" ransom or conflict theories, in which the work of Christ
is interpreted in terms of triumph over cosmic evil powers. While the
classical theory has New Testament support, it is objectionable for many
because it involves the concept of the Devil. Aulén claimed that the
"mythological" language could simply be dropped, but it is then no longer clear what is meant by "cosmic evil powers."[13]

Yoder's understanding of the atonement fits the classical model and

---

12. John Howard Yoder, *The Politics of Jesus: Vicit Agnus Noster,* 2d ed. (Grand
Rapids: Eerdmans, 1994), p. 99.

13. Gustaf Aulén, *Christus Victor: An Historical Study of the Three Main Types of
the Idea of the Atonement,* trans. A. G. Hebert (London: SPCK, 1931). The subtitle of
Yoder's *Politics of Jesus* suggests the centrality of his argument against the standard account of atonement.

fills the gap left by the excision of a "mythical" Devil by means of his interpretation of the "principalities and powers." Yoder follows New Testament scholars such as G. B. Caird and Hendrikus Berkhof in their interpretation of the "powers." Because the New Testament concept of the powers developed from that of the alien gods of other nations in the Old Testament, there is a lingering sense of their being spiritual realities. However, the most significant function of these terms applies not to angelic or mythic beings but rather to sociopolitical forces. These superhuman power structures are the forces with which Jesus came into conflict and from which he freed humankind, both by his example — here the moral influence theory gets its due — and by stripping them of their illusion of absolute legitimacy, in that the most worthy representatives of these powers (the Jewish religion and the Roman state) abused him in his innocence. The cross has as much significance in this theory as in the substitutionary theory, but for different reasons.

Yoder does not ignore personal sinfulness, but he gives it neither the significance nor the inevitability that it has in Augustinian theology. He focuses instead on institutionalized sin, whose remedy is freedom from bondage to the principalities and powers through Jesus' unmasking of the powers and creating of a new social order, the church. His account of justification is also sociopolitical:

> Let us set aside for purposes of discussion the assumption that the righteousness of God and the righteousness of humanity are most fundamentally located on the individual level. . . . Let us posit as at least thinkable the alternate hypothesis that for Paul righteousness, either in God or in human beings, might more appropriately be conceived of as having cosmic or social dimensions. Such larger dimensions would not negate the personal character of the righteousness God imputes to those who believe; but by englobing the personal salvation in a fuller reality they would negate the individualism with which we understand such reconciliation.[14]

Yoder argues that justification — being set right with God — is accomplished when Christians are set right with one another. In Paul's ministry, reconciling Jews and Gentiles was primary. The "new creation" is a new "race" in which the Jewish law no longer distinguishes

14. Yoder, *The Politics of Jesus*, p. 215.

between Jew and Gentile, and in which gender and economic differences are reconciled as well:

> But it is *par excellence* with reference to enmity between peoples, the extension of neighbor love to the enemy, and the renunciation of violence even in the most righteous cause, that this promise takes on flesh in the most original, the most authentic, and most frightening and scandalous, and therefore in the most evangelical way. It is the Good News that my enemy and I are united, through no merit or work of our own, in a new humanity that forbids henceforth my ever taking his or her life in my hands.[15]

This social concept of sin and justification, along with Yoder's politicized version of the conflict theory of the atonement, reinterprets the main features of theology, especially the Pauline corpus, which since Luther has been understood to focus on imputed personal righteousness before God on the basis of faith.

An important thesis for Yoder, as for other theologians in the Anabaptist tradition, is that "the church is not the world." The sixteenth-century Anabaptists' most distinctive feature was their rejection of the state-church arrangement, which identified the church first with empire and later with the nation-state. Anabaptists ("re-baptizers") rejected infant baptism in part because it was the means by which all citizens were incorporated into the state church. When Yoder distinguishes the church from the world, he means to say that a system of interconnected power structures opposes the work of Christ. Within the church, social practices are to some degree healed of their sinfulness. The powers themselves can be redeemed; they can accept their role as servants of God in support of human society. For example, leadership becomes a form of service; economic practices are not to amass wealth but to produce something to share; housekeeping aims at hospitality to the stranger.

In addition, the church has developed unique social practices that aim to maintain and to improve the moral character of the community. One of these is the practice of "binding and loosing" that Jesus taught his disciples in Matthew 18:15-18. This practice has the potential not only to support individuals in their faithfulness to the community's teaching,

---

15. Yoder, *The Politics of Jesus*, p. 226.

but also to offer opportunities for healing personal grievances and for productive discussions on matters of conduct.

These features of the church suggest that conscientious pursuit of the good can and will lead to cumulative moral development, both of Christ-like character among members and of noncoercive, virtue-enhancing institutions and practices. The church acts as an agent of change in the world by demonstrating alternatives to the world's coercive practices. While the world does not and cannot operate as the church does, there are vast differences between the powers in terms of the degree to which they approximate the will of God.

Thus, Yoder believes that moral progress in history is possible. He claims that the New Testament sees our present age, from Pentecost to the *parousia,* as a period when two aeons overlap:

> These aeons are not distinct periods of time, for they exist simultaneously. They differ rather in nature or in direction; one points backward to human history outside or (before) Christ; the other points forward to the fullness of the kingdom of God, of which it is a foretaste. Each aeon has a social manifestation: the former in the "world," the latter in the church or the body of Christ.[16]

The new aeon was inaugurated by Jesus, who is a "mover of history," not merely a teacher of how to understand history's moral ambiguity.[17] The meaning of history is found in the work of the church;[18] by its obedience the church is used by God to bring about the fullness of the kingdom.

The resurrection of Jesus is God's guarantee that the new aeon will ultimately prevail. This implies that the means Jesus chose for participation in history are the right ones: the cross and not the sword, suffering and not brute power determine the meaning of history. One need not choose between *agape* and effectiveness. The ultimate effectiveness of self-sacrificing love is guaranteed; however, it is right not because it is effective but because it anticipates the victory of the Lamb.[19] This ethic

---

16. John Howard Yoder, *The Royal Priesthood: Essays Ecclesiological and Ecumenical* (Grand Rapids: Eerdmans, 1994), p. 146.

17. Yoder, *The Politics of Jesus,* p. 233.

18. Yoder, *The Royal Priesthood,* p. 151.

19. Yoder, *The Royal Priesthood,* p. 151.

makes sense only if Jesus' choice not to rule violently reveals a divine decision or, in other words, if self-emptying is not only what Jesus did but characterizes the very nature of God.[20] Yoder explains:

> This conception of participation in the character of God's struggle with a rebellious world, which early Quakerism referred to as "the war of the lamb," has the peculiar disadvantage — or advantage, depending upon one's point of view — of being meaningful only if Christ be he who Christians claim him to be, the Master. Almost every other kind of ethical approach espoused by Christians, pacifist or otherwise, will continue to make sense to the non-Christian as well. . . . The same is not true for this vision of "completing in our bodies that which was lacking in the suffering of Christ" (Col. 1:24). If Jesus Christ was not who historical Christianity confesses he was, the revelation in the life of a real man of the character of God himself, then this one argument for pacifism collapses.[21]

5. Relating Theology to Ethics

George Ellis and I set out to formulate a "research program" in ethics, consistent with Yoder's theological insights and capable of spanning the gap in the hierarchy of the sciences between theology and the social sciences. This systematic expression of a concept of the ultimate good for humankind served, in particular, to criticize tacit ethical assumptions embedded in the social sciences.

Christians still understand ethics to have a basis (of some sort) in theology, but the modern era saw the development of philosophical approaches to ethics that were specifically designed to free them from theological authority. I mentioned Thomas Hobbes's social contract theory earlier and noted that it is based on an account of human origins sharply at variance with that of the Bible. Utilitarianism and Immanuel Kant's deontological approach to ethics were both intended to base morality purely on *human* reason.

One doctrine shared by modern philosophical ethicists was the

20. John Howard Yoder, *He Came Preaching Peace* (Scottdale, Pa.: Herald Press, 1985), p. 93.

21. Yoder, *The Politics of Jesus*, p. 237.

claim that it is impossible legitimately to derive evaluative statements from statements about the way things are. But consider this example: If we know the *purpose* of something — say, a watch — we can make perfectly legitimate inferences from facts to values. "This watch does not keep good time; therefore it is not a *good* watch."

Alasdair MacIntyre has argued persuasively that the attempt to detach ethics from theology is a failed experiment, and one that was bound to fail because, without an account of the *purpose* of human life, there is no way to adjudicate between differing kinds of ethical arguments. What modern ethicists gave up in rejecting theological tradition was any source of an answer to the question, What is the final purpose or goal of human life? Thus, ethics is essentially dependent upon *some* account of ultimate reality (theistic or otherwise) and of humankind's place in that scheme.[22]

To some readers it may again appear that I am beating my way through an open door. But I think it is important for Christians who *do* base their ethics on their account of God and of God's purposes for our lives to recognize that no special pleading is necessary. All ethical systems are dependent, usually implicitly, on some such account.

What then is the relation between ethics and the Radical-Reformation theological system I have just sketched out? Much of Yoder's ethical thinking is already incorporated into my account of his theology, and in fact he would repudiate any disciplinary boundary between theology and Christian ethics. So let us look specifically at how Yoder's social ethic is related to the hard core of his theology — the claim that the *moral character* of God is revealed in Jesus' vulnerable enemy love and renunciation of dominion. The rationale for ethics, not only for Yoder but for many Christian ethicists, is in fact the character of God. Citing texts from throughout the New Testament, Yoder claims that "sharing the divine nature" is one definition of Christian existence. Because Jesus reveals the moral character of God, the definition of Christian existence can also be expressed as "being in Christ" by loving as he loved and serving as he served.[23] However, Yoder contends that only in one respect are Christians specifically called to imi-

22. Alasdair MacIntyre, *After Virtue: A Study in Moral Theory,* 2d ed. (Notre Dame: University of Notre Dame Press, 1984).

23. Yoder, *The Politics of Jesus,* pp. 115-20.

tate Jesus — in taking up the cross.[24] A crucial issue, then, is how to interpret the cross. For Yoder the Christian's cross is not any and every kind of suffering; it is the price of social nonconformity. Jesus' warning to expect persecution is, in Yoder's words, "a normative statement about the relation of our social obedience to the messianity of Jesus. Representing as he did the divine order now at hand, accessible; renouncing as he did the legitimate use of violence and the accrediting of the existing authorities; renouncing as well the ritual purity of noninvolvement, his people will encounter in ways analogous to his own the hostility of the old order."[25]

So the cost of defying the principalities and powers, especially when it undermines their idolatrous claims, is suffering, sometimes even death. This is the meaning of bearing one's cross:

> What Jesus refers to in his call to cross-bearing is . . . the seeming defeat of that strategy of obedience which is no strategy, the inevitable suffering of those whose only goal is to be faithful to that love which puts one at the mercy of one's neighbor, which abandons claims to justice for oneself and for one's own in an overriding concern for the reconciling of the adversary and the estranged.[26]

In light of Yoder's work, Ellis and I proposed as the hard core of a Radical-Reformation research program in *ethics* the following:

Self-renunciation for the sake of the other is humankind's highest good.

On the one hand, it is probably important to state that this bald thesis is not intended as a denial of everything else that Christian ethics is usually taken to include, but only to state that which is distinctive of Radical-Reformation ethics. On the other hand, it is easy for statements about personal self-sacrifice, renunciation, and other-centeredness to sound platitudinous in a culture widely affected by Christianity. However, the writings of Simone Weil expand on the theme of self-renunciation in a way that makes the claims of such an ethic stand out starkly.[27] She expresses the

24. Yoder, *The Politics of Jesus*, p. 95.
25. Yoder, *The Politics of Jesus*, p. 96.
26. Yoder, *The Politics of Jesus*, p. 236.

connection between the ethical principle of renunciation and its theological grounding as follows:

> Renunciation. Imitation of God's renunciation in creation. In a sense God renounces being everything. (p. 29)

> He emptied himself of his divinity. (p. 12)

> We should renounce being something. That is our only good. (p. 29)

Ellis and I use the term "kenotic" to characterize this ethic. "Kenosis" means self-emptying, and is now widely used by theologians to refer to God's renunciation of divine prerogatives.

So what does this principle entail in terms of ethics? It is wide-ranging in its implications, at both the personal and the social level. Renunciation, according to Weil, involves the following:

> To forgive debts. To accept the past without asking for future compensation. To stop time at the present instant. This is also the acceptance of death. . . . (p. 12)

> To empty ourselves of the world. To take the form of a slave. To reduce ourselves to the point we occupy in space and time. . . . (p. 12)

> To strip ourselves of the imaginary royalty of the world. Absolute solitude. Then we possess the truth of the world. (p. 12)

Further consequences or exemplifications of this kenotic ethic are as follows:

1. Renunciation involves detachment from material possessions:
   - Two ways of renouncing material possessions: To give them up with a view to some spiritual advantage. [Or] to conceive of them and feel them as conducive to spiritual well-being (for example: hunger, fatigue and humiliation cloud the mind and hinder meditation) and yet to renounce them. Only the second kind of renunciation means nakedness of spirit. (p. 12)
   - To detach our desire from all good things and to wait. Experience

---

27. Simone Weil, *Gravity and Grace* (London: Routledge, 1992; first published in English in 1952). Further references to this volume will be made parenthetically in the text.

proves that this waiting is satisfied. It is then we touch the absolute good. (p. 13)

2. Renunciation involves foregoing our rights to rewards:
   - The necessity for a reward, the need to receive the equivalent of what we give. But if, doing violence to this necessity, we leave a vacuum, as it were a suction of air is produced and a supernatural reward results. It does not come if we receive other wages: it is this vacuum that makes it come. (p. 10)

3. Renunciation entails choosing not to harm another person when we have been harmed:
   - To harm a person is to receive something from him. What? What have we gained (and what will have to be repaid) when we have done harm? We have gained in importance. We have expanded. We have filled an emptiness in ourselves by creating one in somebody else. (p. 6)

4. Renunciation calls for nonviolence:
   - We should strive to become such that we are able to be nonviolent. This depends also on the adversary. (p. 77)
   - The cause of wars: there is in every man and in every group of men a feeling that they have a just and legitimate claim to be masters of the universe — to possess it. (p. 77)
   - Whoever takes up the sword shall perish by the sword. And whoever does not take up the sword (or lets it go) shall perish on the cross. (p. 79)

5. Renunciation calls for acceptance of suffering:
   - For men of courage physical sufferings (and privations) are often a test of endurance and of strength of soul. But there is a better use to be made of them. For me then, may they not be that. May they rather be a testimony, loved and felt, of human misery. May I endure them in a completely passive manner. Whatever happens, how could I ever think an affliction too great, since the wound of an affliction and the abasement to which those whom it strikes are condemned opens to them the knowledge of human misery, knowledge which is the door to all wisdom? (p. 31)

6. Renunciation means submission to God:
   - God gave me being in order that I should give it back to him. . . . Humility is the refusal to exist outside God. It is the queen of virtues. (p. 35)

The consequence of this life of renunciation, according to Weil, is that it leads to wisdom, to knowledge of the truth, to the encounter with absolute good.

One additional point that surely follows from the core idea of renunciation is intellectual humility: being willing to give up cherished notions in order to learn from others. This virtue is emphasized by the Quakers in their call to recognize the Light in everyone:

> Do you respect that of God in everyone though it may be expressed in unfamiliar ways or be difficult to discern? . . . Listen patiently and seek the truth which other people's opinions may contain. . . . Think it possible that you may be mistaken.[28]

The paradoxical nature of an ethic of self-sacrifice or renunciation is captured in Jesus' saying that those who try to make their life secure will lose it, but those who lose their life will keep it (Luke 17:33).

I anticipate two major objections to this ethical proposal. The first is that the denial of one's own interests seems negative and destructive — the way to a distorted humanity rather than the way to fulfillment. There are indeed distortions of this ethic that aim more at manipulation of others than at transformation. A serious problem is how to avoid such an ethic being used as an ideology to keep the oppressed in their places. An important issue is how such an ethic applies in cases where people are too oppressed or abused to *have* a self to renounce.[29] I shall take up this issue at the end of the next chapter. I believe the direction to look here will be to the community's role in nonviolently protecting its abused members.

The most potent objection to an ethic such as I have presented is that it is idealistic; it is not possible to implement it in the "real world."[30] Ellis

28. *Quaker Faith and Practice* (Warwick, England: The Yearly Meeting of the Society of Friends in Britain, 1995), Advices and Queries, chap. 1, no. 17.

29. The research on girls' and boys' roles reported in Kimball (Chapter 5, this volume) and on styles of parental discipline (Clements and Mitchell, Chapter 4, this volume) sheds light on factors that may prevent children from developing the moral character that enables them to sacrifice for others without undue harm to themselves.

30. In our *On the Moral Nature of the Universe*, Ellis and I addressed the question of how kenotic action can be sustained in the long term, but we did not believe that our treatment was adequate. Reimer (Chapter 6, this volume) provides evidence of the personal costs involved.

and I attempted to meet this objection in two ways. One was by presenting examples of success — for instance, evidence that restorative justice
systems work better than retributive systems.

Our second move was in line with Yoder's recognition that the
world cannot be expected to operate as the church does, yet the powers
of this world, though fallen, are not all equally distant from God's will.
Thus, Christians acting in the world will generally be presented with a
spectrum of options. No option may be ideal, but if Yoder is correct in
saying that there is the possibility of moral improvement in history, then
consistent choice of the option closest to the will of God can change the
entire social order for the better and produce a better *range* of options
for the future.

It is with regard to the issue of nonviolence that the claim of un-
workability is most often raised. It is possible for an individual to
choose to live nonviolently, both in personal interaction and by refusing
to serve in the military, but, it is argued, social order can be maintained
only by violent coercion. Therefore, the idea of a nonviolent society is
utopian, and nonviolence cannot be a normative part of Christian social
ethics.

What this argument (and others of its kind) leaves out of account is
the wide range of persuasive and coercive measures available. C. J. Cadoux has assembled a list of types of persuasion and coercion, falling
into three major categories: noncoercive, coercive, and injurious. Noncoercive methods range from bribes and rewards through mediation, argument, and arbitration, to a variety of self-renunciatory actions:
prayer, personal example, conciliatory discussion, self-imposed penance,
unmerited suffering, nonresistance, and direct acts of love. At the other
end of the scale, the options include temporarily incapacitating action,
disablement with recoverable damage, pain without permanent harm,
damage to personality, permanent physical disablement, incidental ho-
micide, willful murder, posthumous mutilation, torture, and mutilation.
Cadoux's middle range of coercive yet non-injurious options — non-
cooperation, civil disobedience, threats, bodily obstruction — could be
greatly expanded.[31]

The rationale for using noncoercive and especially self-sacrificial

---

31. Cadoux's list can be found in William Robert Miller, *Nonviolence: A Christian
Interpretation* (New York: Schocken Books, 1964), p. 59.

means of persuasion is that it challenges the opponent to rise to a higher moral level, while the use of violence lowers the opponent's resistance to the use of violence — it justifies retaliation. Ellis and I argue that consistently choosing the least coercive policy that serves the purpose will gradually change the moral climate in such a way as to make more cooperation possible in the future. We are not alone in arguing that Gandhi's effective nonviolent campaign against British rule in India has changed the world forever; it has put nonviolent direct action on the spectrum of effective measures to fight oppression. Since Gandhi's campaign we have seen Martin Luther King Jr.'s peaceful civil rights campaign in the United States, and nonviolent ends to oppressive regimes in former communist countries, the Philippines, and Chile. The struggle against apartheid in South Africa was not entirely without violence, but without nonviolent leadership might have resulted instead in civil war.

Lester Kurtz credits Gandhi with synthesizing two motifs that are present in most religious traditions: the idea of fighting for a just cause and the principle of nonviolence. He argues that all of the nonviolent campaigns mentioned above were facilitated by religious teachings: "Gandhi's nonviolent version . . . was made possible by a religious frame of the world. Gandhi was genuinely convinced that the world was ultimately ruled by a God of love and that the universe was fundamentally nonviolent."[32] Kurtz's claims support two of our central theses: that ethics must be backed by some account of the ultimate nature of reality, and that action in light of such an ethic can change the moral level of society.

6. The Challenge to Psychology

Paul Feyerabend has argued that science makes more progress when there are competing theories in the field. Without theoretical guidance we do not know where to direct our observations, what counts as data worth gathering. Therefore, the presence of competing theoretical view-

32. Lester R. Kurtz, "The Pedagogy of Peace: The Role of Religious Education," in *La Educación Religiosa en un Contexto de Pluralismo y Tolerancia* (Granada: Centro UNESCO de Andalucía, 1998), pp. 245-57; p. 254.

points is likely to lead to the discovery of more facts and thus more progress in understanding the world around us.[33]

Ellis and I have proposed our kenotic ethic — our account of the possibilities for human flourishing — as a theory to guide research in the social sciences. We believe that the availability of such a vision for human life could lead to exploration of topics that otherwise would be overlooked. For example, if one believes that economic behavior is governed by self-interest, then one is not likely to investigate economic activities that are based on sharing. Francis Fukuyama estimates that only 80 percent of economic behavior can be accounted for in terms of enlightened self-interest.[34] If one believes that societies without violent coercion are impossible in principle, one will dismiss examples of such societies as flukes and will not be motivated to understand how they work. If one has no concept of restorative justice, one will never weigh its effectiveness against that of retributive systems.

Thus, we argued that a kenotic view of human flourishing could be understood as a core thesis to be elaborated and tested in the social sciences. Is it in fact possible to create social structures that approximate these ideals? What are the most effective transformative methods? What are the effects of living under such arrangements?

What then about psychology? It is clear that the ethic I have sketched in this chapter has a great deal to say regarding interpersonal relations; I anticipate that confirmation for the ethic could be found at the interpersonal level as well as within the social sciences. Here are some very preliminary suggestions about where to look. The ethic of renunciation proscribes all attempts to coerce or dominate others in interpersonal relations. This entails two sorts of empirical claims: (1) that noncoercive and nondomineering personal relations are an essential aspect of *the good* for human life — that is, they contribute to happiness, success, and ultimate effectiveness; and (2) that noncoercive, nondomineering personal relations are possible. Since it is obvious that *some* noncoercive relations are possible, the interesting question is whether and how the sphere of noncoercion, nonviolence, and cooperation can be widened.

33. Paul K. Feyerabend, *Against Method* (London: New Left Books, 1975).
34. Francis Fukuyama, *The Social Virtues and the Creation of Prosperity* (New York: Free Press, 1995).

There is a wealth of popular literature in psychology and management suggesting that, in fact, successful interpersonal relations depend on an openness to the other person and a willingness that each one involved not dominate the interaction.[35] There is also a growing body of research of a more serious academic nature on topics such as attitude change, prejudice and attribution, competition and aggression, and on the effects both of observing violence and of acting violently. All of these studies are relevant to the question of whether and how noncoercive, cooperative interpersonal relations can replace aggression, coercion, and domination.[36] Such research on the causes and cures of aggression, prejudice, and violence indirectly supports our ethical thesis in that it rebuts any claims that violence is an ineradicable aspect of human nature and therefore not subject to moral sanction.

I hope it is obvious that much more can be done along these lines. I shall put forward a more systematic proposal for psychological research in the following chapter.

7. Sharpening the Contrasts

I have argued that we need to look to theology for a vision of the possibilities for human flourishing, and I have described one such vision, a *radical* proposal in two senses of the word: it is based on the Radical-Reformation tradition in Christianity, and it is also radically different from naturalistic, humanistic, and even many other Christian accounts of the good for humankind. I hope that I have inspired some of my readers to think about the similarities and differences between this vision and their own.

So I end this chapter with a brief glance at alternative, nontheistic accounts of human flourishing. I shall look at some of the better instances of what the secular academy has to say about that which humans can reasonably aspire to attain.

35. See, for example, Anthony Storr, *The Integrity of the Personality* (London: Penguin, 1960); T. Gordon, *P.E.T.: Parent Effectiveness Training* (New York: Plume Books, 1975); R. Fisher and W. Ury, *Getting to Yes: Negotiating Agreement without Giving In* (London: Business Books, 1981).

36. A fine collection of reports on relevant research is found in *Readings about the Social Animal*, 7th ed., ed. Eliot Aronson (New York: W. H. Freeman & Co., 1995).

Iris Murdoch was a very perceptive novelist and an important contributor to current philosophical ethics. She claims explicitly that her ethical system follows from an atheistic metaphysical stance. For her, the modern technological age has demythologized religion and made traditional theological claims unintelligible. Her alternative to traditional religion is a Christianity "without a personal God or a risen Christ, without beliefs in supernatural places and happenings, such as heaven and life after death, but retaining the mystical figure of Christ occupying a place analogous to that of Buddha: a Christ who can console and save, but who is to be found as a living force within each human soul and not in some supernatural elsewhere."[37] The mystic Christ is an image of the Good. As absolute, above all the virtues, it is a pure source, "the principle which creatively relates the virtues to each other in our moral lives."[38]

Despite her denial of the existence of a personal God, Murdoch takes prayer to be an essential exercise. But here prayer is meditation — "a withdrawal, through some disciplined quietness, into the great chamber of the soul."[39] More specifically, prayer is attention to the Good, which allows us to escape self-deception and egocentric attachments.

I venture to state the core theory of Murdoch's ethical system as follows: There is no end, no reward for human life. Thus, morality has no point beyond itself. The goal of life, therefore, must be to recognize and accept this fact, along with the facts of the frailty and unreality of the ego and the emptiness of worldly desires. Or, more briefly, to be moral is to recognize full well that morality, though necessary, has no point. The resignation, the disillusionment, the bowing to necessity that characterize the good life for Murdoch are in sharp contrast to any Christian account of the partial realization of the kingdom of God in this life.

More recently, philosopher Owen Flanagan has set out to debunk claims to the effect that without God, human life is meaningless and morality is pointless. The moral code that Flanagan endorses is not at all out of the ordinary. He argues for the value of friendship, love, kindness, and compassion; for cultivating the virtues of courage, fidelity, and hon-

---

37. Iris Murdoch, *Metaphysics as a Guide to Morals* (London: Penguin Books, 1992), p. 419.

38. Murdoch, *Metaphysics as a Guide to Morals*, p. 507.

39. Murdoch, *Metaphysics as a Guide to Morals*, p. 73.

esty. Murder, assault, rape, and robbery are wrong; hypocrisy and cruelty are vices, as are racism and sexism.[40]

His *arguments*, however, are particularly interesting to me because they have so much in common with mine.[41] The most striking similarity is that he likens ethics to a science — in particular, the science that employs empirical evidence to describe the environments and patterns of behavior that are most conducive to human flourishing. Flanagan helpfully likens ethics to ecology, a science that is both descriptive and normative. He emphasizes (as I would) the fact that humans come into the world with some basic moral equipment in the form of emotions and desires that predispose them to social behavior.

The difficulty Flanagan sees is that two quests are often in tension: the quest to be moral and the quest for a meaningful life. His example of such tension is that between doing philosophy and spending one's salary on living well (meaning) versus turning over half of one's salary or working a second job to help others in need (morals). His analysis of what is necessary for a meaningful life, though, begins with morality itself: "Across cultures one finds that being moral, that is, being a good person, is considered a necessary condition of living a meaningful life. As far as I can tell, it is the only absolutely necessary condition."[42] Good candidates for further conditions are true friendship and what John Rawls calls the Aristotelian Principle: "Other things being equal, human beings enjoy the exercise of their realized capacities (their innate and trained abilities), and this enjoyment increases the more the capacity is realized, or the greater its complexity."[43] The fact, then, that humans have natural dispositions toward morality means that the quest for higher forms of morality is essential to our human flourishing:

> We are conscious beings on a quest, a quest that achieves its aims when we use our minds to flourish and to be good. These are our

40. Owen Flanagan, *The Problem of the Soul: Two Versions of Mind and How to Reconcile Them* (New York: Basic Books, 2002).

41. I mentioned in Chapter 1 that this is due in part to the fact that both Flanagan and I have been much influenced by Alasdair MacIntyre. See MacIntyre's *After Virtue* and *Dependent Rational Animals: Why Human Beings Need the Virtues* (Chicago: Open Court, 1999).

42. Flanagan, *The Problem of the Soul*, pp. 281-82.

43. Flanagan, *The Problem of the Soul*, p. 284.

most noble aims. They involve striving to become better, individually and collectively, than we are. Insofar as we aim to realize ideals that are possible but not yet real, the quest can be legitimately described as spiritual.

This quest suits the human animal well. It is becoming, worthy, and noble.[44]

I find Flanagan's arguments unexceptionable so far. I would not even want to reject his physicalist account of human nature.[45] Where we *do* part company is, of course, that there is no demand in his moral system for self-renunciation of the depth that Weil and Yoder require. There is no paradoxical twist such that she who pursues her own flourishing will lose it, and she who renounces her own flourishing for Christ's sake will find it.

Flanagan's book concludes with the final sentences of the paragraph quoted above:

It [this quest] is the most we can aim for given the kind of creature we are, and happily it is enough. If you think this is not so, if you want more, if you wish that your life had prospects for transcendent meaning, for more than the personal satisfaction and contentment you can achieve while you are alive, and more than what you will have contributed to the well-being of this world after you die, then you are still in the grip of illusions. Trust me, you can't get more. But what you can get, if you live well, is enough.[46]

Perhaps the most illuminating way to frame the difference between my position and Flanagan's is in neuropsychogist and theologian Warren Brown's terms: moral behavior is on a continuum with other forms of adaptive behavior, but its hallmark is that it takes into account a maximal representation of the environment to which one needs to adapt.[47] And Christians know, as Flanagan does not, that their environment — the one in whom we live and move and have our being — is the God of Jesus Christ.

44. Flanagan, *The Problem of the Soul*, p. 319.

45. A central purpose of Flanagan's book is to argue on scientific and philosophical bases against dualistic accounts of human nature.

46. Flanagan, *The Problem of the Soul*, p. 319.

47. This point was made by Warren Brown in personal communication with me.

Chapter 3   **Constructing a Radical-Reformation**
Research Program in Psychology

NANCEY MURPHY

1. Introduction

In the first chapter I made a case in the abstract that it is necessary for
psychologists to assume some theological (or a-theological) account of
human nature: an empirical discipline such as psychology (or the social
sciences) can *describe* human nature as it is, but has no resources in itself
to answer the question of whether humans *ought* to be as they are. I can
restate my claim in terms of the normal distribution curve that is so familiar to psychologists. Psychologists can measure human qualities and
determine the norm. But is it a good thing for humans to fall within the
capacious middle of a normal distribution, or is there some *ideal* state,
out at the right tip of the distribution, that is the true goal of the human
race?

In my second chapter I laid out one particular Christian answer to
the question of the ideal for human life and human relationships — a
kenotic ethic that calls for self-renunciation for the sake of others. Such
behavior is certainly *not* the norm in the world today. Other theological
assumptions that I hold, however, justify the hope that human social
groups can be lured in that direction by means of the prophetic example
of the church at its best.

My question for this chapter is the practical question of what difference this theological and ethical position might make for psychology.
Can there be a Radical Christian research program (or perhaps a cluster
of them) in psychology that makes this thesis about the *telos* of human
life part of its hard core (in Lakatosian terms)?

In this chapter, then, I shall first draw once again from the writings

53

of Alasdair MacIntyre in order to pose the question I wish to put to psychologists. Then I shall try my hand at laying out the basics for such a research program.

2. A Model from MacIntyre

The beginning of MacIntyre's *After Virtue* begins with what he calls a "disquieting suggestion":

> Imagine that the natural sciences were to suffer the effects of a catastrophe. A series of environmental disasters are blamed by the general public on the scientists. Widespread riots occur, laboratories are burnt down, physicists are lynched, books and instruments are destroyed. Finally a Know-Nothing political movement takes power and successfully abolishes science teaching in schools and universities, imprisoning and executing the remaining scientists. Later still there is a reaction against this destructive movement and enlightened people seek to revive science, although they have largely forgotten what it was. But all that they possess are fragments: a knowledge of experiments detached from any knowledge of the theoretical context which gave them significance; parts of theories unrelated either to the other bits and pieces of theory which they possess or to experiment; instruments whose use has been forgotten; half-chapters from books, single pages from articles, not always fully legible because torn and charred. Nonetheless, all these fragments are re-embodied in a set of practices which go under the revived names of physics, chemistry and biology. Adults argue with each other about the respective merits of relativity theory, evolutionary theory and phlogiston theory, although they possess only a very partial knowledge of each. Children learn by heart the surviving portions of the periodic table and recite as incantations some of the theorems of Euclid. Nobody, or almost nobody, realizes that what they are doing is not natural science in any proper sense at all. For everything that they do and say conforms to certain canons of consistency and coherence and those contexts which would be needed to make sense of what they are doing have been lost, perhaps irretrievably. . . .
>
> What is the point of constructing this imaginary world inhabited by fictitious pseudo-scientists . . . ? The hypothesis which I wish to ad-

vance is that in the actual world which we inhabit the language of morality is in the same state of grave disorder as the language of natural science in the imaginary world which I described. What we possess, if this view is true, are the fragments of a conceptual scheme, parts which now lack those contexts from which their significance derived. We possess indeed simulacra of morality; we continue to use many of the key expressions. But we have — very largely, if not entirely — lost our comprehension, both theoretical and practical, of morality.[1]

MacIntyre's conception of ethics as it once was and ought again to become can be represented schematically:

Figure 1

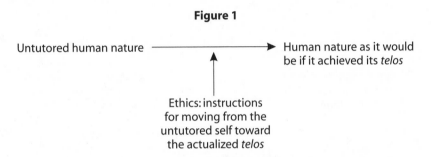

Untutored human nature ⟶ Human nature as it would be if it achieved its *telos*

Ethics: instructions for moving from the untutored self toward the actualized *telos*

That is, the original conception of ethics in the virtue tradition was practical instruction that would serve as a guide for development from the original condition of humans toward their ideal state. With such a conception there is nothing mysterious about the status of the moral "ought." If you want to achieve your *telos,* your true purpose, your final goal, then (as wisdom and experience have shown) you *ought* to do *x.* The anomalous status of moral language in the modern (secular) world is due to the fact that, severed from theology, the whole concept of the purpose of human life has been lost. This, in brief, is why MacIntyre says that current moral discourse is in a grave state of disorder.

I argued briefly in the preceding chapter that the social sciences share in such a disorder. That is, the social sciences began with the goal of studying how society could be morally improved, but when the call came for value-free science, the social sciences became confused about

---

1. Alasdair MacIntyre, *After Virtue: A Study in Moral Theory,* 2d ed. (Notre Dame: University of Notre Dame Press, 1984), pp. 1-2.

their own status. I argued that they ended up clandestinely promoting values that they would not want to own up to.

My question for psychologists is this: If the secular academy has indeed turned away from any theological account of the *telos* of human life, is it not *necessarily* the case that secular psychologists will have confused ideas about what they are supposed to be doing? I propose that the proper task for Christian psychologists is in fact very close to that of ethics as MacIntyre understands ethics. In particular, it is one of the empirical disciplines that tells us how humans can move from their untutored (and, I would add, ungraced) starting point toward the realization of their full potential. Thus, three questions are related in the way indicated in the following diagram:

Figure 2

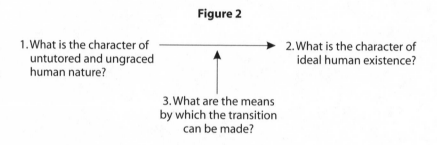

1. What is the character of untutored and ungraced human nature?

2. What is the character of ideal human existence?

3. What are the means by which the transition can be made?

Answers to the first question will come from empirical observation, from biology and theology — for example, one's theological understanding of the fall. Answers to the second will come disproportionately from theological ethics. A brief statement of the ideal human existence (such as my claim concerning the good of self-renunciation) will constitute the hard core of the psychological research program. Notice how different the goal of promoting self-renunciation is from much of secular psychology, especially psychotherapy, where the goal may be to promote adjustment to society — whatever the moral character of that society may be — or self-enhancement. Jerome Kagan says that "the current generation of young adults was socialized to treat the self as the most significant object to enhance. The current ethical imperative demands that each person devote most of their energy to acquiring characteristics that add to the self's accomplishments, beauty, power, or wealth."[2]

2. Jerome Kagan, "Morality, Altruism, and Love," in *Altruism and Altruistic Love:*

If psychology's special role is adding to our body of knowledge about how people and groups can make the transition toward the ideal of self-renunciation, there are a variety of more specific questions and concerns that arise. How does the transition happen in the normal case? What obstacles does mental illness present, and how can they be circumvented? Organizational psychologists could study the effects of democratic rather than authoritarian leadership styles; school psychologists could study techniques for teaching nonviolent conflict resolution. Other questions: How is forgiveness possible? What are the effects of childhood abuse on the developing brain? What are the psychological mechanisms at work in nonviolent resistance and its effects? There are questions that are more particular, such as how to counsel a battered spouse, and broader questions that impinge on the territory of the social sciences concerning means by which society can be changed to support ideal character development.

However much value each of these projects might have, the real goal, I submit, must be a comprehensive view of human nature that is responsive to theology and ethics (the disciplines above psychology in the hierarchy of the sciences) and to biology (below), and is supported by appropriate empirical data. Projects such as those suggested above would contribute to the database for such a program.

The task, therefore, is essentially to rewrite personality theories and theories of social interaction in light of theology.

3. Constructing a Research Program in Christian Psychology

The question now is whether I can pull together the various resources I've been mustering and actually make some usable suggestions to the psychologists among my readers. My goal is more than to list some research topics that might interest a Christian psychologist; it is the much more ambitious goal of sketching the outlines of a *research program* in psychology that is influenced by Christian theology in the manner I have said psychology could and should be influenced.

In my first chapter I did not address the question of whether Imre

---

Science, Philosophy, and Religion in Dialogue, ed. Stephen Post et al. (New York: Oxford University Press, 2002), p. 47.

Lakatos's methodology provides an apt description of psychology. To suggest that it does, consider the close parallels between Lakatos's account of a research program and an account of theory construction written by psychologists Calvin Hall and Gardner Lindzey just before Lakatos's work was published. They point out that the basic assumptions of a theory are conventional — that is, not necessitated by the data but created by the theorist.[3] There should be a cluster of assumptions "systematically related to each other, and a set of empirical definitions" (p. 11). The nature of these assumptions, about the events with which the theory is concerned, represent the distinctive quality of the theory. The logical relations among the theoretical assumptions and definitions must be clear (p. 11). The purpose of the theory is to produce testable empirical hypotheses that lead to "a systematic expansion of knowledge concerning the phenomena of interest" (p. 12). "The capacity of a theory to generate research by suggesting ideas or even by arousing disbelief and resistance may be referred to as the *heuristic influence of the theory*" (p. 13). A second function of a theory is to incorporate known empirical findings within a logically consistent and reasonably simple framework (p. 13).

So Hall and Lindzey's description of psychological theory formation differs very little from Lakatos's account of a research program. It lacks his concept of a hard core — that is, a *subset* of assumptions that one will attempt to save from falsification. It also adds an important requirement of empirical definitions of theoretical terms.

So, putting these two accounts together, we can see that what we need in order to construct a research program are the following:

1. A hard core: specification of the *essential* assumptions of the theory.
2. A positive heuristic: a plan for the development of the rest of the theoretical structure so as to provide a complete account of human nature consistent with the hard core.
3. Definition of theoretical terms in such a way as to relate them to observations or experimental designs.
4. Specification of the appropriate domain of empirical investigation

---

3. Calvin S. Hall and Gardner Lindzey, *Theories of Personality*, 2d ed. (New York: John Wiley & Sons, Inc., 1970), p. 10. Subsequent references to this volume will be made parenthetically in the text.

— in particular, what individuals and groups are most significant
exemplars of the theory.

5. Relation of the theoretical program thus defined to existing empirical research.

6. Development of additional testable hypotheses.

3.1. The Hard Core

In line with my MacIntyrean account of psychology, the hard core of a
program would have to include a summary of one's non-negotiable theories about (1) untutored and ungraced human nature, (2) the *telos* of
human development, and (3) the possibility of assisting individuals and
groups in moving toward that *telos*. Let us first consider briefly the *telos*
and possibilities for its attainment. Then I shall present an analysis of
original human nature.

Telos: I have already, in Chapter 2, devoted considerable space to a
description of the *ideal* for Christian life based on my reading of
Radical-Reformation theology and ethics. I shall state this briefly: Humans reach their highest goal in developing the capacity to renounce
their own lesser goods for the sake of others.

It is necessary, in spelling out this aspect of the core, to be able to
give an account of lesser goods, but this account need not be part of the
core. Such an account would come both from theological ethics and
from empirical research.

Possibilities: There are two ways to regard an ideal such as I have
specified: as attainable in this life; or as attainable only eschatologically,
but nonetheless serving some function in this aeon such as making
Christians aware of the extent of their sinfulness and need for forgiveness. Anabaptists such as John Howard Yoder argue for at least partial
and temporary manifestations of the ideal within history, primarily as a
result of the support that a properly faithful church community can provide. This possibility for transformation is a necessary element in the
hard core of the research program I attempt to sketch here.

Nature: I would want to incorporate a physicalist rather than a
dualist account of human nature into the hard core of my program, even
though I recognize that this may be problematic for many of my readers.
However, my account of the *telos* of human life will also be problematic

to many. I fall back on Hall and Lindzey's claim that a theory can have an important heuristic influence by "arousing disbelief and resistance" (p. 13) as well as by its acceptance and positive development.

My reasons for incorporating physicalism into the hard core rather than attaching it as an auxiliary hypothesis are, first, that dualism allows one to ignore much of biology in one's account of moral possibilities. I believe that evolutionary psychology and some of the developments in the neurosciences make highly valuable contributions to our understanding of the moral character of untutored and ungraced human nature. Second, it serves to distinguish this understanding of human nature and its *telos* from a very different view of the point of religious practice, which is aimed at development and liberation of the soul by means of ascetic discipline of the body. For a well-developed psychological program based on this dualist account of human nature (as found in religions across the spectrum, including Neoplatonic forms of Christianity), see Pitirim Sorokin's book *The Ways and Power of Love,* first published in 1954.[4]

Another aspect of my account of untutored nature comes from theology. Anabaptists in general take a more moderate view of the effects of the fall than do Reformed and Lutheran theologians. The sixteenth-century Anabaptists tended to teach that Christ's atoning death was for all humans, and it served to repair human nature; it restores free will. Christ the Eternal Word illuminates all humans everywhere, whether or not they acknowledge Christ personally.[5] So the effects of sin are not to be found in any innate perversion of the individual intellect, irremediable apart from participation in the community of Christ's followers, but rather in willfully chosen acts on the part of Christians and non-Christians alike. For the Radicals, then, concern for remedy for sin (beyond Christ's universal atonement) turns to practical issues of community discipline — to the practices described in Matthew 18 and 1 Corinthians 14:29. Thus, more significant than the fallen state of the individual is the fact that the church itself — designed by God to provide direction and support — has fallen. Specifically, at the time of Constantine it had fallen into collusion with the

4. Pitirim A. Sorokin, *The Ways and Power of Love: Types, Factors, and Techniques of Moral Transformation,* reprint ed. (Philadelphia: Templeton Foundation Press, 2002).

5. George Hunston Williams, *The Radical Reformation* (Philadelphia: Westminster Press, 1962), pp. 797-800, 840.

powers (a historical event, even if Adam and Eve's defection is symbolic rather than historical).

Jeffrey Schloss has helpfully distinguished among two major Christian positions regarding the relation between self-renunciation and lesser goods; his analysis provides a handy means for me to present the view I propose here. The more common approach he terms the "ordering of loves" tradition. This tradition

> conceives of the biological affinities and affections of human beings as good gifts from God. Like all gifts, especially living ones, they must be tended, disciplined, and cared for. But the view of humanity here is that we are capable of both great selfishness and great other-regard. Fulfillment comes from cultivating the latter. Radically self-relinquishing love is not taken to be necessarily a higher moral obligation than giving or receiving care for near and dear. In fact, if radical altruism involves neglecting or betraying the trust and obligations of personal relationships, it may be immoral. Thus, "enemy love" is affirmed as consonant with and a gracious extension of the natural loves, rightly overseen and ordered.[6]

Schloss notes that this view fits better with biological accounts of un-graced human nature that place more stress on native benevolence.

The other major type of ethic Schloss describes he calls the "agapeist or dialectical perspective." This perspective

> views totally self-disinterested love as the chief moral obligation of human beings. This entails both the intensiveness of caring for others at great personal cost and the extensiveness of caring for those who are remote and even for those who are opposed to one's well-being. Extreme forms of this ethic give no preference to the natural embeddedness of personal relationships and in fact may claim that the natural loves are "carnal" or ultimately selfish.
>
> There are, however, a wide variety of Christian traditions that embrace less extreme versions of the agape ethic, while still holding the central tenet that agape is the highest love and is not an extension of but a supernatural addition to our enhancement of natural loves.

6. Jeffrey P. Schloss, "Emerging Accounts of Altruism: 'Love's Creation's Final Law'?" in Post et al., eds., *Altruism and Altruistic Love*, pp. 212-45; 236.

Some holiness traditions emphasize a second work of grace of "entire sanctification" as the portal to attaining wholly self-disinterested love of God and others. More modest versions simply emphasize a literal interpretation of the Sermon on the Mount as a prescription for right living, entailing the call to move beyond reciprocity to love of enemy.[7]

Schloss associates the more extreme versions of this view with the Anabaptists and a variety of Catholic monastic orders. It is consistent with the more negative accounts of human biological nature since there is usually a strong role for grace.

Schloss points out that it is possible to hold a median position between these two traditions, and this comes closest to my own view:

In this view, the natural loves are good gifts from God, in that they both enrich life and contain hints of a love beyond themselves. They are in no way intrinsically selfish, though they are prone to selfish distortion and, as is all human sentiment, are intrinsically feeble. Therefore, they call us beyond themselves both by virtue of their goodness and by virtue of their need to be sustained by resources greater than the natural affections they entail. . . . Anyone who has spouse, friends, or children knows that "love your enemy" can — and in a virtuous and committed relationship must — apply to the near and dear. Therefore, this third tradition recognizes that self-sacrificial altruism is not something that is extended only to the remote or extended to all without preference.[8]

3.2. *The Positive Heuristic*

The positive heuristic is a plan for developing a research program out of the assumptions provided by the hard core; this is where all the hard work appears. The ingredients that need to go into it are the definitions Hall and Lindzey call for, the specification of the most relevant empirical domain, relating of the theoretical content of the program to existing research, and development of additional testable hypotheses. Essentially

7. Schloss, "Emerging Accounts of Altruism," p. 236.
8. Schloss, "Emerging Accounts of Altruism," p. 238.

what I shall be doing in the rest of this chapter is a first approximation to a positive heuristic for the program I am suggesting.

However, there is another aspect to this mapping and planning exercise. We need a map of the territory that a complete psychological research program ought to address. The parallel here is my claim that a research program in theology needs to address, in light of the hard core, all of the standard topics that theologians regularly address. I am not as well qualified to map the territory of psychology as are many of my readers, but I shall offer a rough list of the subdisciplines that should be relevant in one way or another: personality theory, psychotherapeutic theory and practice; neuropsychology; cognitive psychology; developmental psychology — child, adolescent, adult and aging; family systems; psychometrics; organizational psychology; educational psychology; social psychology; and the study of interracial and interethnic relations.

These subdisciplines in the field all need to be "cross-matched" with the various dimensions listed above that go into spelling out the content of the program. I certainly cannot do this here, so here is my proposal. I shall proceed to discuss the development of a research program on the basis of my own very limited knowledge of the field, and readers who are specialists in one or more of these subdisciplines are invited to think along with me about what I should have included from within their own domain. This will be particularly relevant when I lay out some examples of research already in existence and formulate further hypotheses for testing.

So, the next steps in the development of the positive heuristic are to proceed to consider definitions, empirical models, existing research, and hypotheses for the future.

3.3. Definition of Theoretical Terms

Hall and Lindzey have helpfully reminded us that research requires definitions that relate the terms in the theoretical structure to observable or measurable variables. In my previous chapter I used Simone Weil's thought to begin to give some specificity to what is meant by self-renunciation. This will make a starting point for specifying the meaning of the hard core. I listed the following as aspects of such an ethic:

1. Detachment from material possessions
2. Renunciation of rights to rewards
3. Rejection of retaliation
4. Nonviolence
5. Acceptance of suffering
6. Submission to God

These are still fairly abstract concepts, but I believe that they are specific enough that a researcher would be able to operationalize them. I shall not say more here because my discussion, below, of some relevant research on altruism and forgiveness will enable me to provide some actual instances in which most of these concepts have been operationalized.

3.4. *The Empirical Domain*

All of human life and behavior is, of course, within psychology's proper domain of investigation. However, the account of the ideal form of human life defined by the hard core makes the development and behavior of certain groups and individuals particularly relevant. The Radical-Reformation researcher will want to study groups and individuals who come closest to exemplifying the ideal in order to gain insights into the factors that have facilitated their development. A good instance of a group worth historical study would be the early Quakers.

I turn briefly from saying what one *might* do if one were to pursue this research program to look at an actual instance of a life story that exemplifies the ideal I have been recommending. Iulia de Beausobre was, to begin with, a very ordinary Russian woman. She was arrested in the early 1930s during Stalin's regime. For three months she lived in solitary confinement, followed by three months of intense interrogation. She was then used for medical experiments and finally spent a year at hard labor. Most people subjected to these techniques collapsed in a matter of weeks. Iulia survived, and the person she became in the process provides a model of the six elements of a kenotic ethic that I have drawn from Weil's writings.[9]

9. I first learned of Iulia from a book by Diogenes Allen, *Traces of God in a Frequently Hostile World* (Cambridge, Mass.: Cowley, 1981). It may not be accidental that

Iulia expressed her understanding of the process of change she went through using the Christian concept of redemption. She claims that a victim must try to respond to her tormentors (the examining officers) in a redemptive manner. One does this by making oneself "invulnerable." This does not mean dulling oneself to the pain; rather, it means refusing to be hurt, to be damaged by it. She asks, "Can I experience the acuteness of all this sordidness without hating life and man? Can I possibly bear it with equanimity? The effort of keeping a clear awareness of my surroundings makes me go cold with clammy sweat. I set my teeth hard so they will not chatter."[10]

The victim must attempt to understand the tormentors without becoming sentimental and concealing their responsibility. All passions such as fear, self-pity, and despair must be controlled. Not everyone can do this. But for those who do, such an effort, Iulia claims, has two results:

> You realize that you have been privileged to take part in nothing less than an act of redemption. And then you find that, incidentally and inevitably, you have reached a form of serenity which is, if anything, more potent to counteract sadistic lusts than any barren impassivity could be. But to your mind, now, that is a minor matter. The direct and positive work of an effort applied in this way towards redeeming the deed is far too big and too thrilling for anything else to matter to you very much at the moment.[11]

Iulia explains how this is an act of redemption in a passage where she imagines a conversation between herself and the person she aspires to become. She calls this ideal person Leonardo:

> A great bond is formed, he says, between the man who is tortured day in, day out, and the man who day in, day out, tortures him. . . . If you ponder on this you may find the justification for your apparently absurd suffering.
>
> But, Leonardo, surely there is no justification for a crowd of well-

---

Iulia's story and Weil's ethic are similar, since Allen has written extensively on Weil. I shall follow Allen's synopsis. His quotations are taken from Iulia de Beausobre's *The Woman Who Could Not Die* (New York: Viking Press, 1938) and *Creative Suffering* (Westminster: Dacre Press, 1940).

10. Allen, *Traces of God in a Frequently Hostile World*, p. 62.

11. Allen, *Traces of God in a Frequently Hostile World*, p. 63.

fed, reasonably strong men bullying a weary, under-nourished, half-demented woman who doesn't even know what it is all about.

. . . If you want to understand, to know the truth about this sort of thing, you must rise higher and look deeper. If you do, you can transform the ghastly bond into that magic wand which changes horror into beauty. . . . It is unpardonable that anyone should be tortured, even you — if *you* merely leave it at that. But, surely, when you overcome the pain inflicted on you by them, you make *their* criminal record less villainous? Even more, you bring something new into it — a thing of precious beauty. But when, through weakness, cowardice, lack of balance, lack of serenity, you augment your pain, their crime becomes so much the darker, and it is darkened by you. If you could understand this, your making yourself invulnerable would not be *only* an act of self-preservation; it would be a kindness to *Them*. . . . Look right down into the depths of your heart and tell me — Is it not right for you to be kind to them? Even to them? Particularly to them, perhaps? Is it not right that those men who have no kindness within them should get a surplus of it flowing towards them from without?

The whole of me responds with a "Yes!" like a throb of thundering music. It is so shattering that it makes me stagger. The jailer steadies me. . . . "Oh, Leonardo, what if we are both only mad after all, my dear?"[12]

As the end of the passage indicates, Iulia fears for her sanity. Next she despairs. But it is then that Christ becomes present to her; she finds in him her security, "her invulnerability." She feels joy, serenity, and is empowered to love. The effect of Iulia's transformation was felt throughout the prison. The guards began to treat her with respect; the prison physician commented on the high morale in her cell block.

Iulia's response centered on submission to God and acceptance of suffering. I shall say more about her response in section 3.6.

3.5. Existing Empirical Research

I now turn to the topic of existing research, and I shall briefly survey studies done on altruism and forgiveness. Insofar as the research on altru-

---

12. Allen, *Traces of God in a Frequently Hostile World,* pp. 63-64.

ism makes use of concrete empirical procedures, it exemplifies the operational definition of several aspects of my account of self-renunciation. Some accounts of altruism involve the acceptance of suffering, others the willingness to part with material possessions for the sake of others. One particular piece of research deals specifically with renouncing rights to reward. Forgiveness research operationalizes the rejection of one's rights to retaliation and also, in a sense, the renouncing of one's right to reward.

Altruism is defined in various ways, including definitions so broad as to include bees dying as a result of stinging intruders in their hives. What we are interested in here is a human phenomenon in which a person acts for the benefit of another at cost to himself or herself.

C. Daniel Batson reports on a series of experiments he has done (with a variety of colleagues) to provide evidence for the existence of altruism. His motive is to counter the theory that all (apparently) altruistic action is actually undertaken for the benefit of the actor — in order to gain gratitude and admiration, to avoid guilt, and so on. Batson claims that this hypothesis of universal egoism is the most common assumption about human nature in Western thought. It is a difficult theory to refute because its proponents claim that even *if* one is motivated to increase another's welfare, such a person would be *pleased* by attaining that goal, and so would after all be acting in order to attain pleasure.[13]

Batson's research identified three classes of egoistic motives for helping others: (1) reward-seeking, including self-rewards; (2) punishment avoidance, including social and self-punishments; and (3) aversive arousal reduction — reducing the arousal produced by witnessing another in need. He and his colleagues then designed a series of experiments capable of teasing out each of these egoistic motives. For example, if one is acting in an apparently altruistic manner in order to attain a reward such as social approval, then one will not be much concerned about whether the attempt to help succeeds, since rewards are attached to trying to help even if the helper does not succeed. But if one is truly motivated by altruism, then the success will matter significantly.

Batson tested this in the laboratory by seeing whether individuals induced to act altruistically would report lower mood after an unsuccessful attempt to help. Participants were psychology students who listened

---

13. C. Daniel Batson, "Addressing the Altruism Question Experimentally," in Post et al., eds., *Altruism and Altruistic Love*, pp. 89-105; 89-90.

to a fictitious account of a confederate who claimed to have just experienced a mild electric shock. The participants were told that future shocks for the confederate could be avoided if they performed their assigned tasks successfully. Afterwards participants were informed that they had failed to save the confederate, and their mood after the experiment was compared to that before. Participants reported relatively strong negative mood changes. Other experiments involved asking the participants to take the confederate's place in receiving the shocks.

Reporting on twenty-five such experiments, designed to test for each of the egoistic hypotheses, Batson concludes that with remarkable consistency the results have shown patterns as predicted by the empathy-altruism hypothesis and have failed to support any of the egoistic alternatives.[14]

Notice how Batson's work operationalizes some of Weil's specifications of the meaning of self-renunciation. All of the experiments involved a cost of some sort to the participants, either expenditure of time or willingness to suffer shocks in place of the confederate. Batson tested explicitly whether the students were willing to renounce rewards in the process of helping someone else.

In considering predisposing factors for altruistic behavior, Batson reports that while general religious activity and interest are associated with more stringent moral standards and with *seeing* oneself as more concerned for others' welfare, when it comes to actual opportunities to assist someone in need, individuals who are more religious are not more helpful than the less religious "unless self-presentation concerns have been aroused"![15]

Batson remarks on the limitations of experimental research on altruism, and suggests that a complementary approach would involve interviews and analyses of the life histories of people who are well known for their altruistic behavior.[16] Kristen Renwick Monroe did just that. She conducted intensive interviews with three groups of people: philanthro-

14. Batson, "Addressing the Altruism Question Experimentally," p. 98.

15. Batson, "Addressing the Altruism Question Experimentally," p. 99; referring to Batson et al., "Religious Prosocial Motivation: Is It Altruistic or Egoistic?" *Journal of Personality and Social Psychology* 57 (1989): 873-84. I recall hearing in a sermon of a study involving seminarians who were sent to preach (on the story of the Good Samaritan) and had to pass by a confederate requesting help along the way. They tended to pass by.

16. Batson, "Addressing the Altruism Question Experimentally," p. 102.

pists, recipients of the Carnegie Hero Commission Award, and rescuers of Jews during World War II.

Monroe found that her subjects consistently differed from what the rational choice theory would predict. First, these people tended to act spontaneously rather than after performing a cost-benefit analysis. Second, they claimed not to have had a choice: "But what else could I do?" was their constant reply.[17] The one factor that Monroe found consistently to be determinative of their motivation was the perception of a shared humanity with those they helped.[18] Traditional religious affiliation did not appear to be a significant variable, but a commitment to a "spiritual life" did. Monroe cautions that the content of the spiritual life is critical, since some of the Nazis she interviewed justified their actions in terms of "matters of the spirit."[19]

Some of Monroe's cases provide clear exemplification of what it means to be detached from material possessions — many of those who housed and fed Jews barely had enough to eat themselves. Her subjects also exemplify lack of concern for rewards and willingness to suffer. Some exemplify submission to God as well.

In light of her research, Monroe concludes that the assumption of self-interest, which we might designate as the *core* thesis regarding human nature in the social sciences and in sociobiology, is simply *inadequate* to account for the actions of people such as her subjects:

> I am suggesting that an overemphasis on this one aspect of our complex human nature results in theoretical paradigms that limit our public policies, discourage altruism, and laud selfishness as the norm for human behavior. This is bad science. . . . It will be a major advance for social science to construct new theories that embrace a richer conceptualization of the self.[20]

Samuel Oliner reports on research he has done on Holocaust rescuers, aimed at locating causal factors. Over 700 rescuers were interviewed

---

17. Kristen Renwick Monroe, "Explicating Altruism," in Post et al., *Altruism and Altruistic Love,* pp. 106-22; p. 109.

18. Monroe, "Explicating Altruism," p. 110.

19. Monroe, "Explicating Altruism," p. 113. It would be important to know how she differentiates between religion and spirituality.

20. Monroe, "Explicating Altruism," p. 114.

and tested with scales for self-esteem, social responsibility, locus of control, empathy, and a "commonality scale" developed by him and a colleague.[21] Comparing responders with bystanders, Oliner determined that pity, compassion, and affection made up 76 percent of reasons for helping. Many included religious motivations. For example, Catholic nuns who saved Jewish children said that they asked Jesus for advice and always concluded that rescue was what he would have wanted. Nonetheless, he concludes that parental values and culture were importantly correlated with rescue behavior (for example, rescuers were more likely to have been disciplined by means of reason than by punishment), while religiosity per se was a lesser factor.

A brief report on three research projects that fall directly within the interest of the program I am attempting to promote shows, first, that the ethic of renunciation can be conceptually analyzed and defined operationally in such a way as to be amenable to empirical confirmation, and, second, that there is indeed some confirmation already available.[22] This confirmation consists, first, in showing that the major competing hypothesis of universal egoism is empirically unsubstantiated. Second, Monroe's and Oliner's studies tell us a little about what promotes altruism (and so also self-renunciation) — namely, a sense of one's ties to the whole human race, which has been inculcated by one's parents and culture. It is disappointing from a Christian point of view that the results are ambiguous regarding the causal role of religion. One would have hoped to find a clear correlation between Christian commitment and experience on the one hand and participation in altruistic action on the other.

Another current research effort that supports my program is in the area of forgiveness. Everett Worthington's name may be best known here. Insofar as forgiveness is an essential element of self-renunciation, Worthington's investigations of interventions that promote forgiveness exemplify the claim of my core thesis that empirical investigation of the conditions that facilitate development toward humankind's *telos* is possible.

21. Samuel P. Oliner, "Extraordinary Acts of Ordinary People: Faces of Heroism and Altruism," in Post et al., eds., *Altruism and Altruistic Love*, pp. 123-39; referring to S. P. Oliner and P. M. Oliner, *The Altruistic Personality: Rescuers of Jews in Nazi Europe* (New York: Free Press, 1988).

22. See Post et al., eds., *Altruism and Altruistic Love*, for an annotated bibliography of approximately seventy studies on various aspects of altruism.

Worthington argues that unforgiveness is very much like the effects of fear conditioning:

> Consider an unforgiving person. The person receives a hurt, offense, injustice, or rejection (unconditioned stimulus) from an offender (conditioned stimulus). Afterward, the unforgiving person sees the offender again. First he or she becomes tense, a vestige of orienting and freezing. Second, the stress-response system is activated. Third, the person tries to avoid or withdraw from the offender — to have little or no contact. Fourth, if withdrawal is not possible — because of inclusion in the same family or work unit — then anger, retaliation, and defensive fighting occur. Fifth, if such fighting is unwise, self-destructive, or futile, the person might exhibit the human equivalent of a submissive gesture — depression, which declares that the person is weak and needs succor.[23]

Given that interpersonal hurt is like fear conditioning, extinction is important but does not eliminate the conditioning. Worthington has developed a five-step process that has been shown to be effective:

1. Recall the hurt in an emotionally supportive environment.
2. Attempt to empathize with the person who caused the pain.
3. After recalling one's own need for forgiveness and becoming aware of the extent to which one's own forgiveness by others in the past was a gift, make a resolution to give the gift of forgiveness to the offender.
4. Make a public commitment to forgive.
5. Hold onto the forgiveness by repeating the first four steps if needed.

Worthington has begun to consider the relevance of his method, originally developed for interpersonal situations, for interventions in societies torn by violence and animosity.[24]

23. Everett L. Worthington Jr., "The Pyramid Model of Forgiveness: Some Interdisciplinary Speculations about Unforgiveness and the Promotion of Forgiveness," in *Dimensions of Forgiveness: Psychological Research and Theological Perspectives,* ed. E. Worthington et al. (Philadelphia: Templeton Foundation Press, 1998), pp. 107-37; 113. This volume includes an annotated bibliography of approximately sixty studies on forgiveness.

24. See Everett L. Worthington Jr., "Unforgiveness, Forgiveness, and Reconcilia-

An alternative approach to forgiveness is to study the reasons why people hold grudges. Roy F. Baumeister and colleagues have examined the advantages that motivate one to hold on to the role of victim: it allows one to occupy the moral high ground, it may allow the victim to extract practical or material benefits from the perpetrator, and it may prevent the perpetrator from committing similar acts in the future. So we see that forgiveness involves not only the rejection of retaliation but also may involve renouncing one's rights to rewards and other material benefits.[25]

Another important factor is the different perceptions victim and perpetrator tend to have of the offense. Victims tend to see the act as "possessing severe consequences, as part of an ongoing pattern of misbehavior, as inexcusable and immoral, and as gratuitous." Perpetrators tend to perceive their act as "involving extenuating circumstances and mitigating circumstances, tend to downplay the consequences, [and] divide blame among many parties (including themselves)." Thus, "as soon as one payback makes one party think the two sides are now even, the other party is likely to think that the ledger is egregiously out of balance and that some retaliation is warranted."[26] So retaliation can clearly be shown to be *highly* unlikely to put an end to hostilities.

Thus, empirical studies of forgiveness provide another area in which existing research both operationalizes and confirms (to some small extent) the theses that form the core of my proposed research program.

3.6. Hypotheses for Future Testing

The research on altruism and forgiveness shows how a number of dimensions of self-renunciation can be studied. Of course, there is much

---

tion and Their Implications for Societal Interventions," in *Forgiveness and Reconciliation: Religion, Public Policy, and Conflict Transformation*, ed. Raymond G. Helmick, S.J., and Rodney L. Petersen (Philadelphia: Templeton Foundation Press, 2001), pp. 161-82.

25. Roy F. Baumeister, Julie Juola Exline, and Kristin L. Sommer, "The Victim Role, Grudge Theory, and Two Dimensions of Forgiveness," in Worthington et al., eds., *Dimensions of Forgiveness*, pp. 79-104.

26. Baumeister, Exline, and Sommer, "The Victim Role, Grudge Theory, and Two Dimensions of Forgiveness," p. 83.

more to be done along these lines; the two major volumes I have cited above include many proposals for further research.[27]

The research on altruism touches briefly on the issue of detachment from material possessions. Knowledge of what promotes such detachment would be extremely valuable in our increasingly materialistic and competitive society. Mennonites and other religious communities who live apart from society have found one strategy, but one that is not viable for many of us. Is there research that is relevant here?

Another topic is submission to God. The role of religious commitment in altruism has been investigated, but what leads to religious commitment itself? I suppose that there are conflicting theological perspectives on the question of whether empirical research can contribute to knowledge of how to bring about submission to God. At one extreme are denominations such as the Pilgrim Predestinarian Regular Baptist Church of Jesus Christ that have such a strong doctrine of predestination that they forbid missionary work.[28] The reasonable and surely most common view is that human means provide *formation,* which prepares for but does not compel God's *transformative* action. There is a significant body of literature on Christian formation; however, I am unaware of the extent to which the recommendations have been supported by empirical research. One might have some qualms about assigning some of our children or other seekers to the control group!

The major area where I would like to recommend research is on nonviolence. What factors predispose individuals and groups to choose nonviolent over violent strategies? How, and how well, does nonviolence work? There is in fact a huge body of historical work documenting the variety and prevalence of nonviolent techniques. There is also a respectable body of anecdotal evidence of its effectiveness.[29]

---

27. The work of Clements and Mitchell on parental sacrifice (Chapter 4, this volume) represents another promising line of investigation.

28. Arthur C. Piepkorn, *Profiles in Belief: The Religious Bodies of the United States and Canada,* vol. 2: *Protestant Denominations* (New York: Harper & Row, 1978), pp. 445-47.

29. Gene Sharp's *Politics of Nonviolent Action* (Boston: P. Sargent Publisher, 1973) is a 900-page volume including descriptions of 198 types of action, with a number of historical examples of each. See also Mulford Q. Sibley, *The Quiet Battle: Writings on the Theory and Practice of Non-Violent Resistance* (Boston: Beacon Press, 1963); William Robert Miller, *Nonviolence: A Christian Interpretation* (New York: Schocken Books,

In addition, there are intriguing hypotheses regarding the psychic mechanisms involved. For example, Richard Gregg describes it as moral jiu-jitsu. It throws the attacker off guard and creates feelings in conflict with the aggressive drive: first surprise, then sympathy and respect for the one who has been attacked. While the initial effect of the act of non-resistance may be to bring out a greater degree of sadism on the part of the attacker, the conflicting motives created by patient suffering often eventually bring the violence to an end. The suffering of the nonviolent resister is not incidental to the process; rather, it is a crucial ingredient, since it serves to alter the balance of motives and sympathies on the part of the attacker (and also of bystanders).

The positive reasons for nonviolence have to do with a sense of the moral worth and moral capacities of the attacker. The refusal to resort to violence even when attacked is intended to convey respect for the adversary. It is also expected to be the best way to touch a hardened heart. The goal is to allow the best of the attacker's motives to come to the fore in the hope of reconciliation. Gregg puts it this way:

> As to the outcome of a struggle waged by non-violence, we must understand one point thoroughly. The aim of the non-violent resister is not to injure, or to crush and humiliate his opponent, or to "break his will," as in a violent fight. The aim is to convert the opponent, to change his understanding and his sense of values so that he will join whole-heartedly with the resister in seeking a settlement truly amicable and truly satisfying to both sides. The non-violent resister seeks a solution under which both parties can have complete self-respect and mutual respect, a settlement that will implement the new desires and full energies of both parties. The non-violent resister seeks to help the violent attacker to re-establish his moral balance on a level higher and more secure than that from which he first launched his violent attack. The function of the non-violent type of resistance is not to harm the opponent nor impose a solution against his will, but to help both parties into a more secure, creative, happy, and truthful relationship.[30]

1966); and *Religion: The Missing Dimension of Statecraft,* ed. Douglas Johnston and Cynthia Sampson (New York: Oxford University Press, 1994).

30. Richard Gregg, *The Power of Nonviolence,* 2d rev. ed. (New York: Schocken Books, 1969), p. 51.

One subtle issue that needs to be addressed is highlighted by Iulia de Beausobre's distinction between two different ways of making oneself invulnerable. Iulia says,

> To a sadist you are of interest only for a particular series of reactions which he makes it his business and pleasure to provoke from you. . . . For the victim there is only one way open to save himself, and that is to fail to react at all: then, having ceased to be interesting, he will eventually be left alone.[31]

But there are two ways of failing to react. One is by becoming completely passive, but those who do "become clod-like, indifferent, subhuman."[32] The other is as described above. I venture to suggest that the kind of invulnerability Iulia recommends includes three factors:

1. Keen attention to what is going on.
2. Empathic understanding of the tormentors. This is comparable to Worthington's second step in forgiveness. As noted earlier, Iulia warns that it is not the same as becoming sentimental or passing over the evil of the tormentors' behavior.
3. Control of one's own emotional reactions such as fear and self-pity. On this issue, a valuable book is Marshall Rosenberg's *Nonviolent Communication*. He argues that compassion and nonviolence require that we stop thinking of others as causing our emotions; rather, their actions have an impact on the fulfillment of our needs. People can train themselves to recognize the contribution that they themselves make to the emotional impact and, in fact, take responsibility for their own emotional responses.[33] In Baumeister's terms, this is to give up the rewards that attach to playing the role of victim.

In effect, this response is based on a decision to give the gift to the tormentors of refusing to exacerbate the evil of their actions. For Iulia it was done in part by force of will (and so prior formation is relevant) but also as a result of God's transforming grace.

---

31. Quoted by Allen, *Traces of God in a Frequently Hostile World*, pp. 61-62.
32. Allen, *Traces of God in a Frequently Hostile World*, p. 62.
33. Marshall B. Rosenberg, *Nonviolent Communication: A Language of Compassion* (Encinitas, Calif.: PuddleDancer Press, 1999).

Understanding the difference between these two forms of "invulnerability" is essential for developing an ethic of self-renunciation and nonviolence. It will provide the key to answering the charge that such an ethic is negative and destructive, and the way toward a distorted humanity.

4. Conclusion

I have not said anything to elaborate on the intellectual humility that I mentioned in Chapter 2 as being an implication of an ethic of self-renunciation. I can speak to this issue from experience. I've concluded that there is no better way to instill a sense of humility in oneself than to spend days on end, alone, writing prescriptions for the redirection of a whole discipline that is not one's own. Is all I have written in these three chapters merely a philosopher's fancy? Some of it surely is, but I hope that I have accomplished at least three things:

1. convincing psychologists that their work is "theology-laden" whether they mean it to be or not;
2. persuading Christian psychologists to think about the ways in which their overt theological commitments may conflict with the assumptions embedded in their research; and
3. either by positive example or by "arousing disbelief and resistance" (cf. Hall and Lindzey), calling attention to the issues surrounding an ethic of nonviolence.

TWO   Extensions of the Model

Chapter 4 **Noncoercion, Nonviolence, and Sacrifice:**
Applications in Families

Mari L. Clements and Alexandra E. Mitchell

1. Introduction

In the early 1990s, a whimsical slogan was popular on the T-shirts, tote bags, and key chains of frazzled mothers in the United States. "Because I'm the mother, that's why!" was a lighthearted affirmation of parental authority and a not-so-subtle comment on the stresses of responding to inquisitive toddlers. Such a slogan was humorous not because it reflected what mothers habitually said, did, or thought, but because it reflected a wish that such a response could be used effectively. That is, it was humorous because sole reliance on parental power and authority to regulate children's behavior is a strategy destined to failure. Although in the short run, parents could potentially coerce a child's behavior, for long-term learning and behavior change, the child must internalize standards and master self-regulation. "Because I'm the mother, that's why" does not provide a compelling rationale that would result in lasting behavior change, but rather uses the current differential of power to make the child comply. In contrast, biblical instructions to parents stress the importance of instilling in the child an internal sense of what is right that will endure even after parents no longer wield direct power over the child (Prov. 22:6).

Examining the intersection of individual autonomy and power is important in understanding the long-term adjustment of children and families. In this chapter, we will review the relevant literature, which we argue demonstrates that the respectful use of power within family relationships provides the context in which family members flourish. In contrast, the abuse of power within families may sow the seeds of societal

79

aggression by imperiling the child's sense of self, undermining spousal trust, and destroying a family's ability to care for its members.

Nancey Murphy has argued for the application of a Radical-Reformation theology to psychology. Her formulation of this theology holds self-renunciation as central. Renunciation of the self for the good of the other is viewed as the greatest good to which humans can aspire. Specifically, Murphy cites the importance of noncoercion, nonviolence, and renunciation of rewards (sacrifice) in interpersonal relations, both on individual and global levels. In support of this thesis, she has cited examples of self-renunciation in inspirational acts of historical figures (e.g., Iulia de Beausobre and Mahatma Gandhi) and in research on altruism (e.g., the research of C. Daniel Batson and Kristen Renwick Monroe).[1]

Unfortunately, such a focus on peaceable means of relating has not always characterized the history of the church in the West. Religion has often played divisive and coercive roles in society and in family relations. Specifically, sacrifice has at times been forced upon women and children in the name of religion. Rather than being allowed to choose mutual submission under Christ (Eph. 5:21-22), some women have been coerced into sacrificing their goals, careers, gifts, and identities in the name of the church. Religion has also been used to justify coercive and aggressive forms of parenting, and the popular caricature of conservative Christian parents includes a heavy reliance on physical discipline.

Such coercive and aggressive family practices would appear to stand in direct contrast to Jesus' example of voluntarily laying his life down for the world. If his example and his call are to love one's enemy (Matt. 6:44), how much more should Christians strive to voluntarily sacrifice and support one another in their own families?

The critical roles of sacrifice and nonviolence are evident even in secular society. Human community cannot survive when threatened from within by violence and selfishness. Similarly, families are weakened by domestic violence, child abuse, and self-centeredness. Further, it is in families that children are first socialized, and thus the intergenerational transmission of values, including prizing nonviolence, noncoercion, and sacrifice, must be understood in the context of the family.

Murphy's tenets of self-renunciation in noncoercion, nonviolence, and sacrifice are thus examined in this chapter in the context of family rela-

1. See Murphy, Chapter 3, section 3.5, this volume.

tionships. The application of a Radical-Reformation theology in families is considered in the light of relevant research and theory in psychology. Such examination also allows for an investigation of Peacocke's hierarchy of the sciences as advanced by Murphy,[2] as the theoretical importance of theological constructs is tested in the application of psychological data and investigation. It is our position that the meaning and effects of coercion, violence, and sacrifice in families must be understood contextually, but that in each case, research supports striving for interactions that involve respectful uses of power that balance individual and communal needs to achieve desired ends through the least coercive methods available.

2. Self-Renunciation in Families

Examining self-renunciation in family relationships brings special challenges. Although the goals of noncoercion and nonviolence are laudable, their application is least ambiguous in relations among equals. Parent-child relationships, in contrast, are inherently hierarchical, and this hierarchy may give rise to intentional and unintentional coercion. For example, successful child socialization can be argued to include some degree of coercion. Furthermore, the prevalence of corporal punishment in American society means that many children are introduced to some level of violence in their own homes.

The hierarchy of parent-child relationships serves, in part, to advance children's socialization. For instance, children's wants and desires are at times incompatible with socially acceptable behavior or even with their own best interests. When a child wants to eat only chocolate chip cookies for breakfast, to chase a ball out into a busy street, or to climb out a window onto the roof, parents bear the responsibility for exerting power sufficient to derail the child's attempts to obtain those desires. Similarly, parents bear the responsibility for teaching their children the appropriate behaviors to display in social situations, even when their children would prefer to act in socially unacceptable ways. Indulging a child's unbridled curiosity (e.g., "Mommy, why is that lady so fat?"), untempered responses (e.g., "Yuck! Why'd you give me that stupid present?"), and unschooled behavior (e.g., running and shouting in situa-

2. Murphy, Chapter 1, section 4, this volume.

tions more suited to sitting and being quiet) may lead to inadvertent pain inflicted by the child and to social rejection of the child. In other words, responsible parents occasionally exert their will over their children's will; such behavior is, at least on some level, coercive.

Just as the hierarchy of parent-child relationships has an inherent degree of coercion, the use of corporal punishment prevalent in both churched and unchurched families in the U.S. introduces a level of violence in family relationships. Specifically, epidemiological research suggests that 94 percent of parents of preschool children have used corporal punishment,[3] and for nearly half of all children, physical punishment of some sort continues into the teen years.[4]

Parents in the church are not immune to the use of aggression, and in fact, it has been widely held that Christian families may use more physical punishment than do unchurched families. The actual research on this topic, however, reveals a more complex association. In a comprehensive review of the psychological and sociological literature, Annette Mahoney, Kenneth Pargament, Nalini Tarakeshwar, and Aaron Swank found that although conservative Christian parents endorsed the use of corporal punishment at higher rates than did non-Christian parents, the association between religion and actual use of corporal punishment was significantly weaker. That is, conservative Christian parents spanked their young children more frequently, but they were also likely to discontinue such punishment at high rates. In fact, by the time children reached adolescence, Christian parents did not differ from non-Christian parents in rates of physical punishment.[5]

Thus, if American familial contexts expressly include coercion, power, and even aggression, how do children develop into adults with

3. Murray A. Straus and Julie H. Stewart, "Corporal Punishment by American Parents: National Data on Prevalence, Chronicity, Severity, and Duration, in Relation to Child and Family Characteristics," *Clinical Child and Family Psychology Review* 2 (1999): 55-70.

4. Murray A. Straus and Glenda K. Kantor, "Corporal Punishment of Adolescents by Parents: A Risk Factor in the Epidemiology of Depression, Suicide, Alcohol Abuse, and Wife Beating," *Adolescence* 29 (1994): 543-62.

5. Annette Mahoney, Kenneth L. Pargament, Nalini Tarakeshwar, and Aaron B. Swank, "Religion in the Home in the 1980s and 1990s: A Meta-Analytic Review and Conceptual Analysis of Links between Religion, Marriage, and Parenting," *Journal of Family Psychology* 15 (2001): 559-96.

the capacity for self-renunciation as Murphy has described it? It is our premise that the respectful use of power within family relationships forms a model for children's exercise of their own power, both within the family and in their later individual and corporate relationships. Learning to respectfully use power provides the foundation from which coercion and violence may be eschewed and sacrifice may be chosen.

To this end, our treatment of noncoercion, nonviolence, and sacrifice in family relationships examines both respectful and abusive uses of power in parent-child and marital relationships. Specifically, the literature on parental warmth and control, on coercive family processes, on child abuse and domestic violence, and on interpersonal sacrifice seem directly relevant to the roles that noncoercion, nonviolence, and sacrifice may play in families.

3. Parental Warmth and Control

Parents' warmth and control are critical to their relationship with their children. The effective combination of parental warmth and control fosters the healthy psychological, social, and moral development of children and enables them to develop the ability to use their own power correctly in relationships with others.

Diana Baumrind's classic work on parenting styles examined parenting on the two dimensions of warmth and control.[6] Subsequent to Baumrind's initial introduction of the concept of parenting style, other researchers have extended and refined these ideas.[7] Most conceptualizations of Baumrind's parenting styles include four types of parenting: authoritative, authoritarian, permissive, and neglectful. Authoritative parents exhibit high levels of both behavioral control and warmth; authoritarian parents exhibit high levels of behavioral control but low levels of warmth; permissive (or indulgent) parents exhibit low levels

6. See Diana Baumrind, "Effects of Authoritative Parental Control on Child Behavior," *Child Development* 37 (1966): 887-907, and "Current Patterns of Parental Authority," *Developmental Psychology* 4 (1971): 12.

7. Eleanor Maccoby and John Martin, "Socialization in the Context of the Family: Parent-Child Interactions," in *Handbook of Child Psychology*, vol. 4: *Socialization, Personality, and Social Development*, ed. E. Mavis Hetherington and Paul H. Mussen (New York: Wiley, 1983), pp. 1-101.

of behavioral control but high levels of warmth; and neglectful (or laissez-faire) parents exhibit low levels of both behavioral control and warmth.

An examination of the authoritative and authoritarian styles is most relevant for the present discussion of the appropriate use of power in parenting. As noted above, authoritative and authoritarian styles are both characterized by high levels of parental control of children's behavior. However, authoritative parents, although firm, are also involved with, affectionate toward, and respectful of their children. Equally firm, authoritarian parents place a strong emphasis on obedience. In contrast to authoritative parents, however, authoritarian parents show little warmth in their interactions with children. Susie Lamborn, Nina Mounts, Laurence Steinberg, and Sanford Dornbusch described children of authoritarian parents as "overpowered into obedience,"[8] thus highlighting the coercive undertones of the authoritarian parenting style. Although the levels of parental control of children's behavior are similar in authoritarian and authoritative families, this control may be experienced as less negatively coercive by children of authoritative parents because of the warmth of the relationship in which the control is experienced.

Research has supported the theorized importance of the combination of parental warmth and control. As compared to other parenting styles, authoritative parenting has been shown to lead to healthy psychological development of children.[9] Authoritative parenting styles have been shown to be associated with healthy adjustment[10] and better school performance.[11] Of particular note, the benefits of authoritative parenting style have been shown to be similar across most ethnic groups, socio-economic

8. Susie D. Lamborn, Nina S. Mounts, Laurence Steinberg, and Sanford M. Dornbusch, "Patterns of Competence and Adjustment among Adolescents from Authoritative, Authoritarian, Indulgent, and Neglectful Families," *Child Development* 62 (1991): 1062.

9. Lamborn et al., "Patterns of Competence and Adjustment among Adolescents from Authoritative, Authoritarian, Indulgent, and Neglectful Families."

10. Dagmar Kaufmann, Ellen Gersten, Raymond C. Santa Lucia, Octavio Salcedo, Gianna Rendina-Gobioff, and Ray Gadd, "The Relationship between Parenting Style and Children's Adjustment: The Parents' Perspective," *Journal of Child and Family Studies* 9 (2000): 231-45.

11. Sanford M. Dornbusch, Philip L. Ritter, P. Herbert Leiderman, D. F. Roberts, and M. Fraleigh, "The Relation of Parenting Style to Adolescent School Performance," *Child Development* 58 (1987): 1244-57.

power (i.e., punishments that are overly harsh and motivated as much by parental anger as by child misbehavior).

Coercive family processes function to increase the probability of child aggression and child coerciveness. Both by being rewarded for their own aggression and by learning from their parents' explosive aggression, children in these families learn that aggression and coercion are effective means to desired ends. In this way, coercive family processes both teach children antisocial behaviors and fail to teach prosocial behaviors.[17]

In the absence of an adequate prosocial repertoire, it is not surprising that children in coercive families generalize their aggression outside the family context into the peer context.[18] The neglect of parental power coupled with periodic abuses of that power may lead children to use coercion in their own relationships.

In contrast, when parents appropriately use power to socialize their children — to train them in the ways that they should go — and when this power is accompanied by love, warmth, and concern for their children's well-being, children may learn empathy, compassion, self-reliance, and self-control. Such positive outcomes require that parents not rely upon brute coercion to socialize their children, but rather attend to their children's behavior and correct misbehavior in a timely and measured fashion (i.e., before such behavior has escalated out of control or has become an entrenched part of the child's repertoire).

5. Violence in Family Relationships

Intrafamilial violence represents a particularly noxious and coercive abuse of power. Violence in American families has reached such epidemic proportions that Jan Stets and Murray Straus suggested that the marriage license might well be renamed a hitting license.[19] Although re-

---

17. Capaldi and Patterson, "Interrelated Influences of Contextual Factors on Antisocial Behavior in Childhood and Adolescence for Males."

18. Rolf Loeber and Thomas J. Dishion, "Boys Who Fight at Home and School: Family Conditions Influencing Cross-Setting Consistency," *Journal of Consulting and Clinical Psychology* 52 (1984): 759-68.

19. Jan E. Stets and Murray A. Straus, "The Marriage License as a Hitting License: A Comparison of Assaults in Dating, Cohabiting, and Married Couples," *Journal of Family Violence* 4 (1989): 161-80.

search has demonstrated that corporal punishment, child abuse, and domestic violence tend to be correlated,[20] the issues surrounding parent-child violence and partner violence are sufficiently distinct that they will be reviewed separately.

5.1. Corporal Punishment and Child Abuse

The use of corporal punishment in families remains a controversial topic in the field of psychology. There are those who would call for a blanket injunction against its use,[21] there are those who would argue that it is an effective tool in parenting, and there are those who suggest that it is a complex phenomenon that may only be understood by examining intensity, frequency, consistency, and the nature of the parent-child relationship in which it occurs.

Although there is little consensus about the role that corporal punishment should play in family discipline, a greater consensus exists on its definition and its prevalence in American culture. Diana Baumrind, Robert Larzelere, and Philip Cowan note that the consensus in the field defines spanking, the most widely used form of corporal punishment, both in terms of what it is — an open-handed striking of buttocks or extremities administered with the intent to modify behavior — and what it is not — physically injurious.[22] That is, by definition, spanking does not inflict physical injury on the child. By extension, if corporal punishment cannot be child abuse, then child abuse cannot fall under the category of corporal punishment.

This separation of child abuse and corporal punishment is critical to

20. Elizabeth T. Gershoff, "Corporal Punishment by Parents and Associated Child Behaviors and Experiences: A Meta-Analytic and Theoretical Review," *Psychological Bulletin* 128 (2002): 602-11.

21. As an example of those who reject corporal punishment, see Gershoff, "Corporal Punishment by Parents and Associated Child Behaviors and Experiences." Among Christians, James Dobson is a well-known advocate of punishment. See his book *The New Dare to Discipline* (Wheaton: Tyndale House, 1992). For the complexity view, see Ross D. Parke, "Punishment Revisited — Science, Values, and the Right Question: Comment on Gershoff (2002)," *Psychological Bulletin* 128 (2002): 596-601.

22. Diana Baumrind, Robert E. Larzelere, and Philip A. Cowan, "Ordinary Physical Punishment: Is It Harmful? Comment on Gershoff (2002)," *Psychological Bulletin* 128 (2002): 580-89.

the understanding of corporal punishment and its effects on children. As noted earlier, 94 percent of American parents have spanked their preschool child,[23] and these numbers have remained relatively stable since the middle of the twentieth century.[24] The use of corporal punishment has been identified as a risk factor for child abuse,[25] and in fact, there are those who would argue that corporal punishment and child abuse are essentially the same entity, distinguished only by degree.[26] The relation between corporal punishment and child abuse, however, is something like the relation between rectangles and squares. Just as all squares are rectangles but not all rectangles are squares, parents who are physically abusive have used corporal punishment, but not all parents who use corporal punishment become physically abusive. Much of the research on corporal punishment has failed to screen out overly harsh and abusive practices,[27] and thus has inadvertently confounded corporal punishment with child abuse.

Making clear the distinction between child abuse and corporal punishment is critical to understanding the effects of corporal punishment on children. As Baumrind and her colleagues noted, unintentionally including parents who are physically abusive in a study of corporal punishment would necessarily distort the findings of the study, potentially leading to more negative conclusions about corporal punishment than are actually warranted.[28] For instance, Ronald Rhoner, Shana Bourque, and Carlos Elordi found that corporal punishment was related to children's maladjustment only if it was experienced in a relationship that the children viewed to be rejecting.[29] That is, corporal punishment by itself did not

23. Straus and Stewart, "Corporal Punishment by American Parents."

24. Robert R. Sears, Eleanor E. Maccoby, and Harry Levin, *Patterns of Child Rearing* (New York: Harper & Row, 1957).

25. Straus and Kantor, "Corporal Punishment of Adolescents by Parents."

26. Gershoff, "Corporal Punishment by Parents and Associated Child Behaviors and Experiences."

27. Baumrind et al., "Ordinary Physical Punishment"; Parke, "Punishment Revisited."

28. Baumrind et al., "Ordinary Physical Punishment."

29. Ronald P. Rhoner, Shana L. Bourque, and Carlos A. Elordi, "Children's Perceptions of Corporal Punishment, Caretaker Acceptance, and Psychological Adjustment in a Poor, Biracial, Southern Community," *Journal of Marriage and the Family* 58 (1996): 842-52.

predict children's adjustment. Rather, corporal punishment in the context of lack of parental acceptance predicted children's adjustment.

The arguments for a ban on corporal punishment are founded in part on the conclusion that corporal punishment carries the risk for escalation into physical abuse.[30] This risk is certainly real and nontrivial; parents who never hit their children cannot hit them too hard, for instance. However, a comparison of the prevalence rates of corporal punishment and physical abuse clearly implies that the vast majority of "rectangles" are not in fact "squares": most American parents seem able to make the appropriate distinctions between punishment and abuse. At the same time, completely nonviolent parenting is sufficiently rare in the United States as to be extraordinarily difficult to study.

For the children of those parents who cross the line separating corporal punishment from physical abuse, the results are significant and sobering. Physically abused children are at significantly increased risk for such outcomes as lower self-esteem, poorer prosocial functioning, greater peer withdrawal, greater depression, more externalizing behavior problems, more psychological symptoms, and more borderline personality features.[31] College students who reported abuse in childhood were also less likely to engage in problem-solving strategies that involve collaboration with or deferring to God.[32] Further, children who are abused are more likely to abuse their own children.[33]

30. Gershoff, "Corporal Punishment by Parents and Associated Child Behaviors and Experiences"; Murray A. Straus, *Beating the Devil out of Them: Corporal Punishment in American Families and Its Effects on Children* (New Brunswick, N.J.: Transaction, 2001).

31. Melora Braver, Jeanne Bumberry, Kimberly Green, and Richard Rawson, "Childhood Abuse and Current Psychological Functioning in a University Counseling Center Population," *Journal of Counseling Psychology* 39 (1992): 252-57; Kenneth A. Dodge, Gregory S. Pettit, John E. Bates, and Ernest Valente, "Social Information-Processing Patterns Partially Mediate the Effect of Early Physical Abuse on Later Conduct Problems," *Journal of Abnormal Psychology* 104 (1995): 632-43; Joan Kaufman and Dante Cicchetti, "Effects of Maltreatment on School-Aged Children's Socioemotional Development: Assessments in a Day-Camp Setting," *Developmental Psychology* 25 (1989): 516-24.

32. Marcia Webb and Kara J. Otto Whitmer, "Abuse History, World Assumptions, and Religious Problem Solving," *Journal for the Scientific Study of Religion* 40 (2001): 445-53.

33. Richard E. Heyman and Amy M. Smith Slep, "Do Child Abuse and Interparental Violence Lead to Adulthood Family Violence?" *Journal of Marriage and the*

The presence of such pervasive effects and intergenerational transmission should not be surprising either to those who understand social learning theory or to those have taken seriously the admonition of Exodus 34:7 that the sins of the fathers are visited on children and grandchildren. In this way, the perversion of parental power and authority through abuse leaves a legacy of pain and suffering that children are far too likely to re-enact in their own relationships as adults.

5.2. Domestic Violence

Richard Heyman and Amy Smith Slep found that the risk of both domestic violence and child abuse in families was increased incrementally by the exposure to different types of violence in the family of origin. Specifically, women who both were abused as children and observed interparental violence were more likely to abuse their own children, to perpetrate domestic violence, and to be abused by their partners. Men in this study who were both abused and witnesses to interparental violence were twice as likely to be victims of domestic violence. Exposure to either type of family violence placed men at increased risk for both abusing their children and abusing their partners.[34] The flip side of these statistics is, of course, that men and women who were neither victims of child abuse nor observers of interparental violence were far less likely to abuse their own children or to be involved in domestic violence as either perpetrators or victims.

The effects of witnessing interparental violence are not limited to difficulties in later relationships, however. Mari Clements and her colleagues found preschool children of physically aggressive marriages to evidence heightened behavioral dysregulation, poorer self-esteem, and greater teacher-, parent-, and self-reported behavior problems as compared to children of nonaggressive marriages.[35]

Family 64 (2002): 864-70; Joan Kaufman and Edward Zigler, "Do Abused Children Become Abusive Parents?" *American Journal of Orthopsychiatry* 57 (1987): 186-92.

34. Heyman and Smith Slep, "Do Child Abuse and Interparental Violence Lead to Adulthood Family Violence?"

35. Mari L. Clements, David W. Randall, Sarah E. Martin, and Karen G. Lim, "The Utility of Child and Parent Perceptions of Marital Conflict in Predicting Preschool Children's Adjustment," manuscript submitted for publication (2004); Sarah E. Martin

Taken as a whole, the literature on domestic violence suggests that children of violent marriages are at increased risk for being abused as children, for developing a variety of emotional and behavioral difficulties, for perpetrating abuse on their own partners and children, and for being victims of domestic violence as adults.[36] In a very real sense, violence in families appears to feed upon itself, spilling over from one relationship into another.

Given the abundant evidence for the negative consequences of child abuse and domestic violence, it is clear that such violence has no place in Christian marriages and families. We would argue that those who translate "He who withholds his rod hates his son, but he who loves him disciplines him diligently" (Prov. 13:24, NASB) as authorization from God to abuse their children have misunderstood the purpose and meaning of discipline, which is ultimately to instruct. Violence, we would argue, teaches fear and distrust and promotes a perversion of parental power that is far removed from the loving parents Christians are called to be.

Further, we see no room for domestic violence in a relationship where husbands are called to love their wives as Christ loved the church (Eph. 5:25). Violence would seem to desecrate the "living and holy sacrifice" we as Christians are called to make (Rom. 12:1, NASB). If the animal sacrifices offered to the Lord were to be without blemish or spot (cf. Deut. 17:1), must God not be more grieved by bruises and broken bones in the living sacrifices of his people?

Thus, it is our position that although corporal punishment in the context of a warm and loving parent-child relationship may be an effective component of a broader stance toward discipline, actual violence in families is unacceptable on both psychological and theological grounds. Corporal punishment should be, at most, a small part of the parents' disciplinary repertoire and should be phased out as children grow and gain greater reasoning skills.

Violence demeans both the aggressor and the victim, and thus has no place in families. Both child abuse and domestic violence represent

---

and Mari L. Clements, "Marital Aggression and Child Adjustment: The Role of Children's Emotional and Behavioral Responding to Marital Conflict," *Journal of Child and Family Studies* 11 (2002): 231-44.

36. George W. Holden, Robert Geffner, and Ernest N. Jouriles, *Children Exposed to Marital Violence: Theory, Research, and Applied Issues* (Washington, D.C.: American Psychological Association, 1998).

dramatic misuses of power and lead to negative consequences for both the perpetrator and the victim. Parents who misuse their power in this manner fail to provide children with models of the respectful use of power, and children without effective and appropriate models often have significant difficulties in managing their own power.

6. Interpersonal Sacrifice in Family Relationships

Sarah Whitton, Scott Stanley, and Howard Markman defined sacrifice within couple relationships as referring to acts in which the individual gives up something of value in the interest of benefiting either the relationship or the partner.[37] That is, the immediate self-interest is foregone in the service of some greater good. This definition, although developed in work with couples, is also applicable to parent-child relationships.

For instance, an avid golfer might choose to give up a round of golf in favor of attending a jazz fest that is important to the partner. In couples with disparate work schedules, the partner with the later schedule may choose to get up early to spend time with the other before work. In parent-child relationships, a parent may choose to go to the child's baseball game, postponing work until after the child's bedtime. A parent may choose to forego a promotion because the concomitant long hours are perceived as a threat to family relationships. All of these sacrifices, both large and small, share three important similarities. First, the person is giving up something of value to the self in order to benefit the relationship or the relationship partner. That is, a sacrifice that does not matter to the person is not, in this conceptualization, a sacrifice at all. Second, the sacrifice is a choice. Such a point is important, given the history of sacrifices forced upon women and children in the history of the church. Compelled forfeitures, although perhaps no more or less painful than chosen sacrifices, are not sacrifices but rather results of coercion. Third, sacrifices are for the good of the other, not for the good of the self. In other words, the person is giving up something out of a genuine

37. Sarah W. Whitton, Scott M. Stanley, and Howard J. Markman, "Sacrifice in Romantic Relationships: An Exploration of Relevant Research and Theory," in *Stability and Change in Relationships,* ed. Anita L. Vangelisti, Harry T. Reis, and Mary Anne Fitzpatrick (New York: Cambridge University Press, 2002), pp. 156-81.

desire to help the other rather than out of any desire to induce guilt or to coerce future sacrifices.

In their review of the broader psychological literature on sacrifice, Whitton and her colleagues noted that the likelihood of sacrifice increases as degree of relation increases.[38] That is, just as coercion and violence appear to characterize family relationships, so does sacrifice. That is, sacrifice is more likely to occur in relationships that are loving and committed, such as spousal or parent-child relationships, as compared to those that are more transitory, such as casual dating or roommate relationships.[39]

In fact, some degree of sacrifice is necessary to ensure long-term human community. When people form a community, their individual needs necessarily conflict over time. Voluntary relinquishment of one's right to rewards is important for sustained harmonious interaction. In a society in which all members continually insisted on having their own way, chaos and conflict would inevitably result. Lasting associations and societal order depend upon the willingness to subjugate individual needs for the greater good at times.

Despite these apparent benefits, the role of sacrifice in relationships is controversial in the literature. Views of sacrifice range from viewing it as transcendent and important to seeing it as devaluing and risky. Criticisms of sacrifice have focused on the hazards of asymmetrical sacrifice. For instance, feminist theorists have held that women are socialized to sacrifice in relationships.[40] This socialization may lead them to sacrifice even when it is harmful to them to do so.[41]

---

38. Whitton et al., "Sacrifice in Romantic Relationships."

39. Paul A. M. Van Lange, Caryl E. Rusbult, Stephen M. Drigotas, Ximena B. Arriaga, Betty S. Witcher, and Chante L. Cox, "Willingness to Sacrifice in Close Relationships," *Journal of Personality and Social Psychology* 72 (1997): 1373-95; Whitton et al., "Sacrifice in Romantic Relationships"; Sarah W. Whitton, Scott M. Stanley, and Howard J. Markman, "If I Help My Partner, Will It Hurt Me?: Perceptions of Sacrifice in Romantic Relationships," manuscript submitted for publication (2003).

40. Positive interpretations of sacrifice include Howard M. Bahr and Kathleen S. Bahr, "Families and Self-Sacrifice: Alternative Models and Meanings for Family Theory," *Social Forces* 79 (2001): 1231-58. On the negative side, see Nancy C. Atwood, "Gender Bias in Families and Its Clinical Implications for Women," *Social Work* 46 (2001): 23-36.

41. Dana C. Jack, *Silencing the Self: Women and Depression* (Cambridge, Mass.: Harvard University Press, 1991).

Although this risk exists, both theoretical and empirical work has suggested alternate understandings of sacrifice. Howard Bahr and Kathleen Bahr wrote that although sacrifice could certainly be taken to unhealthy extremes, this did not undermine the importance of sacrifice in relationships. They viewed the sincere giving of self as more important than the giving of material objects.[42] Interestingly, this is the aspect of sacrifice that has been most criticized by feminist theorists as silencing the self.[43]

Empirical work has examined the links between sacrifice and individual and relationship functioning. Whitton and her colleagues found that the perception of sacrifice as harmful to the self was associated with higher levels of depressive symptoms and with lower levels of relationship satisfaction. However, two important points about this association bear noticing. First, these relations were observed for both men and women, suggesting that the gender of the person making the sacrifice is less important than the perception of harm. Second, perceptions of sacrifice as harmful to the self were related to the success of the relationship. That is, for both men and women, perceptions of sacrifice were associated with relationship quality, with individuals in stronger relationships more likely to be satisfied with sacrificing for their partner or for the relationship.[44] Similarly, Paul Van Lange and his colleagues found that willingness to sacrifice was associated with both relationship commitment and relationship stability.[45]

Research about sacrifice in parent-child relationships is far scarcer than research about sacrifice in adult relationships. In the absence of empirical data, it is impossible to draw firm conclusions. However, some of the principles extracted from couples research likely extend to parent-child relationships.

Specifically, as already discussed, the definition of sacrifice is likely to be similar in family relationships as in couple relationships with potentially few exceptions. Parental sacrifice, for instance, may be similar to, but potentially even more frequent than, partner sacrifice.[46] Parents often choose to forego their own best interests for the sake of the child.

42. Bahr and Bahr, "Families and Self-Sacrifice."
43. Jack, *Silencing the Self.*
44. Whitton et al., "If I Help My Partner, Will It Hurt Me?"
45. Van Lange et al., "Willingness to Sacrifice in Close Relationships."
46. Bahr and Bahr, "Families and Self-Sacrifice."

In fact, it could be argued that being a good parent is inherently a self-less act. Infants, for instance, are completely dependent upon their care-givers, and taking care of infants entails sacrifices. These sacrifices are sufficiently frequent and routine that they may not even be experienced as sacrifices, but they do require the renunciation of the parents' self-interests. As examples, parents would almost certainly prefer to sleep than to get up for three A.M. feedings, and few individuals find changing diapers inherently rewarding.

On the other hand, the very nature of parental sacrifices may create the biggest problem for the definition outlined above. Their routine and necessary nature may run counter to the idea of choice required in the three-part definition of sacrifice. That is, although the parents clearly subjugate their own desires to the needs of the child, these sacrifices may be made out of a sense of necessity rather than any clear sense of choice.

The issue of choice also creates difficulties when considering children's sacrifices. The hierarchy of parent-child relationships may create barriers to (though not completely preclude) children's free choice to sacrifice. That is, children may perceive pressure to give up their own best interests for the good of others. Such pressure in a hierarchical relationship may make it difficult for a child to truly and freely choose to sacrifice. If a child chooses to sacrifice out of a desire to please the parent and thus be rewarded with the parent's affection or regard, then the goal of benefiting the other was not truly met. Nonetheless, parental valuing and modeling of sacrifice are crucial to children developing their own sacrificial proclivities.

In addition to definitional similarities, sacrifice in parent-child relationships may well function similarly to the way it functions in couple relationships. However, issues of perceived duration of the relationship may be less relevant to parent-child relationships than they are to couple relationships. In this sense, the parent-child relationship is by default long-lasting. Even in the case of marital dissolution, noncustodial parents may remain active and involved in their children's lives.[47]

However, other aspects of sacrifice may reasonably be expected to perform similarly in parent-child and couple relationships. Specifically, perceptions of sacrifices as harmful to the person would be expected to be associated with poorer individual and relationship outcomes. In a

---

47. Amato and Gilbreth, "Nonresident Fathers and Children's Well-Being."

similar manner, sacrifice in stronger relationships would be expected to be perceived as more satisfying for both parents and children.

In addition to having empirical and theoretical support, sacrifice also has biblical support. The most obvious example is Jesus' sacrificial life and death, but Christians also have been exhorted to bear each other's burdens (Gal. 6:2), to go the second mile (Matt. 5:41), and to forgive those who repeatedly wrong them (Matt. 18:22). The clear expectation is that Christians are to be a sacrificial people. This bearing of burdens implies a giving of self that Bahr and Bahr argued to be the purest form of sacrifice.[48]

Perhaps even more so than noncoercion and nonviolence, sacrifice represents an affirmative example of the respectful use of power. Whereas noncoercion and nonviolence represent the restraint of power, sacrifice reflects an active giving up of power. In sacrificing, the person chooses to give up something of value in order to improve the functioning of the relationship partner or the relationship itself. It is perhaps in sacrifice that parents best model for their children the respectful use of power. Both in their parents' sacrifice for each other and in their parents' sacrifices for them, children observe self-renunciation in action. Such sacrifices may play critical roles in enabling children to respectfully exercise their own power, both in sacrificing for others and in eschewing coercion and violence in their interactions with others.

In this, we would heartily agree with Murphy's hypothesis that the use of the least possible coercive strategy will enable future interactions to be even less coercive.[49] Further, we believe that the data suggest that whereas coercion breeds increased coercion,[50] decreased coercion creates the environment in which children may flourish. That is, children who are reared in atmospheres that are minimally coercive, minimally violent, and appropriately sacrificial are expected to become adults who will both value and practice noncoercion, nonviolence, and sacrifice.

However, as we have said above, "least coercive" does not imply the absolute absence of coercion. The respectful use of parental power demands that parents neither abuse nor abdicate their power. Effective child-rearing involves exerting parental control in the context of a warm

48. Bahr and Bahr, "Families and Self-Sacrifice."
49. Murphy, Chapter 2, this volume.
50. Patterson, *Coercive Family Process.*

and loving relationship, establishing limits with both clear expectations for adherence and appropriate consequences for violation, and respecting the gifts of the child with careful attention to the need for parental guidance and discipline.

In the context of such effective parenting, children may grow into adults who will in turn model noncoercion, nonviolence, and sacrifice in their own families, communities, and nations. The impact on the world of a generation of such adults is potentially enormous, and would indeed constitute a radical reformation.

Chapter 5 ## Radical-Reformation Theology and the Recovery of the Proper Incarnational View of the Self

CYNTHIA NEAL KIMBALL

1. Introduction

Self-actualization and self-fulfillment have been the goal of many a therapeutic outcome as well as a theoretical ideal for personality development. Indeed, more ink has been spilt in the past century extolling the virtue of self-fulfillment and self-esteem than on self-sacrifice. By contrast, Nancey Murphy extols the kenotic self. She asserts, "The paradoxical nature of an ethic of self-sacrifice or renunciation is captured in Jesus' saying that those who try to make their life secure will lose it, but those who lose their life will keep it (Luke 17:33)."[1] With this she presents us with a kenotic ethic of self-renunciation as the ultimate good for human life. Taking up the cross is the way to imitate Christ. She charges psychologists to apply this ethic to protect those who have been oppressed and abused, who have no "self" to renounce.

I will explore this question by asserting that the early view of Christology, without intending to, has led to a distorted view of the Incarnation and, subsequently, a distorted view of the self. This distortion has rendered the kenotic notion of self-renunciation irrelevant when considering the notion of human flourishing. Too much emphasis has been placed on individualistic views of self, sanctification, and how these affect gendered roles and rules. In contrast, a Radical-Reformation Christology, particularly the strong conviction of the call to nonviolence, provides a proper incarnational vision for understanding self-renunciation. Self-renunciation requires a nonviolent view that intrinsically avoids

1. See Murphy, Chapter 2, section 5, this volume.

placing arbitrary gendered roles and rules upon people based on their anatomy. The purpose of this chapter is to show ways in which we can begin to understand how the "loss of self" can be properly redeemed. I will analyze how loss of self (based on gendered roles and rules) affects women and men differently.

First, I will explore the scholarship contributed from feminist psychology, and in particular, the self-in-relation model.[2] Radical-Reformation Christology is relevant to this work. Recent empirical studies on women's development have established that many adolescent girls confront a significant developmental crossroad. While traditional theories argued that the adolescent years were ones of separation and independence, these studies show the importance of connections and strong relationships. As a result, adolescent women face contradictory developmental tasks. Many of these young women choose to silence the self in an effort to maintain relationships. This phenomenon is called the "lost voice," in which "some girls, who in pre-adolescence demonstrate a strong sense of self, begin in adolescence to renounce and devalue their perceptions, beliefs, thoughts, and feelings."[3] Against the background of a kenotic Christology, such a girl would grow up to be a woman unable to renounce a self, because she has no self to renounce. By "self" I mean an articulate view of values, beliefs, perceptions, and so forth that is represented in her "voice." One who has no "voice" doesn't really feel safe or secure in relationship but gives herself up because connection has become so important. I will talk about how the cultural myth (often prevalent in the church) of the "perfect girl" (or "perfect Christian girl or woman") plays a critical role in this. A Radical-Reformation Christology is particularly relevant to this issue because of its incarnational view that prohibits violence played out in gendered roles and rules.

Second, the current work on boys' and men's development yields a similar conclusion. William Pollack, a Harvard psychologist well known for his work with boys and men, believes that boys, feeling ashamed and

2. See C. N. Kimball, V. Creighton, and H. DeVries, "Self-in-Relation: An Anabaptist, Feminist Theological and Psychological Model of Agency and Connection," in *Religion, Marriage, and Family,* ed. Mary Stewart Van Leeuwen and Don Browning (Grand Rapids: Eerdmans, forthcoming).

3. Lori Stern, "Disavowing the Self in Female Adolescence," in *Women, Girls, and Psychotherapy: Reframing Resistance,* ed. Carol Gilligan, Annie G. Rogers, and Deborah L. Tolman (New York: Harrington Park Press, 1991), p. 109.

frightened of vulnerability, mask their emotions and ultimately their true feeling selves.[4] This unnecessary disconnection — from family and then from self — causes many boys to feel alone, helpless, and fearful. Yet society's prevailing myth that "boys don't cry" essentially leaves them with the notion that boys don't feel. When a boy finds himself feeling fear or vulnerability, he worries about not being "man enough." He feels ashamed, but must mask that shame. Over time, he risks losing touch with his emotions — not only the ability to express them but, more importantly, the ability to even feel them. Pollack talks about boys using these masks to hide their deepest thoughts and feelings — their real selves — from everyone, even the people closest to them. This mask of masculinity enables the boy to make a bold (if inaccurate) statement to the world: "I can handle it. Everything's fine. I am invincible." Pollack labels this the Boy Code. I will explore the implications of the Incarnation for this distorted and gendered role and rule.

2. Girls and Women

Feminist clinical theorists have traced in girls' voices a developmental transition during early adolescence from a view of self as strong and confident to a view of self that is dissociated from experience. Thus, the young girl who has the "capacity to speak one's mind with all one's heart" becomes the girl who no longer recognizes the authority of her own voice. She doubts that she knows what she knows. As she loses her voice, she loses her courage.

Lyn Mikel Brown and Carol Gilligan describe the development of the "perfect girl" who maintains silence rather than speak her true feelings, which she comes to consider "stupid," "selfish," "rude," or just plain irrelevant.[5] A repudiation of self emerges as the perfect girl, who must be both perfectly nice and perfectly smart, suppresses her own desires in order to meet the needs of others and make them happy. At the threshold of adolescence, the eager young woman learns that to be a

4. William S. Pollack, *Real Boys: Rescuing Our Sons from the Myths of Boyhood* (New York: Random House, 1998).

5. Lyn Mikel Brown and Carol Gilligan, *Meeting at the Crossroads: Women's Psychology and Girls' Development* (Cambridge, Mass.: Harvard University Press, 1992).

"good" woman, she must get along with everyone and never reveal particular feelings, such as anger, passion, sadness, or even excessive excitement. She is taught that the experiential knowledge that comes from within oneself is not safe to talk about because it may express something that is less than "perfect" or "normal." Brown and Gilligan call the trap of trying to live up to this oppressive idealized image the "tyranny of nice and kind."[6] These girls silence themselves and police each other. This policing also comes from well-intended, "good" older women.

Girls and women strive for these standards because they feel that this is the kind of girl/woman with whom everyone wants to be. The perception is that her perfect qualities make her worthy of inclusion.[7] Consistently, these clinical theorists found young women who cared so much about relationships of love and acceptance that they sacrificed their voices, their selves, for the sake of those relationships. Relationships are held out as the ultimate goal, but the image of the perfect girl is an unattainable ideal.

Karen Horney wrote about this when she asserted that we are all born with a "real self."[8] Christians may, perhaps, identify this real self with the self that God created. With others' appraisals and disapprovals, we may learn to despise this real, created self, and begin to develop an "ideal" and artificial self that everyone will love and accept. We fall under what Horney calls the "tyranny of the shoulds." We think that if we follow all the "shoulds" written by the others in our lives, we will be loved and feel secure.

Gilligan and her colleagues use the example of Sheila, who was interviewed several times between the ages of fourteen and sixteen.[9] At fourteen, Sheila makes decisions for herself, knowing that others' love for her is not dependent upon her choices to go along with them or not. She is confident in her subjective knowledge and trusts it. By the age of sixteen, however, Sheila has decided to disavow herself in order to "pro-

---

6. Brown and Gilligan, *Meeting at the Crossroads,* p. 53.

7. Elizabeth Debold and Lyn M. Brown, "Losing the Body of Knowledge: Conflicts between Passion and Reason in the Intellectual Development of Adolescent Girls." Paper presented at the annual meeting of the Association for Women in Psychology, Hartford, Connecticut, March 1991.

8. Karen Horney, *Neurosis and Human Growth* (New York: W. W. Norton, 1950), p. 17.

9. Gilligan et al., eds., *Women, Girls, and Psychotherapy.*

tect her feelings, thoughts and beliefs from the criticism she feels certain would follow if she expressed them." She shuts out those who criticize her by agreeing with them while knowing the truth — that is, that they do not know her. She succeeds in defeating them, but defeats herself in the process and eliminates the possibility of being "honest in relationships."[10]

Sheila fully understands her choice to disavow herself. She knows that she is harming herself and is not allowing herself to enter into the relations that are so important to her, yet feels helpless. She cannot reveal her true, well-articulated self to anyone, and cannot let it into relationships. She uses the metaphor of the sinking ship to describe this inherent dichotomy that results when "relationships are sacrificed in hopes of preserving the self which depends on its relationships."[11]

Sheila has a new boyfriend and has decided not to voice her own wishes. In this case, she is certain that it is not in her best interest to continue her relationship with him, as he is several years older and involved with drugs. However, she expects that she will abandon her resolve to break up with him. She is having migraines because of her troubling dilemma but fears she would upset him if she were to bring up her true feelings. In this case, she feels both that she must speak and that she cannot. She describes her dilemma with startling clarity: "It is like two people standing on a boat that they both know is sinking. I don't want to say anything to you because it will upset you and you don't want to say anything to me because it will upset you. And we are both standing here in water up to our ankles watching it rise and I don't want to say anything to you."[12]

Thus, in an effort to become "perfect girls," these young girls not only silence themselves but also act contrary to their internal voice for the sole purpose of maintaining relationships. This, again, is the "lost voice" phenomenon. "Voice" is conceived of as the core of a person's self. Dana Jack believes that a person's voice is an indicator of the self and observes that the loss of voice often coincides with the loss of self.[13] On the one hand, when a person speaks her feelings and thoughts, she is

---

10. Gilligan et al., eds., *Women, Girls, and Psychotherapy,* p. 107.

11. Gilligan et al., eds., *Women, Girls, and Psychotherapy,* p. 112.

12. Gilligan et al., eds., *Women, Girls, and Psychotherapy,* p. 108.

13. Dana Jack, *Silencing the Self: Women and Depression* (Cambridge, Mass.: Harvard University Press, 1991).

"creating and maintaining" her voice and exhibiting her authentic self. On the other hand, when a person devalues or does not use her voice, she is portraying a false self and instilling a perpetual sense of self-doubt about the legitimacy of her true thoughts and feelings.

Lyn M. Brown argues that during this developmental stage, an adolescent female faces the dilemma between needing to stay connected to others and needing to use her voice.[14] If the young adolescent chooses to avoid conflict in her relationships by silencing herself, she risks herself and her feelings. Alternatively, she can remain true to herself and her voice while staying involved in a conflict, but she risks losing the relationship and must suffer the subsequent feelings of isolation, rejection, and abandonment.

In other words, young women may experience extreme distress if the use of their voice costs them a relationship or, conversely, if they maintain the relationship at the cost of their genuine "voice." On a similar note, Brown and Gilligan found that young women who have lost their voice often end up doing things they do not want to do and stay in relationships that are not beneficial to them.[15]

In research that I conducted with Michael Mangis, we found that adolescent girls who had engaged in unwanted sexual experiences to avoid conflict and disruption in the relationship were more likely to exhibit a silencing of their voice in relationships.[16] Consistent with the research reported above, the category of greatest significance, from our findings, was the category of the "lost voice." We were struck by the numbers of stories in which the women did not tell of rape or physical coercion, but gave accounts of finding themselves in situations where they were sexually involved to a greater degree than desired, without a voice to bring a stop to the situation. For example, in many of the stories the women indicated that they were saying "No" on the inside but could not muster the voice to verbalize to the other person how they actually felt. A 21-year-old college senior said, "I found it hard to say no. NO! was running through my mind but I just couldn't say it till afterward."

14. Lyn M. Brown, "Telling a Girl's Life: Self-Authorization as a Form of Resistance," in Gilligan et al., eds., *Women, Girls, and Psychotherapy*, pp. 71-86.

15. Brown and Gilligan, *Meeting at the Crossroads.*

16. Cynthia J. Neal and Michael W. Mangis, "Unwanted Sexual Experiences among Christian College Women: Saying No on the Inside," *Journal of Psychology and Theology* 23 (1995): 171-79.

In their own descriptions these women would often say that they simply felt paralyzed, or that they had no right to stop what was happening. Some of these stories were linked to explanations that males were given certain prerogatives or authority over women or that they carry the brunt of the responsibility for behavior within the relationship. Here is a sampling of these stories:

> I was involved in a serious dating relationship with a boy two years older than me who I viewed as a spiritual mentor (at the time he wanted to be a youth pastor). He convinced me that everything other than actual intercourse before was all right. I didn't really feel the same but I figured he knew more than I did since he was older. (19-year-old college freshman)

> At age 15 I became sexually involved with my youth pastor. There was heavy petting but no intercourse. I knew it was wrong but I was emotionally dependent on him. (22-year-old college senior)

> There have been a few times when I felt like I couldn't say no to my boyfriend. I was afraid he'd get mad at me. (20-year-old college senior)

> I guess I have been manipulated into physical intimacy because of my terrible fear of being rejected by a man or of not being loved by him. I am luckily still a virgin, but I feel like some of my rights have been taken away from me, in relationships, that shouldn't have been played with. (19-year-old college freshman)

> Once something like this happens, it's very hard to say no to it later, even if you really want to (like I did). Each time it happens I feel cheaper, but it's hard to say no when you want to hold on to someone and you think this is the only way to keep them. (19-year-old college freshman)

> Just the fact that I couldn't say no to a guy even though I knew I should. I was not forced to do anything — I just didn't have the strength to say no. (21-year-old college senior)[17]

17. Neal and Mangis, "Unwanted Sexual Experiences among Christian College Women," p. 178.

These and other stories clearly reflect a common experience of women who feel they have lost their voices. In other words, these women were unable to voice their fears, desires, and conflicts, and hence were unable to act with their own authority. They spoke as if their will was subjugated to that of the male with whom they were relating. Young women like these grow up unable to renounce a self properly (as Christ calls us to) because they have lost a true sense of self. Again, by the loss of self, I am referring to a disavowal of personal views and beliefs in an effort to be loved and accepted.

3. Boys and Men

Boys learn very early from our culture that anything other than the masculine script is viewed as feminine and is unacceptable. This script describes certain ways to think, feel, and behave as a man. As Ronald Levant has argued, the fear of femininity and feminine values is a common result of male socialization.[18] Becoming a man entails learning not only what endeavors are consistent with being masculine, but what activities are considered feminine. As boys begin to consolidate their identity, they develop an acute sensitivity and ability to discriminate between masculine and feminine behavior, and they typically avoid anything associated with femininity.[19] Many conclude that being "masculine" is equivalent to not doing the kinds of things one would expect a woman to do.[20]

This too results in a loss of voice. As mentioned earlier, William Pollack believes that boys learn to mask their emotions.[21] He believes that the origin of this lies in the unnecessary emotional/parental disconnection expected of little boys. Both fathers and mothers are concerned that their boy will become a mama's boy, too dependent upon those early emotional ties. He must break away from mom in order to become a man. Pollack believes that the opposite is really true. A boy will separate from mom when he is ready, "but he will do better if he feels that there

18. *A New Psychology of Men,* ed. Ronald F. Levant and William S. Pollack (New York: Basic Books, 1995), p. 60.
19. Levant and Pollack, eds., *A New Psychology of Men,* p. 11.
20. Levant and Pollack, eds., *A New Psychology of Men,* p. 12.
21. Pollack, *Real Boys.*

is someone there to catch him if he falls."[22] When a boy feels disconnected from his family, he often begins to feel disconnected from his sense of self. These feelings of aloneness, helplessness, and fear are real and yet unacceptable by society's gendered illusions. This leaves a boy with the confusing message that these are not "male" emotions. Therefore, the boy has no way to articulate his sense of vulnerability. He begins to feel ashamed for not measuring up to the male standard, yet cannot talk about that either. "Over time, his sensitivity is submerged almost without thinking, until he loses touch with it himself. And so a boy has been 'hardened,' just as society thinks he should be."[23] In essence, the loss that the boy experiences is the "lost emotional self" and parallels the girls' lost sense of voice.

Pollack stresses the strength of the unwritten "Boy Code" of which all boys and men are aware. This code, learned early in life, gives the rules of conduct, the appropriate language that boys are to use, and so on. There are four injunctions that make up the framework of the Boy Code:

1. The "sturdy oak": [the imperative that] "a man never shows weakness."
2. "Give 'em hell": "the misconception that somehow boys are biologically wired to act like macho, high-energy, even violent super-men."
3. The "big wheel": "the imperative men and boys feel to achieve status, dominance, and power . . . the way in which boys and men are taught to avoid shame at all costs."
4. "No sissy stuff": "the literal gender straitjacket that prohibits boys from expressing feelings or urges seen (mistakenly) as 'feminine.'"[24]

Shame is the tool that powerfully forces boys and men to adhere to this code: "The isolation and humiliation we feel — and the feelings of emotional disconnection that result — are what psychologists call shame."[25] While girls may be shame-sensitive, boys are shame-phobic: "They are exquisitely yet unconsciously attuned to any signal of 'loss of

22. Pollack, *Real Boys,* p. 12.
23. Pollack, *Real Boys,* p. xxii.
24. Pollack, *Real Boys,* pp. 23-24.
25. Pollack, *Real Boys,* p. 32.

face' and will do just about whatever it takes to avoid shame."[26] Shame is an indicator of vulnerability and exposure, and men will go to great lengths to keep this masked.

The quest for manhood, to prove one's masculinity, is pervasive and formative in the early life of boys. They learn the Boy Code and strive to fulfill every injunction. In their effort to follow the code, boys begin to mask their emotions and thus their real selves. The emotional voice goes underground in an effort to prove one's manhood. Michael Kimmel writes,

> Manhood is less about the drive for domination and more about the fear of others dominating us, having power or control over us. Throughout American history American men have been afraid that others will see us as less than manly, as weak, timid, frightened. And men have been afraid of not measuring up to some vaguely defined notions of what it means to be a man, afraid of failure. . . . It's other men who are important to American men; American men define their masculinity, not as much in relation to women, but in relation to each other.[27]

Stephen Bergman offers another way to view male identity.[28] He suggests that men, like women, desire relationship and are unhappy when disconnected from others. They are dissatisfied with relationships that are less than mutually empowering. He presents us with a male self-in-relationship model that goes a step beyond Pollack's caution against the disconnection of boys from their mothers. This disconnection is more than maternal separation; it is a separation from a mutually empathic relationship. The self is disconnected from that early self-in-relation, disconnected from the ability to listen to the self's and/or others' feeling states. Bergman argues that the cultural pressure to disconnect in order to achieve maleness is essentially a disconnection from the very process of growth in relationship, a turning away from the whole relational mode.[29]

26. Pollack, *Real Boys,* p. 33.

27. Michael Kimmel, *Manhood in America: A Cultural History* (New York: Free Press, 1996), pp. 6-7.

28. Stephen J. Bergman, "Men's Psychological Development: A Relational Perspective," in Levant and Pollack, eds., *A New Psychology of Men,* pp. 68-90.

29. Bergman, "Men's Psychological Development," p. 75.

In this light, Bergman also talks about shame as being a familiar childhood experience for boys:

> It can begin with being teased for playing a girls' game or for being "chicken," and it becomes the companion of every soldier who, facing battle, dreads his own terror and the possibility that his unmanly fear will cause him to act like a coward. Boy culture is competitive, insensitive, and often cruel. Being chosen last, or not at all, is a vivid memory for many men. Being picked on, afraid to fight, or forced to fight generates a welter of intense feelings, with shame at the core.[30]

I remember my own son as he traversed the middle-school years. The most effective weapon that boys could use on other boys was to call them "faggot." It was the weapon of choice and feared by all. No wonder boys become shame-phobic, masking their real emotions and attempting to appear in control, hiding their vulnerability and fear of exposure.

4. Self-in-Relation Model

At this point I will briefly describe a model that gives empirical evidence for the need to retain one's voice (or sense of self) while also maintaining relationships. The self-in-relation model is a two-dimensional typology that allows us to operationally define the constructs of "sense of self/voice" and "relationship quality."[31] In a pilot study, 110 women from a liberal arts college were interviewed and categorized into one of four types:

1. The self out of relation is the adolescent girl who scores high on her sense of self yet is disengaged from others. She uses her voice regardless of the consequences.
2. The self-in-relation is the adolescent girl who has a strong sense of self and is able to maintain her voice while staying connected in relationships.

30. Bergman, "Men's Psychological Development," p. 93.
31. Kimball et al., "Self-in-Relation."

3. The invisible self is the adolescent girl who has no developed sense of self or significant relationships.

4. The self defined by relation is the adolescent girl who values relationships and will sacrifice her voice/self to avoid conflict. She has a poorly developed sense of self.

Participants were categorized based on their scores on measures of "sense of self/voice" and "relationship quality." These four groups were then compared on standard measures of different domains of psychological health — for example, satisfaction with life, self-esteem, and depression. Results indicated that women who had achieved "self-in-relation" had the highest scores on measures of well-being. Those classified as "invisible self" had significantly lower scores. The mean well-being for those who were classified as "self out of relation" was higher than that of those classified as "self defined by relation." This model may prove a useful tool for understanding adolescent girls and boys and their needs. The challenge here will be to understand this model with regard to a kenotic ethic. I believe this challenge can be met with a Radical-Reformation theology.

5. The Church and Loss of Voice

To what degree has the church supported this "lost voice" phenomenon? Historical and contemporary analyses can help us understand some of the reasons that churches are ill-equipped to answer the question of self and self-renunciation. In the past, families governed with absolute authority over their children. Girls and boys were required to respond with unquestioning obedience and submission. Such control tends to encourage the stilling of the voice in adolescent girls and boys.

Numerous writings of church leaders from the seventeenth century forward evidence the same themes about discipline and family governance.[32] In ideal evangelical families, parents had exclusive control over their children. These households were isolated and self-contained; authority and love were to be found in the parents. This control was so

---

32. Philip Greven, *The Protestant Temperament: Patterns of Child-Rearing, Religious Experience, and the Self in Early America* (New York: Alfred A. Knopf, 1977).

absolute that grandparents were often suspected of indulgence that would undermine parental authority. John Wesley gave mothers this warning:

> Your mother, or your husband's mother, may live with you; and you will do well to shew her all possible respect. But let her on no account have the least share in the management of your children. She would undo all that you have done; she would give them their own will in all things. She would humour them to the destruction of their souls, if not their bodies, too. . . . In four-score years I have not met with one woman that knew how to manage grand-children. Give up your will to hers. But with regard to the management of your children, steadily keep the reins in your own hands.[33]

Another early evangelical, John Witherspoon, advised absolute submission from children. He urged like-minded parents to enact, very early, an unmitigated and total authority over their children:

> I would have it early . . . that it may be absolute, and absolute, that it may not be severe. If parents are too long in beginning to exert their authority, they will find the task very difficult. Children, habituated to indulgence for a few of their first years, are exceedingly impatient of restraint; and if they happen to be of stiff or obstinate tempers, can hardly be brought to an entire, at least to a quiet and placid submission; whereas, if they are taken in time, there is hardly any temper but what may be made to yield, and by early habit the subjection becomes quite easy to themselves.[34]

Obviously, this assumes that the emerging will must be controlled and broken in the early years of life. John Wesley also urged, "Break their wills, that you may save their souls."[35] He went on to explain,

> A wise parent . . . should begin to break their [children's] will, the first moment it appears. In the whole art of Christian education there is nothing more important than this. The will of a parent is to a little child in the place of the will of God. Therefore, studiously teach them

33. Wesley, cited in Greven, *The Protestant Temperament*, p. 27.
34. Witherspoon, cited in Greven, *The Protestant Temperament*, p. 35.
35. Wesley, cited in Greven, *The Protestant Temperament*, p. 35.

to submit to this while they are children, that they may be ready to submit to his will, when they are men.[36]

Breaking the child's will was not just about total submission but also about conformity. Parental control over all aspects of life, including their children's diet, dress, and manners, mattered acutely to the parents of Wesley's day. One's outward appearance and behavior were observed and judged as reflections of one's inner values. The church was able to assess how well the parents were doing based upon their children's behavioral display. Wesley was clear in his rebuke to parents who permitted their children to deviate from their model: "Whenever . . . I see the fine-dressed daughter of a plain-dressed mother, I see at once the mother is defective either in knowledge or religion. . . . In God's name why do you suffer them to vary a hair's breadth from your example?"[37]

How different is the ethos of contemporary evangelicalism on this matter? Research I have conducted with Jennette Lybeck sought to examine how the concept of the "lost voice" (for women) functioned in contemporary evangelical circles.[38] Utilizing Gilligan and Brown's interview and coding criteria, we interviewed thirty girls and young women from a well-known conservative church and a well-known egalitarian church. The respondents were divided into three age groups: ages 8 to 10, ages 12 to 14, and ages 20 to 30. Because the egalitarian churches permitted greater leadership roles for women, it was hypothesized that the respondents from the egalitarian church would exhibit less loss of voice than those from the conservative church.

The results, however, indicated that the majority of the respondents from both churches showed some evidence of a loss of voice. One troubling finding was that some of the youngest girls were already experiencing the "tyranny of the nice and kind." They were worried about how others felt about them, they tried to be nice to avoid conflict, and they behaved in ways that would maintain their relationships.

The most significant difference between the two churches was found in the 20-to-30-year-old group. In both churches, most of the young

36. Wesley, cited in Greven, *The Protestant Temperament*, p. 37.
37. Wesley, cited in Greven, *The Protestant Temperament*, p. 45.
38. Jennette Lybeck and Cynthia J. Neal, "Do Religious Institutions Resist or Support Women's 'Lost Voice'?" *Youth and Society* 27 (1995): 4-28.

women described themselves as more confident, both in themselves and in their relationships. They described their friendships as more honest and authentic. However, they differed in their perceptions of their developing voice and how they *should* be developing. The women from the egalitarian church were celebrating their emergent voices and subsequent confidence, finding the ability to balance their own expression with the sensitivity needed in relationships. In contrast, the women from the conservative church were troubled by their emergent voices, worried that they were selfish, proud, and disobedient Christians for considering their own needs. Although these women were beginning to trust their instincts and opinions, there was a discrepancy between how they lived and how they felt they *should* live.

While Lybeck and I did not study spirituality, one might expect that the loss of voice and subsequent emergence would have implications for one's relationship with God. Although not empirically tested, it would be very important to consider how men experience the loss of their emotional voice in the current evangelical world.

I will move now to the discussion of the proper understanding of kenosis and servanthood. I believe that as our church communities practice "becoming like Christ," they will become the nutrient soil out of which our girls, women, boys, and men might grow in their ability to freely choose self-emptying and servanthood.

6. Kenosis and Relational Nonviolence

Nancey Murphy has proposed an ethic of kenosis as an integral part of the journey toward human flourishing. Christ "emptied himself" and took on human likeness in the form of a servant. Many examples of this "self-emptying" are evident throughout the New Testament. Christ grew in wisdom as he spent time with the elders in the temple (Luke 2:40-52); he relinquished the knowledge of the last days (Mark 13:32); he emptied himself of power and wealth and became poor that we might become rich (2 Cor. 8:9); he served as a high priest who could understand our weaknesses and temptations (Heb. 4:15); and perhaps most profoundly, he suffered the cross and the separation from God (Matt. 27:46). Jesus' act of kenosis is described in a well-known passage from Paul, thought by many to be an early Christian hymn:

Let the same mind be in you that was in Christ Jesus,
who, though he was in the form of God,
did not regard equality with God as something to be exploited,
but emptied himself,
taking the form of a slave,
being born in human likeness.
And being found in human form,
he humbled himself
and became obedient to the point of death —
even death on a cross.   (Phil. 2:5-8)

The narrative is preceded by Paul's call to the believer for unity, humility, servanthood:

> If then there is any encouragement in Christ, any consolation from love, any sharing in the Spirit, any compassion and sympathy, make my joy complete: be of the same mind, having the same love, being in full accord and of one mind. Do nothing from selfish ambition or conceit, but in humility regard others as better than yourselves. Let each of you look not to your own interests, but to the interests of others. (vv. 1-4)

Christ is the norm, and all believers are called to share in his humility and servanthood. John Howard Yoder asserts that our imitation of Christ is bound up in the cross: "Servanthood replaces dominion, forgiveness absorbs hostility. Thus — and only thus — are we bound by New Testament thought to 'be like Jesus.'"[39]

I am intrigued by this call to "be like Jesus." Jesus exhibited a powerful presence and a strong will, was seemingly independent, and never feared reprisals from those who policed the rules and traditions of the law. This is certainly not the conventional view that many are taught about self-denial. The girls and women who have lost their voices, and hence their selves, often believe that thinking more highly of the other prohibits one thinking of the self at all. Boys and men learn to mask their selves, thus denying their vulnerability. Yet Jesus had a strong identity, a self, albeit one formed by the God he served. We too are called to

---

39. John Howard Yoder, *The Politics of Jesus*, 2d ed. (Grand Rapids: Eerdmans, 1994), p. 131.

have our identities formed by traveling on the journey toward making Jesus' story our story.

One critical feature of this journey is the need for self-awareness. When we require a silencing of voice, we are participating in a form of violence. The theme of peace in Radical-Reformation theology posits that we must become more aware of the violence that lives in our hearts, a violence that plays a role in our relationships as well as in larger social structures. Too often and without true malice, we visit violence upon others when we prescribe roles and rules that force them to lose their selves, rendering kenosis or faithful relinquishment difficult. Violence permits illusions of control, both for our own self and for the others in our life. Stanley Hauerwas writes,

> Violence results from our attempting to live our lives without recognizing our falsehoods. Violence derives from the self-deceptive story that we are in control — that we are our own creators — and that only we can bestow meaning on our lives, since there is no one else to do so.
>
> We mightily fear giving up our illusions; they are as dear to us as our selves. We fear if we learn to make the story of God our story, we may have no self, no individuality left. Or that we will lose our autonomy. But the blessing lies in the irony that the more we learn to make the story of Jesus our story, the more unique, the more individual, we become — thus, the example of the saints.[40]

Relational violence that imposes control and coercion over self and others while maintaining the inevitable self-deception fuels an increasing identification with individualism rather than community. This particular form of violence wreaks havoc in two distinct ways. First, the resulting self-deception and subsequent (illusion of) self-sufficiency obviates the need (or indeed even the logic) for self-renunciation. Second, relational violence can diminish the other's sense of self, either through the lost voice or the lost emotional voice.

The Anabaptist, Radical-Reformed view differs significantly from that of the other Reformers. As Robert Friedman writes of the current Protestant movements,

---

40. Stanley Hauerwas, *The Peaceable Kingdom* (Notre Dame: University of Notre Dame Press, 1983), pp. 94-95.

Everybody still remains alone, seeking his personal salvation, and he only enjoys the sharing of edification with the like-minded co-religionists. Or to put it in other words: the brother is not absolutely necessary for the salvation of the individual, which rests alone in the possession of one's faith. It is but one further step from this position to the liberal concept of individualism of the last hundred years, [which] almost atomized society and destroyed church life at large.[41]

Friedman contrasts the Protestant way with the Anabaptist way:

Now then, the central idea of Anabaptism, the real dynamite in the age of Reformation, as I see it, was this, that one cannot find salvation without caring for his brother, that this "brother" actually matters in the personal life. . . . This interdependence of men gives life and salvation a new meaning. It is not "faith alone" which matters (for which faith no church organization would be needed) but it is brotherhood, this intimate caring for each other, as it was commanded to the disciples of Christ as the way to God's kingdom. That was the discovery which made Anabaptism so forceful and outstanding in all of church history.[42]

In the Anabaptist tradition, the freedom of the Christian (self) is shared with the life of the community (in-relation). This leads us to ask how a proper understanding of kenosis might come to mean choosing freely while also flourishing within caring communities.

7. Self-in-Relation as the Call to Servanthood

Jesus' call to servanthood (Matt. 20:25-28) is the only way we can properly understand and live this self-in-relation. Jesus obeyed and served because he loved. He images for us how we might practice kenosis and learn to love and serve as he did so faithfully. When girls and women, boys and men, lose their sense of self, they are not able to practice

41. Friedman, cited in Franklin H. Littell, "The Anabaptist Concept of the Church," in *The Recovery of the Anabaptist Vision*, ed. Guy F. Hershberger (Scottsdale, Pa.: Herald Press, 1957), p. 123.

42. Friedman, cited in Littell, "The Anabaptist Concept of the Church," p. 123.

kenosis or servanthood as a choice that emerges from a strong sense of identity, purpose, and the freedom to love. Thomas Finger, an Anabaptist theologian, writes,

> We emphasize that servanthood . . . is above all the fruit of a loving relationship. Servanthood is possible only as mutual servanthood — as service is to the One, and to that One's followers, who also serve us. . . . As long as one's deepest self is not loved, affirmed and nourished, one really has nothing to give.[43]

The call to servanthood must involve, in some fundamental way, the call to participate in a servant community:

> When one speaks of servanthood today, it is important to specify: to whom or to what? If one seeks to practice Jesus' "strenuous" ethics solely in relation to oppressive social structures or the mandates of a negative self-image, one's behavior will often become legalistic. The repressed hurt and rage will find destructive outlets in other ways. But if servanthood involves mutual service within a community of servants, servanthood will function as an integral dimension of each person's self-actualization . . . [which] occurs only through self-surrender to God and mutual self-giving with others.[44]

Consequently, what the psychological community characterizes as self-actualization is not the kenotic understanding of self-actualization. If we are to take on the message of Christ, our self-actualization will be formed from our self-emptying and service to others in a serving community.

Nancey Murphy argues that "humans can move from their untutored (and, I would add, ungraced) starting point toward the realization of their full potential."[45] She continues with questions of forgiveness, healing from childhood abuse, supporting those who do not have a voice or self to renounce. The self-in-relation model has both empirical and clinical evidence which shows that women and men who value both a strong sense of self and relationships enjoy greater well-being than

43. Thomas N. Finger, *Christian Theology: An Eschatological Approach*, vol. 2 (Scottsdale, Pa.: Herald Press, 1998), p. 101.

44. Finger, *Christian Theology*, p. 101.

45. Murphy, Chapter 3, section 2, this volume.

those whose lifestyle emphasizes one over the other. This model clearly relates to the Anabaptist conviction of self-in-community. Communal support is absolutely necessary to live a life of self-renunciation and achieve God's good for us. Thus, I end this chapter with these profound and challenging words of Dietrich Bonhoeffer, which emphasize the difficult struggle of achieving self and self-emptying:

> Let him who cannot be alone beware of community. He will only do harm to himself and to the community. Alone you stood before God when he called you; alone you had to struggle and pray; and alone you will die and give an account to God. You cannot escape from yourself; for God has singled you out. If you refuse to be alone [e.g., to be an individual] you are rejecting Christ's call to you, and you can have no part in the community of those who are called.
>
> But the reverse is also true: Let him who is not in community beware being alone. Into the community you were called, the call was not meant for you alone; in the community of the called you bear your cross, you struggle, you pray. You are not alone, even in death, and on the Last Day you will be only one member of the great congregation before Jesus Christ. If you scorn the fellowship of the brethren you reject the call of Jesus Christ, and thus your solitude can only be hurtful to you.[46]

46. Dietrich Bonhoeffer, *Life Together* (New York: Harper & Row, 1995), pp. 77-78.

Chapter 6 **Mere Humanity: The Ordinary Lives**
of Ambivalent Altruists

Kevin Reimer

1. Introduction

In the opening of his *Varieties of Moral Personality*, Owen Flanagan invokes William James on the special influence of saints upon humanity:

> The saints are authors, *auctores*, increasers of goodness . . . they are impregnators of the world, animators of potentialities of goodness which but for them would lie forever dormant. It is not possible to be quite as mean as we naturally are, when they have passed before us. One fire kindles another; and without that over-trust in human worth which they show, the rest of us would lie in spiritual stagnancy.[1]

For Flanagan, the psychological study of altruism and morality must, for reasons of integrity, grapple with the extraordinary achievement of saints. This does not, however, imply that perfection should serve as a primary study variable. In all likelihood, the fallibility of the saint is as psychologically significant as exemplary behavior, a point that is commonly overlooked in contemporary behavioral and social scientific research. The promiscuity of Martin Luther King and the hedonism of Oskar Schindler boldly illustrate this saintly paradox. At the end of the

---

1. Owen Flanagan, *Varieties of Moral Personality: Ethics and Psychological Realism* (Cambridge, Mass.: Harvard University Press, 1991), p. 277.

This chapter arises from an article entitled "Natural Character: Psychological Realism for the Downwardly Mobile," first published in *Theology & Science* 2 (2004): 3-32.

day, humans are inevitably human, bound to natural limitations of experience and moral ambivalence.

In her symposium lectures on the integration of psychology and theology, Nancey Murphy identified an ethic of altruistic *self-renunciation* as the core theory for psychological research.[2] In Murphy's view, self-renunciation consists of altruism based on the kenotic example of Jesus Christ, a view that pushes deeply into the essence of human nature. Her work intersects with current psychological debate over the degree to which lofty theories of altruism and morality should be constrained by real-world examples of caring people, a concern known as *psychological realism*.[3] Two key questions emerge from this encounter. First, can self-renunciation realistically serve as the core theory of psychology? Second, how should altruism be psychologically understood as an extension of human character?

To address these questions, I will use self-renunciation as a catalyst for thinking about character in a manner that is psychologically realistic. First, I will argue that Murphy's criteria for self-renunciation unfairly burden mere humans in the absence of grace. This is evident in the lives of caregiver assistants involved in my ongoing study of altruistic love in L'Arche communities. L'Arche assistants are widely considered to be living altruists, given their choice to embrace founder Jean Vanier's idea of *downward mobility* — renouncing social status and financial security to live in community with the developmentally disabled.[4] Whereas L'Arche assistants in many instances demonstrate self-renunciation based on their Christian faith, there is self-conscious recognition of the costs of altruism in alcoholic and other compulsive behaviors. Given the lives of these everyday exemplars, self-renunciation may be less about achieving Christlike perfection and more about the altruist's experience of grace in self-understanding. It is in self-understanding that the altruist learns to test personal life habits against the well-lived lives of others. I will outline this in terms of *natural character.*

2. Murphy, Chapters 1-3, this volume.

3. Flanagan, *Varieties of Moral Personality.* See also Lawrence J. Walker, "The Perceived Personality of Moral Exemplars," *Journal of Moral Education* 28 (1999): 145-62.

4. Stephen Post, "The Tradition of Agape," in *Altruism and Altruistic Love: Science, Philosophy, and Religion in Dialogue,* ed. Stephen Post, Lynn Underwood, Jeffrey Schloss, and William Hurlbut (Oxford: Oxford University Press, 2002), pp. 51-64. See also Jean Vanier, *Becoming Human* (New York: Paulist Press, 1999).

Second, I will argue that an adequate psychological understanding of self-renunciation is principally a methodological concern. Rather than locate a preferred philosophical or theological framework for the study of natural character (e.g., Kohlberg's deontology), psychologically realistic research balances empirical goals with the exemplar's own perceptions of altruism. Thus, the purpose of this chapter is to consider new methods that support a psychologically realistic study of human altruism and, by extension, natural character. The self-understanding process of natural character is a storied event. Consequently, self-understanding of natural character might be explored in the cognition of narratives. Narratives are mentally represented in symbols of the self and other. I will conclude by proposing a method for empirical study of natural character through the mapping of symbolic representations for self and other using computational linguistics.

2. Self-Renunciation and Psychological Realism

It turns out that Murphy's self-renunciation thesis bisects a lively debate over how altruistic behavior should be understood psychologically. Her proposal is useful for a moral psychology field that currently suffers from philosophical indigestion. Daniel Hart notes that in the years since Kohlberg, moral psychology has become stuck in a morass of philosophical problems involving the study of altruism and morality.[5] I will briefly review two contemporary perspectives on altruism in order to understand specific implications of Murphy's argument. My primary focus is the field of moral psychology, with the disclaimer that while "moral" does not entirely capture the self-renunciation concept as defined by Murphy, elements of altruism implied by her theory are commonly (but not exclusively) taken up by psychologists in this camp.

It is a distinct possibility that the malaise affecting moral psychology was created through the growing self-awareness of social scientists in the field. Because of its broadly inclusive scope, Kohlberg's theory of moral development provoked criticism that stirred the philosophical pot, a problem made worse by the abstract nature of caring motivation in human be-

5. Daniel Hart, "Can Prototypes Inform Moral Developmental Theory?" *Developmental Psychology* 34 (1998): 420-23.

havior. The decline of Kohlberg as the unopposed champion of moral psychology was applauded by those who noted that his preference for a single philosophical tradition overlooked aspects of human caring.[6] But Kohlberg's preference for Kantian justice gave pause to researchers who might eventually take his place and, by clinging to a pet philosophical theory, suffer a similar fate. As a result, moral psychologists were forced to grapple with their own philosophical subjectivity in understanding altruistic behavior. The field was faced with the uncomfortable prospect of figuring out how to describe altruism while limiting the influence of philosophical biases on method and interpretation.

Consequently, two poles became visible along a continuum of strategies designed to preserve the scientific integrity of research into altruistic and moral behavior. One pole signified a powerful minimalism. C. Daniel Batson and colleagues worked to isolate caring behavior around domains that could be studied experimentally.[7] A minimal realist, Batson argued that empathy provided the simplest and most forthright explanation for care. Batson saw his *empathy-altruism* theory as a hedge against evolutionary arguments for ego-centered motives such as reward seeking, punishment avoidance, and aversive-arousal reduction. Batson's approach to empathy typically involved the intentional deception of human participants. Accurate assessment of empathy required that the participant be convinced that dilemmas requiring a caring response were authentic. Only within a controlled, experimental regimen would the researcher find what initiates altruism in a sample population. While influential, Batson's studies have been criticized for oversimplifying caring behaviors.[8] In addition, laboratory approaches to altruism are limited to the reflexive responses of participants confronted with stimuli. Thus, it is difficult to understand how altruistic commitment becomes established and sustained over time in human character.

6. Augusto Blasi, "Moral Identity: Its Role in Moral Functioning," in *Morality, Moral Behavior, and Moral Development,* ed. William Kurtines and Janet Gewirtz (New York: Wiley, 1984), pp. 128-39.

7. C. Daniel Batson, "Addressing the Altruism Question Experimentally," in Post et al., eds., *Altruism and Altruistic Love,* pp. 89-105.

8. S. Neuberg, R. Cialdini, S. Brown, C. Luce, B. Sagarin, and B. Lewis, "Does Empathy Lead to Anything More than Superficial Helping? Comment on Batson et al.," *Journal of Personality and Social Psychology* 73 (1997): 510-16; see also Murphy, Chapter 3, section 3.5, this volume.

The other pole was strongly idealistic, premised on the study of exemplars nominated for exceptional altruistic and moral commitment. The phenomenological approach of Anne Colby and Bill Damon's classic *Some Do Care* outlined altruism through the stories of modern saints. Exemplar narratives sparkled with accounts of civil rights advocacy, work with the urban poor, and protection of voiceless children in the developing world.[9] The accomplishments of this small sample were extolled for their exemplarity, making it difficult to establish connections to the psychological functioning of everyday people. In a sense, the exemplars of the study were nearly too good to be true. Their personal narratives, while useful as a window into moral commitments, were still subject to the artistic license of the storytellers. The subjectivity of the researcher interpreting exemplar narrative is easily aligned with points of intersection between story and the recalled achievements of the interviewed saint. Qualitatively speaking, the researcher may overstate idealistic interpretations of saintly behavior. The coding of behavior in a selectively positive manner neglects the conflicted internal states of those who produce noteworthy accomplishments on behalf of humanity. This is evident in exemplar autobiography, a reminder that exemplarity should continually be reassessed in light of ordinary human experience.[10]

In crudely outlining these two poles of a continuum, I have unfairly excluded other positions in moral psychology that strike a compromise between minimal realism and idealism. Yet these perspectives highlight a significant tension in the psychological study of altruism. To reduce care to the jurisprudence of empathy is to risk creating a fragmented understanding of altruistic motivation removed from the real world. On the other hand, to idealize caring in the lives of saints places such extraordinary demands on human behavior that psychologists are "compelled to create persons so different from themselves that if they and the kinds of

9. Anne Colby and Bill Damon, *Some Do Care: Contemporary Lives of Moral Commitment* (New York: Free Press, 1992).

10. Gandhi is candid regarding his own shortcomings and the very human tendency to embellish subjective experiences in memory. See Mohandas Gandhi, *Gandhi: An Autobiography: The Story of My Experiments with Truth* (New York: Beacon, 1993). See also Lawrence J. Walker, "Moral Exemplarity," in *Bringing in a New Era in Character Education*, ed. William Damon (Stanford, Calif.: Hoover Institution Press, 2002), pp. 65-84.

persons they were trying to create were to coexist, they would be so dissimilar that they would not in all likelihood relate very well to each other."[11]

In response to this conundrum, Flanagan proposes that *psychological realism* should govern the moral ethos of the researcher. Psychological realism implies that philosophical and theological theories of caring should be limited by the understanding of real people who wrestle with everyday struggles, yet manage to behave altruistically anyway. Because of his commitment to psychological realism, Flanagan acknowledges the futility of advocating another philosophical mandate for the study of altruism, and the improbability of research without a priori bias. Instead, this bottom-up approach makes space for mundanely human concerns, particularly for people who evidence a "good enough" existence.

Understood on the basis of altruism study, psychological realism is organized around the following theses:

1. We ought to treat the common-sense reactions and intuitions of persons we pre-theoretically believe are reasonable as a powerful constraint on normative theorizing.
2. The motivational structure — the personality — required by a credible theory should not normally demand that the actual persons to whom the theory is addressed aspire to become, or to create, persons they themselves could not reasonably be expected to become without undergoing complete character transformation — without, that is, becoming radically different persons.
3. Once a personality is above a certain threshold of decency, there are particular psychological goods, such as integrity or commitment to the projects that give one's life meaning, which need not yield in the face of more impersonal demands.[12]

Given my purpose to examine Murphy's vision for self-renunciation in the study of human altruism, I will offer two observations informed by psychological realism. First, Murphy's core theory of self-renunciation is Christological. The psychological realist must therefore ask a difficult question: Which Jesus should serve as the example of self-renunciation?

11. Flanagan, *Varieties of Moral Personality,* p. 57.
12. Flanagan, *Varieties of Moral Personality,* p. 79.

Christ's unique nature as human and divine may specify the mundane circumstances of humanity, indicate an impossible vision of divine perfection, or leave the assumptions of self-renunciation painfully ambiguous. The fact of Christ's humanity is unarguable for Christians, yet the example of self-renunciation that he gave on earth was unprecedented. Mortals who model themselves after Christ will struggle to come close to his example, and may in their efforts sink into depths of messianic narcissism. For the purposes of psychological research into altruism, Murphy's Christological notion of self-renunciation may require further clarification.

Second, Murphy's core theory of self-renunciation is itself an ethic. The psychological realist must consider how self-renunciation will reflect moral positions and biases in research. Exemplar narratives hold great promise in terms of outlining the motivational bases of self-renunciation and altruism. But the subjective imposition of the researcher's ethic is a risk when handling the interpretation and systematic examination of these narratives. Consequently, psychologically realistic constraints on self-renunciation should be premised not only on research findings in a general sense, but also on the methods used to make meaning from exemplar narratives.

From this discussion, two questions are visible in the interest of exploring altruistic care in a manner that is psychologically realistic. First, should unqualified self-renunciation, given its Christological basis, serve as the core theory for psychological study? Second, how should altruism be psychologically understood as an extension of human character? True to Flanagan's argument, the next sections will use research examples to establish boundaries for self-renunciation in the study of altruistic behavior.

3. Self-Renunciation in the Trenches: Ambivalent Altruists

In response to the first question, I assert that authentic self-renunciation requires grace, at least for mere humans. This is a psychologically realistic premise based on life experiences of real human exemplars from a current psychological study. Because it is my intent to use actual human subjects to reflect upon self-renunciation theory, it is imperative to verify that the study sample incorporates the six criteria of self-renunciation identified in Murphy's argument. The sample must demonstrate self-renunciation that (1) involves detachment from material possessions, (2) renounces rights to rewards, (3) entails choosing not to harm another person when harm has been done, (4) calls for nonviolence, (5) calls for acceptance of suffering, and (6) means submission to God.[13]

What group of exemplars is characterized by these criteria? Recently I received a grant to study altruistic love in L'Arche. L'Arche (French for "the ark") is an international federation of more than a hundred communities in twenty-nine countries that cares for persons with developmental disabilities.[14] Although officially multidenominational, L'Arche is predominantly Christian in ethos and Roman Catholic in practice. L'Arche is the genius of Jean Vanier, a Canadian philosopher, religious leader, statesman, and activist. In 1962 Vanier established a residential community for the disabled that was marked by relational commitments of altruistic love, not simply from caregiver assistants to the core members, as the disabled are known, but in mutual exchange between assistants and core members. Vanier's mission with the developmentally disabled led to a praxis of agape as a redemptive element wherein

> everyone is of unique and sacred value, and everyone has the same dignity and the same rights. People with a mental handicap often possess qualities of welcome, wonderment, spontaneity, and directness . . . [and are] able to touch hearts and call others to unity through their simplicity and vulnerability. In this way they are a reminder to the wider world of the essential values of the heart without which knowledge, power, and action lose their meaning and purpose.[15]

In L'Arche communities, assistants and core members live peacefully together, sharing faith and everyday experience. L'Arche assistants are invited to participate in community on the basis of theological commitments. Individuals are asked to carefully weigh their commitment in terms of a calling, which is typically ratified in year-long increments that require periods of spiritual discernment prior to recommitment. In his

---

13. See Murphy, Chapter 2, section 5, this volume.

14. I am grateful for grant #1658.3 from the John Fetzer Institute of Kalamazoo, Michigan, for supporting my study of L'Arche.

15. Vanier, *Becoming Human*, p. 27.

many books outlining the philosophy and spirituality of L'Arche, Vanier describes a *downward mobility* of care and compassionate commitment:

> We live in a world of competition, where importance is given to success, a good salary, efficiency, distractions, and stimulations. Our world, however, needs to rediscover what is essential: committed relationships, openness and the acceptance of weakness, a life of friendship and solidarity in and through the little things we can do. It is not a question of doing extraordinary things, but rather of doing ordinary things with love.[16]

In terms of the criteria of Murphy's self-renunciation theory, L'Arche assistants are (1) asked to live simply, renouncing (2) excessive commitment to material possessions. In my study venue of American L'Arche communities, assistants are nearly volunteers, receiving a small stipend of 400 dollars per month. Peace, nonviolence, and conflict mediation (3 and 4) are practiced in L'Arche as outlined in its charter. Assistants are made aware that their time in L'Arche at some point will (5) involve painful self-reflection upon realizing the broken state of the human condition. As a consequence, L'Arche positions itself to be a sign of hope and healing within the community and to the world. Assistants are encouraged to grow more deeply in their knowledge and experience of God, a commitment (6) supported in many communities by the presence of residential priests, therapists, and spiritual directors.

How do the lives of L'Arche assistants constrain Murphy's core theory of self-renunciation? It is helpful to briefly review the study protocol as a means of addressing this question. Following resolution of ethics and consent issues, assistants were asked to complete the *Interpersonal Adjectives Scale Revised, Big 5* (IASR-B5) and the *Spiritual Strivings Scale* prior to my arrival.[17] Assistants then participated in an audiotaped, semi-structured interview that included sections on self-understanding, interpersonal relatedness with core members, and identity narrative.[18] Assis-

---

16. Vanier, *Becoming Human*, p. 65.

17. Jerry Wiggins, *Interpersonal Adjectives Scales: Professional Manual* (Odessa, Fla.: Psychological Assessment Resources, 1995); Robert Emmons, *The Psychology of Ultimate Concerns* (New York: Guilford, 1999).

18. S. Drigotas, C. Rusbult, J. Wieselquist, and S. Whitton, "Close Partner as Sculptor of the Ideal Self: Behavioral Affirmation and the Michelangelo Phenomenon," *Jour-*

tants were given 25 dollars for their time and effort. In order to accomplish the sampling phase of the study, I was invited to visit L'Arche communities in various regions of the United States. Beyond the immediate benefit of completing many interviews over brief periods of time, my residence in L'Arche communities provided the advantage of participant-observer ethnography, a kind of check on altruistic commitment in its ecology.

It was in the experience of living in L'Arche that I was struck by the depth of altruistic commitment in assistants and the unexpected costs of their calling. In one location with a high number of long-term assistants (those with more than three years' service), a variety of compulsive behaviors were evident. Several assistants struggled with eating disorders, and many members of the community would spend evenings in a local tavern drinking heavily. I was invited on one of these excursions, informed by assistants that I should experience firsthand how people "compensate" for their lives in L'Arche. These compensatory activities spilled over into the regular routine of the community and became a significant feature in the ethos of L'Arche. Community narratives were forged around tavern trips as a fixture in daily life — a rite of passage for new assistants entering the community, and an identity for those within. For L'Arche assistants in this particular instance, alcohol figured prominently in self-understanding related to altruistic commitment.

It is not my desire to pass judgment on these assistants and their behavior. In no way should this account dull the remarkable stories of personal healing, transformation, and altruism that are typical of their identity narratives. Yet despite their achievements, these were ambivalent altruists, openly acknowledging in themselves places where goals collided with what one assistant referred to as "the dark places in my soul." In this instance, altruism is framed by the recognition of its considerable requirements of people of high spiritual and moral commitment. Alcohol was an unfortunate but widely affirmed companion for many of these assistants. The high standard of care achieved by these people is, in a psychological sense, even more interesting given the prev-

nal of Personality and Social Psychology 77 (1999): 293-323; Dan P. McAdams, *The Stories We Live By* (New York: Guilford, 1993). Also, Kevin Reimer and David Wade-Stein, "Moral Identity in Adolescence: Self and Other in Semantic Space," *Identity: An International Journal of Theory and Research* 4 (2004): 229-49.

alence of compensatory behaviors, a point of departure for future study on the shape of human altruism.

During one tavern trip, an assistant told me about an important lesson she had recently learned in becoming "gentle" with herself. She explained that gentleness included a personal admission that her humanness was frail and prone to hurting others. Conversely, she recognized her own hurts at the hands of others in the community and the need for God to reconcile these conflicts with love. I believe that this insight constrains self-renunciation on the basis of its gentle and honest affirmation of human weakness. Self-renunciation as a theory may comprise certain exemplar behaviors that are at least partly feasible within the milieu of human possibility. But the criteria for self-renunciation in Murphy's theory are derived from the historical person of Jesus. In Christ's example, self-renunciation is incarnated in a way given to the eschatological purpose of his ministry on earth, a *telos* for the reconciliation and healing of humanity. In a psychologically realistic view, Christ's self-renunciation should function not as a theoretical absolute for human care and conduct, but as evidence of the grace of God available for wounded humanity — past, present, and future. This grace or "gentle" admission of reconciliation reflects an altruism that is both already and not yet, premised on divine rather than human initiative.[19]

Given the lives of these L'Arche assistants, can self-renunciation legitimately function as a core theory for psychological research? I believe that it can, but only within the bounds of what is realistic for admittedly ambivalent altruists. The altruism of self-renunciation is, for the L'Arche assistant, a continuing process of self-understanding — drafting a coherent narrative of the self in relation to others. For assistants in at least one location, alcohol is an important confederate in this process. The altruist is chalking up insights into relationships and personal failures relative to whatever ideological commitments are central to his or her L'Arche experience. The centrality of this self-understanding process and the challenges

---

19. Of course, it may be pointed out that Jesus was subjected to moments of weakness and human inadequacy, particularly on the cross. The passion of Jesus is eminently human and immediately evident within the tavern narrative. However, Murphy's self-renunciation mandate does not specify which Jesus exemplifies self-renunciation, nor does she provide a specific Christological framework for interpreting altruistic behavior. It is this ambiguity, rather than the Christological basis of her argument, that is of greatest concern.

intrinsic to it require flexibility and forgiveness, not only with others, but also with the self. Consequently, self-renunciation should be clarified to reflect the full measure of grace that is embedded within the eschatological purpose of Christ's kenosis.[20] The notion of *natural character* attempts to capture self-renunciation that is "already," describing the process of self-understanding and the frail exemplars that animate it. Natural character suggests that the L'Arche altruist, whether conscious of it or not, is enabled to care by the grace of God. I do not intend natural character to be used as a universal statement on the objective composition of human altruism. Rather, natural character, as a process of self-understanding, implies moral casuistry whereby each individual engages in the imaginative testing of life habits against the well-lived lives of others.[21]

4. A Question of Scientific Method

It is useful and perhaps imperative to consider the role of scientific method at this point, largely because the rubric of psychological realism places a new burden of responsibility on the way in which stories of altruists are interpreted and, consequently, used to shape theory. I have argued that exemplar narratives provide important insights into the altruistic motivation of natural character. The trick is to figure out how to let exemplar narrative stand, philosophically speaking, on its own feet with

20. It is worthwhile to note that Murphy's self-renunciation proposal is teleological in its commitment to a Christian eschaton. This is a theologically realistic emphasis. Grace is also grounded in the reality of the present, while emphasizing reconciliation and healing implied by Christ's future return. My argument is meant to extend and clarify Murphy's argument on the basis of my own Reformed perspective. I am aware that in so doing, I invoke Augustinian language that is absent in Murphy's Anabaptist theology.

21. Stanley Hauerwas, *The Peaceable Kingdom: A Primer in Christian Ethics* (Notre Dame: University of Notre Dame Press, 1983). Natural character implies imperfection related to human neediness and dependence. Because of limited space, I will confine further consideration of natural character to the psychological processes evident in L'Arche assistants. A detailed discussion on the moral underpinnings of natural character may be found in Alasdair MacIntyre, *Dependent Rational Animals: Why Human Beings Need the Virtues* (Chicago: Open Court, 1999). Natural character is also evident in local, particular narratives that emerge in the context of psychotherapy. See Alvin C. Dueck and Kevin Reimer, "Retrieving the Virtues in Psychotherapy: Thick and Thin Discourse," *American Behavioral Scientist* 47 (2003): 427-41.

a minimum of researcher imposition. This methodological challenge to an *unsupervised* analysis of narrative has plagued psychological research into complex, cognitively emergent behaviors such as altruism.

What are narratives, psychologically speaking? This is a cognitive issue, for only the brain is capable of telling stories, particularly in a manner representative of natural character. Terrence Deacon provides a framework for understanding the basic structures through which narratives are created.[22] Deacon recalls the semiotic scheme of Charles Sanders Peirce, who distinguished three categories of referential associations in the brain. *Icon* refers to associations of similarity between sign and object. *Index* implies physical or temporal connections between sign and object. *Symbol* is understood by formal or previously agreed-upon links irrespective of physical characteristics of either sign or object. These modes of cognitive association are hierarchically organized, in order implying (a) similarity, (b) contiguity or correlation, and (c) law, causality, or convention. Deacon argues that it is symbolic representation that distinguishes humans from other animals, as it is in tandem that symbolic language and the brain co-evolved.[23]

These three modes of referential association in human cognition are simply illustrated. Consider a gold wedding ring. The immediate, iconic resemblance of the wedding ring is to a washer or a doughnut. Iconic relationships are based on similarities in the shape and form of a particular object. Along with shape, the physical properties of the ring such as its metallic luster are reminiscent, in an iconic sense, to the color and texture of other golden objects such as a picture frame. An indexical understanding of the ring requires additional learned experience in order to construct the right correlation from memory. Mentally, we represent the ring's indexical meaning by its correlation with a human finger. Indexical meaning is specified in the fact that we know that the ring, when compared to other rings represented in memory, is the correct size for a finger as opposed to a toe. Several iconic comparisons must be indexically correlated in the mind in order to make the best referential association. But this does not constitute the highest form of meaning as-

22. Terrence Deacon, *The Symbolic Species: The Co-Evolution of Language and the Brain* (New York: W. W. Norton, 1998).

23. I am grateful to colleagues of the John Templeton Oxford Seminars in Science and Religion for suggestions to help clarify and strengthen this section of the argument.

sociated with our perception of the ring. Many Americans understand the ring within the social and cultural conventions of marriage. The ring symbolizes a covenant between two individuals, reflecting the laws and taboos of a coupled human relationship. Symbolically speaking, this might include a mandate for monogamy. Interpretation of the ring as indicative of a monogamous relationship implicates several indexical correlations based on represented memories of rings with prior individuals, religious teachings on marriage, and personal experience of divorce. Indexical meanings are themselves organized into symbolic beliefs regarding the conventions of marriage.

Deacon notes that words reflect the same hierarchy of association. For example, the word "trout" is iconic in that the sign or image of t-r-o-u-t on this piece of paper looks similar to "spout." This is only an iconic resemblance, as we understand that a trout has little if any meaning association with the spout on a teapot. At a higher referential level, we know that "trout" is indexically correlated with an animal — in this case, a cold-blooded vertebrate that lives in freshwater streams and lakes. Finally, we have symbolic representations of "trout" in our minds, perhaps related to aesthetics, concern for the environment, and as a quarry for outdooor enthusiasts who enjoy fly-fishing. In sum, trout are remarkably beautiful fish that are intolerant of pollution and available to the angler using artificial flies. Each of these symbolic interpretations is built upon indexical correlations that may include past memory of nature photography, consequential knowledge of human pollution, and learned behaviors associated with the sport of fly-fishing. Ultimately, symbolic referential meaning is constructed within the language "community" of mainstream American culture, where the image of the trout is assigned specific rules or boundaries for interpretation. The relationship between representations and words is bidirectional, creating symbolic meaning on the basis of iconic and indexical associations in cognition.

How does Deacon's scheme relate to personal stories, including the narratives typical of self-understanding in natural character? I would suggest that a single word is iconically associated with past occurrences of similar utterances, which in turn is indexically connected with a represented object known in memory from prior experience. Correlations between words and objects can form direct associations such as between a trout and a fishing rod, but also include particular occasions, people, and places. The brain is capable of creating fantastically complex repetitions of these correlations in stories. Indexical correlations between words and objects are assembled into higher-order abstractions that include elaborate, symbolic representations of characters, plots, themes, and dilemmas. To achieve this, associations of symbols are combined into *conceptual blends* that form novel meaning.[24] The meaning of these blends can be diverse and varied, applied through characters or other participants in narrative. Narrative is rich with data regarding the individual's symbolic self-understanding, based on how the self is mentally represented relative to other people.

As an example, take an adolescent boy's story about catching a big trout. On the phone with his friend, the boy recounts the tale of a treasured fishing trip with his father. After an entire day without a bite, he hooks and lands a three-pound brown trout at dusk. Many iconic relationships are accessed as a basis for indexical correlations that in turn provide the setting for the symbolic landscape of the story, evident in the boy's recollections of the cold water temperature, the huge cedars of the forest stream, the weather conditions, and his emotional state after a day without a fish. Upon sharing the moment of hooking the fish, the boy blends these symbolic references as he describes the victorious moment when it comes to the net. Sophisticated symbolic implications emerge through blended narrative, including the yells of the boy's father (pride), the taking of pictures (accomplishment, trophy), and the knowledge that, in the retelling, the fish will grow larger (embellishment). The meaning of the landed brown trout is not just "fishy" in its essence and intent — the boy uses the account to illustrate how he understands the self in relation to his father, a relationship of primary significance.

The "gap" between symbolic representation and natural (spoken or written) language at any level along Deacon's hierarchy may be understood in term of *semantic space*. Semantic space is cognitive shorthand for the meaning associations that are generated by the brain between symbols expressed in language. Assuming that natural character is present in exemplar self-understanding, it follows that narratives will yield secrets about how self and other are symbolically configured in cognition.

Recently, we conducted a pilot computational semantic-space analysis of self-understanding in L'Arche assistants. Based on a prior study with

---

24. Gilles Fauconnier and Mark Turner, *The Way We Think: Conceptual Blending and the Mind's Hidden Complexities* (New York: Basic, 2002).

exemplary adolescents, we theorized that symbolic self-understanding could be "mapped" at a representational level. Specifically, we wanted to know if representations of self and other are organized differently for fifteen *experienced* assistants (those with more than three years' service) than they are for fifteen *novice* assistants (those with less than a year's experience).

To accomplish this, we used a computational language program developed at Bellcore Laboratories and the University of Colorado, Boulder.[25] Latent Semantic Analysis (LSA) can be used to make meaning comparisons for words and narrative from participant responses to a clinical interview. LSA is both a human knowledge theory and a computational method for the extraction and representation of word meaning from a large text corpus. LSA compares a test parcel of language responses with a large (eleven-million-word) library of text knowledge. By using a matrix decomposition technique similar to factor analysis (singular value decomposition), LSA is able to compare a target word, phrase, or paragraph within the test parcel of language in order to generate an estimate of meaning similarity.[26]

LSA does not make any use of word order; thus syntax and morphology are not considered in the construction of meaning. Instead, test data are represented in terms of words and the narrative episodes in which they occur. LSA has been successfully used in two applications relevant to the mapping of natural character. LSA demonstrated that human metaphors are understood where categories of nonliteral and literal meaning are distinguished in order to facilitate comprehension.[27] For example, the metaphor *My lawyer is a shark* contains a nonliteral, meta-

25. I am grateful to Dr. Warren Brown at the Travis Research Institute, Fuller Graduate School of Psychology, for the invitation to find an empirical solution to natural language responses in human subjects during my second doctoral year.

26. LSA is accessible online at http://lsa.colorado.edu. Detailed review of LSA can be found in the following articles: Darrel Laham, "Latent Semantic Analysis Approaches to Categorization," in *Proceedings of the Nineteenth Annual Conference of the Cognitive Science Society*, ed. M. Shafto and P. Langley (Hillsdale, N.J.: Erlbaum, 1998), p. 979; T. Landauer, P. Foltz, and D. Laham, "An Introduction to Latent Semantic Analysis," *Discourse Processes* 3 (1998): 259-84; B. Rehder, M. Schreiner, M. Wolfe, D. Laham, T. Landauer, and W. Kintsch, "Using Latent Semantic Analysis to Assess Knowledge: Some Technical Considerations," *Discourse Processes* 25 (1998): 337-52.

27. Walter Kintsch, "Metaphor Comprehension: A Computational Theory," *Psychonomic Bulletin and Review* 7 (2000): 257-66.

phorical word (shark) that refers to a superordinate category of living creatures renowned for their ferocity. The metaphorical properties of shark (vicious, aggressive, tenacious) are directly attributed to the lawyer, and were identified by LSA in assigning meaning to that phrase. By contrast, the literal properties of the shark (gills, fins, teeth) are not applicable to the metaphor and similarly were not noteworthy in LSA output data. Thus, LSA can ascertain metaphorical meaning in natural language on the basis of either nonliteral or literal categorizations. In the narratives of L'Arche assistants, representational meaning of self and other is sustained at both nonliteral and literal levels. If a L'Arche assistant says *My best friend cares for me like Mother Teresa,* we may presume that she is articulating a metaphor of social influence. In the same interview, she might concretely refer to the same friend as a *mentor.* By virtue of its ability to distinguish categories around uses of metaphor in natural language, LSA offers a nuanced assessment of meaning.

5. Mapping Natural Character

The computational semantic-space method is useful in providing an unsupervised, visual picture of how social influences are potentially indicated for the development of natural character in L'Arche. Responses from experienced and novice L'Arche assistants corresponded with interview questions designed to access representations of *actual self* along with *partner, parents, best friend,* and *God.* Narrative data were prepared for LSA by extracting all words used by each individual to describe the actual self. In LSA these self-descriptor words were compared to combined narrative responses for the experienced and the novice sample group to the interview questions corresponding with each of the five study representations (actual self, partner, parents, best friend, God). This resulted in a matrix of LSA output data that compared the meaning of self-descriptor words to the actual self and other people as described in narrative responses. To put this in a slightly different way, the "distance" between the actual self and various other people was calculated in semantic space based upon the meaning similarities of participant narratives.

Matrix data from LSA were then subjected to multidimensional scaling analysis (MDS). Briefly, MDS is an exploratory, multivariate technique that attempts to find structure in a set of distance measures be-

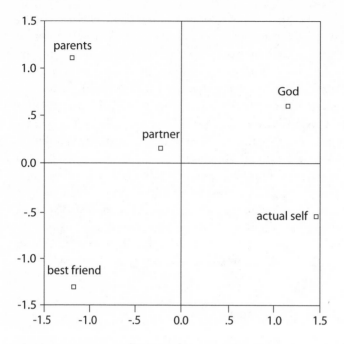

Figure 1. MDS perceptual map illustrating experienced L'Arche assistant representations of self and other derived from LSA

tween objects. MDS is able to identify dimensions affecting the objects under study when the bases of comparison are unknown or undefined. The MDS technique results in a perceptual "map" of the data matrix. In this application, the ALSCAL multidimensional scaling model was selected and used with the Euclidean distance measure, an approach suitable for data matrices of group samples.[28] This method specified the selection of the smallest possible number of dimensions in order to obtain the best fit. Generally, the researcher's selection of dimensions for MDS must simultaneously balance the number of objects under study (minimum of four objects necessary per dimension), along with Kruskal's stress value equal to or below .20, and the preservation of a R^2 value at or

28. A detailed review of multidimensional scaling can be found in J. Hair, R. Anderson, R. Tatham, and W. Black, *Multivariate Data Analysis*, 5th ed. (Saddle River, N.J.: Prentice-Hall, 1999).

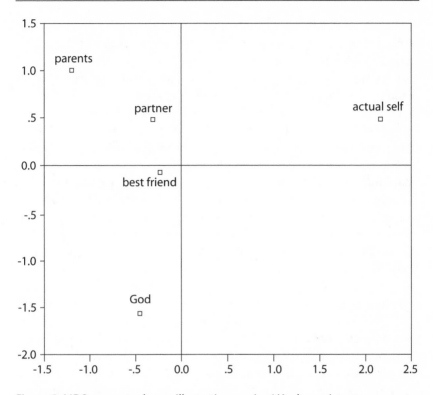

Figure 2. MDS perceptual map illustrating novice L'Arche assistant representations of self and other derived from LSA

above .60. Given these criteria, ALSCAL MDS was used to create two-dimensional perceptual maps of expected social influences for both experienced and novice assistant groups. That is, the actual self was compared to various others on the basis of *what those people expect* of the L'Arche assistant. For the experienced L'Arche assistants, Kruskal's stress of .03 and R^2 value of .98 indicated a strong model fit. Further, Kruskal's stress of .10 and R^2 of .93 indicated good model fit for the novice assistants. MDS perceptual maps for experienced and novice L'Arche assistant groups are given in Figures 1 and 2, respectively.[29]

29. Kevin Reimer and Lawrence J. Walker, "Social Cognition of Altruistic Love and Compassionate Care in L'Arche Assistants." Paper presented at the Association for Moral Education Annual Conference, 12-17 July 2003, Krakow, Poland.

What do these maps tell us about natural character? Assuming that natural character is forged in the context of relationship with others, the maps show a fairly isolated actual self for both experienced and novice assistants. However, in Figure 1 the representation of God is close to the actual self. This means that experienced assistants use language to describe the actual self that is similar to the language used to describe "what God expects of me." This is noteworthy for several reasons. First, experienced assistants powerfully identify their altruistic commitment with their spiritual experiences of God. God's expectations for their goals and conduct are at the forefront of their thinking about the self. Second, novice assistants lack this kind of representational affiliation in cognition. This was qualitatively evident in novice responses. In the main, novices were much less interested in spirituality and tended to demonstrate uncertainty as to who God is or what God does. Third, these observations suggest that experienced assistants perceive themselves as spiritually empowered agents, but do this from a firmly established, foundational self-understanding. To be blunt, experienced assistants have better-formed identities, knowing who they are in the context of relationship with others. We would expect this, given their altruistic longevity and enthusiasm in L'Arche.

The use of a computational language model to provide unsupervised analysis of L'Arche assistant narratives potentially alters the landscape of the altruism research project in psychology. In the interest of providing a psychologically realistic portrait of caring behavior, we are obligated to avoid minimal realism or idealism in the assessment of human motivation. If LSA is even remotely accurate in its meaning inferences, we can use the narratives of ambivalent altruists to demonstrate implicit relationships in symbolic representation that may not immediately be evident to the individual study participant. Indeed, in a prior study of exemplary adolescents, everyday comparison youth demonstrated a social-cognitive profile of unformed identity. That is, despite the efforts of these adolescents to present themselves as "having it together," their own use of language demonstrated an actual self that was inexorably isolated from representations of self and other.[30] It is important to note that the L'Arche social-cognitive data presented here are preliminary, as is the use of LSA with natural language responses from human subjects.

30. See Reimer and Wade-Stein, "Moral Identity in Adolescence," p. 33.

Inferences drawn from these data should be treated tentatively until further work is done to establish the construct validity of the model and, more particularly, its efficacy with a full L'Arche sample set.

6. Conclusion

Murphy's self-renunciation thesis, while requiring qualification in psychological research, represents an important stimulus for the field of moral psychology. This chapter has attempted to outline one potential direction for altruism research understood in terms of natural character. As understood on the basis of psychological realism, the natural character project implies a social science of grace — accepting what is in order to know what might be. Consequently, Murphy's proposal requires that the psychological realist think deeply regarding the generation of meaning from research data. I have argued that this raises the importance of narrative data taken from the lives of real, potentially ambivalent altruists. Much work remains in establishing the credibility of this perspective as expressed in an unsupervised, computational methodology applied to human speech. Yet the story of self-understanding in exemplars such as L'Arche assistants makes this a worthwhile effort, and a hedge against philosophical hegemony in the task of moral psychology.

Chapter 7

Unequally Yoked? The Role of Culture in the Relationship between Theology and Psychology

J. DEREK McNEIL

1. Introduction

There is little evidence that culture or ethnic identity have played a significant role in the dialogue between theology and psychology.[1] However, there continues to be a growing call for a broader conversation that might draw on diverse perspectives and backgrounds.[2] Moreover, any new model of integration must consider the global nature of the dialogue between theology and psychology, and invite those who have been on the periphery of the conversation to come closer to the center. This appeal toward inclusion can be seen biblically, in the parable of the great banquet (Luke 14:12-24). Jesus uses the banquet as a kingdom metaphor to suggest that God is also interested in those who dwell on the outside and in those whose value is questionable. Moreover, he is willing to displace the privileged who resist his invitation to an inclusive banquet table. I remain convinced that we must still create places at our "integration" table for other voices, worldviews, and philosophical assumptions.

1. Sally S. Canning, Paul W. Case, and Sandra L. Kruse, "Contemporary Christian Psychological Scholarship and 'The Least of These': An Empirical Review," *Journal of Psychology and Christianity* 20 (2001): 205-23.

2. Trey Buchanan, "Historically Grounding the Practice of Psychology: Implications for Professional Training," *History of Psychology* 5 (2002): 240-48; Canning et al., "Contemporary Christian Psychological Scholarship and 'The Least of These'"; Peter C. Hill and Duane R. Kauffmann, "Psychology and Theology: Toward the Challenge," *Journal of Psychology and Christianity* 15 (1996): 175-83; Hendrika Vande Kemp, "Christian Psychologies for the Twenty-First Century: Lessons from History," *Journal of Psychology and Christianity* 17 (1998): 197-209.

Nancey Murphy has been very thoughtful in her attempts to move us beyond the present "research program" in the integration of theology and psychology. In this volume, she has put forth ideas worthy of deeper examination and has approached the task with admirable faithfulness. I am encouraged by her willingness to challenge the (hegemonic) assumptions of a "generic Christianity" in what I believe is an attempt to expand the integrative dialogue. Her choice to put forth an Anabaptist tradition as the core theology has considerable potential. However, I don't believe Dr. Murphy has gone far enough in her integrative exercise. She recognizes the reforming nature of offering a particular view of theology as the core of her integration, but in the coupling neglects to question the privileged assumptions of a modern Euro-American psychology. Consequently, this chapter is not so much a critique of her work as it is an attempt to join her and extend the dialogue.

As an African American with formal theological and psychological training, I have valued the richness of the dialogue within the integration discourse. I must confess, however, that I have bristled at the narrow scope of human experiences that have been examined. My early forays into (evangelical) Christian psychology, in the late 1980s, certainly convinced me that examining the relationship between Christian theology and psychology was an important pursuit. But after a brief introduction during graduate school, I walked away from the integration conversations with the distinct feeling that I would never be a significant partner in the dialogue. My identity as an evangelical Christian was affirmed, but other identities (ethnic and cultural) and loyalties, and the contexts in which they were lived out, were dismissed or ignored. I don't believe this indifference was malicious or fully conscious, but simply evidence that ethnic identity was less relevant (or apparent) to the concerns of those people to whom Christian psychology was appealing. Moreover, this seemed to be reconfirmed in the tacit assumption that an evangelical Christian identity freed of particularity was the exclusive lens with which to interpret the world. This posture has been the privilege of European Americans, but less that of ethnic minorities, who, as in all other social sectors, have been addressed first via minority status. Consequently, for a person who has lived his life as a social "other," culture and ethnicity matter. In truth, this chapter has emerged out of some frustration, but more significantly, out of a hunger for a more inclusive conversation.

More recently, Christian psychology has increased its sensitivity to the experiences and contexts of ethnically and culturally diverse populations,[3] and race and ethnicity have been given more attention as clinical variables. But the relatively young (modern) enterprise of "integration" has been centered largely in the context of the Western theological tradition[4] and Euro-American psychology.[5] These two worldviews have significantly influenced the parameters of the dialogue and shaped the roles that culture and ethnic identity have played in the discussion. Consequently, culture and ethnic identity[6] are topics that have generally been absent in the integrative dialogue between psychology and Christian faith.[7] Our present conceptual horizons are still quite "culture-bound," and Christian psychology runs the risk of being "ghettoized" if it is unable to engage Christians of differing ethnic identities and cultural worldviews and draw them into the conversation.

In the face of globalization, Western societies are now confronted with rising voices from within, such as the "politics of difference," the "politics of recognition," and the resurgence of ethnic, cultural, and religious discontinuities. In addition, there are a growing number of voices from the outside, expressed in the escalating tensions and conflicts between modern (Western) ideologies and technologies and traditional cultures.[8] Here in the West, we tend to frame these conflicts as resistance to Western progress and Western ideals (freedom, democracy, rule of law, and so on), while others in the world describe it as resistance to Western imperialism. All indications suggest that the complexity and the tensions

---

3. Siang-Yang Tan, "Cultural Issues in Spirit-Filled Psychotherapy," *Journal of Psychology and Christianity* 18 (1999): 164-76.

4. Trey Buchanan, "Historically Grounding the Practice of Psychology."

5. Kenneth J. Gergen, Aydan Gulerce, Andrew Lock, and Girishwar Misra, "Psychological Science in Cultural Context," *American Psychologist* 51 (1996): 496-503.

6. "Ethnic" or "ethnic identity" is often used interchangeably with "race" and "culture"; however, "ethnicity" is generally used in reference to groups characterized by a common nationality, geographic origin, culture, or language. See, e.g., Hector Betancourt and Steven R. Lopez, "The Study of Culture, Ethnicity, and Race in American Psychology," *American Psychologist* 48 (1993): 629-37.

7. Canning et al., "Contemporary Christian Psychological Scholarship and 'The Least of These'"; Hill and Kauffmann, "Psychology and Theology"; Vande Kemp, "Christian Psychologies for the Twenty-First Century."

8. Judith M. Gundry-Volf and Miroslav Volf, *A Spacious Heart: Essays on Identity and Belonging* (Harrisburg, Pa.: Trinity Press International, 1997).

of the global context will increase before they stabilize. Moreover, the social disruptions will increase the need for psychosocial services around the world. While Western *psychologies* are beginning the struggle to meet these realities, Western theologies have generally not been as responsive.[9] In addition, Christian psychology, a progeny of both, seems quite inexpert and unsure of its ability to respond. Because our conversations have been focused more domestically, we lack the awareness and the tools to engage in a more global conversation. We must further broaden and "thicken" the dialogue that has already begun,[10] if a Christian psychology will be able to negotiate the complexity of a culturally diverse (global) milieu and an increasingly postmodern (late modernity) context. I believe we are facing a crisis of relevance, and I desire to see a Christian psychology that is able to take bolder steps toward being salt in a world that is teetering on the edge of dramatic — and possibly traumatic — change.

Murphy doesn't use the construct of culture, but she implies the concept when she engages the particularities ("thickness") of a historical theological tradition. With this choice she brings into focus the classic tensions between the "global" and the "local,"[11] or the etic (universal) and emic (group-specific) distinction found in the respective literatures of anthropology and cross-cultural psychology. A very helpful tool (metaphor) in understanding this tension is the notion of "thickness" and "thinness" employed by Alvin Dueck and Kevin Reimer.[12] Thickness represents the cultural density of a discourse, while thinness represents those more common elements that can be found across various groups. Dueck and Reimer suggest that the thicker the discourse, the more it is bound to a particular group and historical tradition.[13] The metaphor is helpful because it allows us to understand the value of the universal and the particular, but also the paradoxical nature of their relationship.

Culture is a complex subject with ambiguous boundaries, but I believe a greater understanding will help us avoid becoming an intellec-

9. Robert J. Schreiter, *The New Catholicity: Theology between the Global and Local* (Maryknoll, N.Y.: Orbis Books, 1997).

10. D. John Lee and Mark Kane, "Multicultural Counseling: A Christian Appraisal," *Journal of Psychology and Christianity* 11 (1992): 317-25.

11. Schreiter, *The New Catholicity.*

12. Alvin Dueck and Kevin Reimer, "Retrieving the Virtues in Psychotherapy: Thick and Thin Discourse," *American Behavioral Scientist* 47 (2003): 427-41.

13. Dueck and Reimer, "Retrieving the Virtues in Psychotherapy."

tual enclave. Therefore, I have organized this chapter to maintain a dialogue with Dr. Murphy's ideas. In the next section, I will develop a workable definition of culture. In the following section, I will interact more directly with her ideas from a different vantage point. In the final section, I will briefly look at the biblical narratives of Babel and Pentecost as potential resources for considering culture in a Christian psychology dialogue.

2. Culture as a Construct

As I have stated, part of the dilemma in applying the notion(s) of culture is that its meanings are multifaceted. Culture is variously defined across the social sciences and examined as a multilevel phenomenon. It can be described as the property of an individual, group, or society. In a real sense, this ubiquitous quality makes it quite difficult to distinguish and conceptualize. Moreover, the relationship that it has with such movements as "multiculturalism," "diversity," and "postmodernity" further muddies the conceptual waters.[14] Therefore, before we begin, it is necessary to provide a context for our discussion and clarify my use of the term.

We are most aware of culture in its manifestations (language, ritual, artifacts, food, and so forth) and during the awkwardness of intercultural interactions.[15] Culture in this sense is more "shallow," external, objectified, and categorical (thin), often associated with racial and ethnic characteristics.[16] However, the culture of a group is dynamic, and its core assumptions change (slowly) over time, in interaction with the context. These changes are manifested in artifacts, stylistic expectations, group identification, and analytical and conceptual tools for interpreting experience. Understanding these last two aspects (analytical/conceptual) of culture would serve us in developing a more global Christian psychology. Hence, we can think of culture as being the product (artifacts), the customs (mores), and the interpretative lens (metaframe) by which members of a group interact in their environment.

14. Kevin Avruch, *Culture and Conflict Resolution* (Washington, D.C.: United States Institute of Peace, 1998).

15. David R. Matsumoto, *Culture and Psychology,* 2d ed. (Belmont, Calif.: Wadsworth/Thomson Learning, 2000).

16. Matsumoto, *Culture and Psychology.*

In truth, we continue to be so strongly influenced by our political views of culture and race that scholarly treatments have less salience. Generally, in the "national consciousness," we appear to talk about culture in two broad ways. In our social discourse, we seem to hold a communal understanding of these meanings, even if we are at odds with their use.

They are not our only public notions of culture, but they have particular sociohistorical salience. First, we employ the term "culture" when we are speaking of changes in the milieu or shifts in the national ethos related to attitudes, values, and moral beliefs. Often these changes are thought to be negative or disruptive trends, supported by a particular ideological struggle (e.g., religious right versus liberal left; "culture wars"). We usually treat this form of culture in societal terms, more in the domain of sociology than psychology.

The second notion of culture is considered an aspect of one's racial or ethnic identity, minority status, or "otherness." Many will consider this as an outgrowth of the "politics of difference"; consequently, this cultural form is thought to be the product and customs of a particular group and its identity. This approach views culture more psychologically, as a personal or group attribute.

Both of these forms can be defined as culture, and are more prominent in our collective meaning because of the present sociopolitical context. However, these forms are not as helpful in viewing how culture influences our processing, metaphors, and meaning-making as a lens for viewing reality. Our conscious ideas of the concepts of culture are determined by the dominant "modes" of culture that we have already unconsciously employed. Hence, we are never able to avoid having a priori assumptions about culture.

I have found Kevin Avruch's brief treatment of culture, in his book *Culture and Conflict Resolution*,[17] very helpful in managing the concept for this type of exercise. I would like to talk about three notions, or "modes," that have generally been accepted within our collective consciousness. I'm using the term "modes" here to suggest the form in which culture is understood. The first is what can be called an "aesthetic" view of culture. Culture in this mode is a product of the intellectual or artistic endeavors of a particular society. When we speak of "high culture" or "pop culture," we are utilizing this notion of culture.

---

17. Avruch, *Culture and Conflict Resolution*.

The second, an evolutionist view of culture, is often connected to developmental notions about civilization and societal progress. Culture is envisioned on a continuum of primitive to progressive, and seen as advancing over time. All people are assumed to have culture as acquired through their society; in other words, they have beliefs, art, laws, moral standards, capacities, and customs. However, all societies are not in possession of the same degree of civic complexity, differing in their degree of development along a universal continuum from "primitive" to "developed" cultures. Also known as "unilineal cultural evolution," this theory of human progress was most prolific in Western ideologies. It assumed that "Western civilization" was the superior cultural form based on its morality, rationality, technology, and institutions, and ranked all other cultures in accord with their similarity to Western ideals. While unilineal cultural evolution has lost much of its scholarly appeal, this thinking is still evident in much of Western thought (ideology) and posture in the global context. This view dominated anthropology until the twentieth century. Anthropologist Franz Boas and his students, for example, reacted negatively to the valuation and ranking of people groups.[18] Consequently, the last of our three modes of culture, "anthropological," emerged in response to the "evolutionist."[19] In contrast to the previous perspective, this view of culture focused on the uniqueness of various people groups and societies.[20] Later developments in this mode have emphasized relativism and plurality, but they have been less broadly appealing, becoming the source of ideological debate.

These three "generic" ways of thinking about culture in the Western context help us see how we apply cultural notions tacitly, or even unconsciously. I have highlighted these three modes because while each is an influential part of the Western worldview, each also holds a different kind of significance and importance in our assessment of the world. All three modes remain meaningful in the present social context as part of a historically transmitted (socialized) set of ideas, but they are relevant in varying degrees. We appear to draw on contextual cues to determine which modes are most salient, while our group membership(s) serves to supply

18. This is referenced in Eloise H. Meneses, "No Other Foundation: Establishing a Christian Anthropology," *Christian Scholars Review* 29 (2000): 531-49.

19. Avruch, *Culture and Conflict Resolution*.

20. Avruch, *Culture and Conflict Resolution*.

us with the modal options, and personal attributes determine a particular approach. Of course, I have oversimplified a complex process, but my hope is that we will begin to see how cultural modes can influence our perceptions and concepts below the level of conscious awareness.

For this project, I will employ culture as an "analytical tool" or a lens ("metaframe") by which to make our cultural assumptions about integration a bit more explicit. I must begin by acknowledging that my own perspective is from a particular vantage point and complex history. I recognize that there are modes that I hold that are more universal (generic) across groups, but there are also aspects of my religio-cultural community that are quite particular (e.g., a theological emphasis on "celebration" and "suffering"). In some ways, Murphy's explicit use of her tradition encourages us to make our hermeneutical horizons more explicit. This has not been a part of our generic tradition (evangelical Christian psychology) since we have emphasized a universal Christianity, but it invites us to place our conversation about a new Christian psychology in the midst of a broader global Christian community.

3. Murphy's Integration

While I differ with Dr. Murphy's integrative treatment of theology, I find her Radical-Reformation integration to be a refreshing notion. I appreciate her attempts to catapult us free of the gravitational pull of a scientism that has drawn psychology into either emulating the natural sciences or struggling with its scientific legitimacy. Christian psychology has been compelled to follow suit, since we are committed to gaining legitimacy as a subset in the field of psychology as well as in the Christian church. All truth may be God's truth, but increasingly, in Christian psychology, the prevailing method to validate this truth is empirical evidence. Our present attempts to integrate an increasingly scientific psychology with a modern theology appears to work to the degree that both are modern exercises and assume a similar logic that values rationalism and objective methods.[21] Our theological methodology may have some

---

21. Eric L. Johnson and Stanton L. Jones, "A History of Christians in Psychology," in *Psychology and Christianity*, ed. Eric Johnson and Stanton Jones (Downers Grove, Ill.: InterVarsity Press, 2000), pp. 11-53.

compatibility with a scientific methodology, but I'm not convinced we have retained the "good news." Murphy's work actually renews my questions about the compatibility of a Christian theology or any other "particular" theology that draws on other sources of knowledge (scripture, tradition, and so on) and a modern science ideology that devalues nonmaterial resources.

Murphy introduces us to Imre Lakatos as a resource for "reforming theological methodology." She invites us into a process of theoretical (metaphorical) change as we examine her proposal for a Christian psychology. With a background in counseling/clinical psychology, I am less familiar with the philosophy of Lakatos than that of Thomas Kuhn and his classic text, *The Structure of Scientific Revolutions*,[22] and hence less comfortable relinquishing his "idea set." However, both Kuhn and Lakatos are concerned with the methods of theory change in science and the role of history in the emergence of new ideas. Kuhn, responding to Karl Popper and the neopositivist movement, challenges the assumption in their philosophy of science that knowledge emerges in a rational fashion. As Murphy acknowledges, Kuhn's "paradigm shifts" are a critique of Popper's falsification method where he introduces the idea that scientific progress was influenced by sociohistorical or "irrational" (versus rational) factors. Lakatos's work attempts to move Popper's method into a more competitive position to respond to Kuhn's notions of irrational theory change in the scientific community by offering a developmental rationale.[23] However, it seems relevant for us to ask again the classic question for this enterprise: What is the role of history and culture in theory change and in the development of a new Christian psychology?

Murphy tries to find a new direction by constructing a model that alters our metaphors for theology, by providing a quintessential ("proper") role for theology in the relationship with the sciences, and offering a particular "tradition" to anchor the discourse. It is this last overture that invites us to consider the role of culture or other particularities. Moreover, in her "positive heuristic," or her research program plan, Murphy suggests the importance of "interracial and interethnic relations."[24] How-

22. Thomas S. Kuhn, *The Structure of Scientific Revolutions*, 2d ed. (Chicago: University of Chicago Press, 1970).

23. See Murphy, Chapter 1, section 2, this volume.

24. See Murphy, Chapter 3, section 3.2, this volume.

ever, she takes her cues from a psychology that has not adequately addressed culture beyond the clinical context and that holds a number of the assumptions of modern science. The traditional goal of scientific psychology is to strengthen existing theoretical models, their assumption of universality and their claims of explanatory capacity. A second goal is to understand and explain existing variations in performance among individuals from varying races, ethnic groups, genders, and other demographic categories.[25] Both goals are focused on universal theory application while clarifying the exceptions. Traditional science and psychology have utilized culture most often as a distinguishing variable. It is the cultural detachment of psychology that is thought to provide it with its explanatory authority. Any suggestion that it is embedded within a culture is tantamount to denying it this authority.[26]

In fairness to Murphy, we cannot accuse her of ignoring human complexity in her positive heuristic, but her lack of contextual treatment (global or local) leaves me wondering if her framework can be lived out. Her focus on methodological compatibility and rational consistency has allowed her to overlook related sociohistorical movements that are likely to have a significant impact on the future of a Christian psychology, both in how we do psychology and in the ways we think about theology. The sociocultural context has changed in dramatic ways as well. We can no longer ignore the philosophical influence of postmodernity or the shifting demographic realities of globalization. In tandem, both challenge our notions of truth and epistemological authorization. They also challenge the universality of our theology and the global utility of our psychology.

I think there are two examples that may help to highlight the point. The first major sociohistorical movement is the globalization of Christianity and the demographic shifts in Christendom. The second movement is the re-emergence of the importance of religion, culture, and ethnicity in a globalizing context. The first example is likely to be less

25. Catherine R. Cooper and Jill Denner, "Theories Linking Culture and Psychology: Universal and Community-Specific Processes," *Annual Review of Psychology* 49 (1998): 559-84.

26. David Ingleby, "Problems in the Study of the Interplay between Science and Culture," in *The Culture and Psychology Reader*, ed. Nancey R. Goldberger and Jody B. Veroff (New York and London: New York University Press, 1995).

familiar to most readers than the second, so I'll highlight the major points made in this argument.

The Western theological tradition has yet to acknowledge the southward and eastward movement (Africa, Asia, and South America) of the Christian church, or recognize the impact of this phenomenon on theological inquiry. Philip Jenkins argues in his book *The Next Christendom* that while there is a decline of Christians in the Western world, Christianity in the Southern Hemisphere is on the rise.[27] He suggests that by the year 2050, only one Christian in five will be white (non-Latino) and born in Europe or America. Jenkins proposes that the emerging world Christianity is more traditional, orthodox, evangelical, and supernaturally oriented than that of the Western church. It can be argued that if we are to understand the emerging Christian world, we must look increasingly to non-Western contexts and culture. The Western dominance of Christianity has meant that debates over faith and culture have often focused specifically on European and American (contextual) matters.[28] The dramatic demographic shifts in the church certainly raise many questions about the changing "face" of Christendom over the next fifty years.

Theologies of liberation, ecology, human rights, and feminism have all emerged on the global scene in the last thirty years, and may have been the first wave of the coming global changes we must address. Robert Schreiter argues that these "contextual (thick) theologies" arose because the universal (thin) and more Western theologies were unable to speak effectively to issues of poverty, oppression, alienation, postcolonialism, de-traditionalization, and commodification that were more idiosyncratically expressed in local circumstances.[29] However, these early theological forms have been resisted and dismissed by many Western theologians (especially evangelicals) as not being "orthodox" theology, or as being subcategories of mainstream theology. It seems now that we will have to revisit the issue of orthodoxy as we are faced with finding our (Christian psychology) role in this new global mix. This is not to suggest that we can ignore the challenges of syncretism,

27. Philip Jenkins, *The Next Christendom: The Coming of Global Christianity* (New York: Oxford University Press, 2002).
28. Jenkins, *The Next Christendom.*
29. Schreiter, *The New Catholicity.*

but that we must take seriously the influence of culture, context, and identity in the process of "doing" theology. A new Christian psychology cannot ignore the questions raised by a global context if it is to remain relevant to a global Christendom. As Westerners, we have thought of ourselves and our culture as producing the missionaries to the world. Hence, we have more clearly understood the flow of the global to the local (globalization), but we have had less appreciation for the "reflexivity" or the "outflowing" of Western ideology as it curves back to the West.[30] Schreiter argues that it is not just Christendom but the rise of religious fundamentalism, acts of terror, resistance to the Western intrusion, global demographic shifts, and postmodernity that all might be explained by this aspect of globalization.

We are in need of a sociohistorical perspective that treats culture and context as significant factors in the integrative dialogue.[31] This is neither a new nor a revolutionary idea; others in Christian psychology have suggested that we need to consider ethnicity and culture as "differential" variables.[32] However, with this approach, culture is usually limited to a demographic category and examined as an individual-level phenomenon, with little philosophical or historical depth. While we have just begun to examine cultural differences and consider the nature of intercultural interactions, there is less sophistication in considering cultural influences or the a priori assumptions we hold about our methods and conclusions. It is important not just to respect cultural differences but to understand the ethnocentrism of our own philosophy and worldview. This may sound a bit overstated, but I would argue that our inability to see ourselves (Christians) and our tools (psychology) as embedded in our cultural setting will mean that we risk offering a (Christian) psychology that is "universalizing" but not universal.

This was never brought home to me more clearly than it was in my experience in India a few years ago. I was with a team of psychology faculty and two students, one of whom was from India. We had been invited to teach a group of Indian evangelists basic counseling and listening skills. We all understood this was something of a grand experiment, but with a sense of trepidation and adventure, we embraced the mission.

---

30. Schreiter, *The New Catholicity.*
31. Vande Kemp, "Christian Psychologies for the Twenty-First Century."
32. Vande Kemp, "Christian Psychologies for the Twenty-First Century."

However, there was a moment that was quite profound for all of us, trainees and trainers alike. It came during a presentation by one of our team members about a classic suicide intervention strategy. She was offering the standard methods for assessing the risks and suggested that the trainees should ask about suicidal ideation. An uneasiness came over the trainees, but it took a few minutes before our Indian students were willing to risk offending us. Then one trainee asked, "What about Karma?" We as a team were confused by the question and assumed that maybe we weren't communicating very well. Though we all spoke English, American English is not Indian English. Nervously, the team member presenting started to repeat the standard procedures as if she had not been clear, and then another trainee asked, "But what about Karma?" We stopped the session and decided to try to understand Karma and the question. Painfully, our students explained to us that one's Karma emerges from one's deeds, and if we were to ask someone about suicidal thoughts, it would suggest that suicide was their Karma, their destiny. In other words, the standard intervention in a Western context was a pronouncement of death in theirs. We quickly suggested that this was not a useful strategy and worked together to identify a better intervention. Together we decided that Christ had died to take on someone's Karma and provide an alternative to suicide. The level of excitement from this synergy was quite invigorating and contagious. While we came to an agreement on the universals, the prevention of suicide, the particulars were quite different, and we momentarily shared a co-constructed worldview. I cannot begin to suggest that we understood their worldview(s), or they ours, but we understood how differently we saw the world.

Schreiter suggests that Western theology, as practiced in the academy and presented globally, is also prone to devaluing the cultural and contextual issues relevant to its intended audience for those issues thought to be more universal.[33] However, this is a method and an ideology that extends from modernity and Western culture. Hence, when it was exported to Asia, Africa, South America, and the South Pacific, the question was, Does one need to be Western in order to become Christian? Schreiter argues that what Christians presented globally were *universalizing* theologies rather than a universal theology.[34] In other words,

---

33. Schreiter, *The New Catholicity.*
34. Schreiter, *The New Catholicity.*

they extended the results of their theological reflection beyond their own contexts to other settings with little awareness of the rootedness of their theologies within their own cultural context.

We have borrowed heavily from Western philosophical ideas and tradition to construct our psychology (or psychologies) and to interpret theology. Moreover, it has become the *lingua franca,* and it has provided the ideological assumptions of our integrative dialogue. However, just as we should not assume that the extensive use of the English language around the world is indicative of universality, so we should not assume that our psychology is in a purely universal form. While speakers of "American English" and (East) "Indian English" are able to overcome their different "accents" to interact, they are not always communicating compatible ideas about the world. We must consider the church in the world beyond its Western boundaries and take into account the diversity of worldviews. How else can we have a "Christ-like" psychology that extends beyond the American church?

Shifting our hermeneutic of culture is clearly a significant challenge for the Christian psychological movement, particularly since much of the evangelical church has yet to acknowledge the importance of the dialogue concerning cultural and ethnic diversity,[35] and the field of psychology lacks the philosophical will to do so. American evangelical thinking, for its own reasons, has been quite reserved in its validation of other cultural frameworks or worldviews, and therefore has offered little theological affirmation of cultural differences at any level of depth.[36] Consequently, as American evangelicals attempting to "integrate" in a diverse cultural context, we lack ideological self-awareness and have limited tools.[37] This critical lack of awareness is likely the main factor in culture being excluded from the dialogue. It would be difficult for me to conceive of any conversation about "integration" or the future relationship between theology and psychology without some conversation and awareness about the impact of culture and context.

The central issue that many evangelical theologians are concerned with is the erosion of the universal truth claims of Christianity and

35. Michael O. Emerson and Christian Smith, *Divided by Faith* (New York: Oxford University Press, 2000).

36. Emerson and Smith, *Divided by Faith;* Jones and Johnson, "A History of Christians in Psychology."

37. Emerson and Smith, *Divided by Faith.*

their replacement by "culture-specific systems of shared meaning."[38] There is also a growing concern that diversity equals diversity of Christian interpretations, communities, and structures, thereby leading to competition and divisiveness. Few American Christians have been offered a biblical model that affirms cultural distinctiveness or metaphors of unity in diversity; indeed, it is more likely that the opposite has been affirmed. This throws evangelical Christians into a quandary. How do we ethically embrace culture and diversity while resisting the postmodern erosion of modernity and the challenges of pluralism? The results are, at best, an ambivalent support; at worst, an ethnocentric backlash.

Evangelicals have been reticent to blaze new trails and are more content to defend entrenched positions, since novelty is often associated with heresy.[39] However, I would suggest that we are in need of new biblical metaphors for culture. The following treatment of Babel and Pentecost offers an alternative approach to understanding how God preserves our cultural distinctiveness and presents a universal appeal.

4. Biblical Narratives for a Hermeneutic of Culture

While the scope of this chapter does not allow us to develop a more systematic theology of culture, it is necessary to offer a more biblical perspective. The biblical narratives of Babel and Pentecost provide two such perspectives of language and culture that may offer a framework by which to address unity and diversity. The Tower of Babel account is a brief narrative that emphasizes the introduction of linguistic diversity and ethnic identity. The story of Pentecost emphasizes the emergence of the persona of the Holy Spirit and the beginning of the church. It is more likely to be scrutinized regarding the issues of glossolalia rather than the re-introduction of diverse languages by God. It would be a hermeneutical error for me to argue that either of these passages is simply about language and culture, but they do offer a biblical context for us to catch

---

38. R. Albert Mohler, "The Integrity of the Evangelical Tradition and the Challenge of the Postmodern Paradigm," in *The Challenge of Postmodernism: An Evangelical Engagement,* ed. David S. Dockery (Wheaton, Ill.: Victor Books/SP Publications, 1995).

39. Gerald Bray, *Biblical Interpretation: Past and Present* (Downers Grove, Ill.: InterVarsity Press, 1996).

a glimpse of divine intentionality.[40] Our examination of these two texts allows us to explore other understandings that would better serve a theology of language and culture.

At first glance, the Babel narrative can be looked at as a functional story, explaining how humankind gained diverse languages and became scattered across the earth. However, this does not tell the whole story. With a closer look, God and humanity can be seen as protagonist and antagonist in a drama in which humanity is in rebellion against the wishes of God. In contrast, Pentecost reveals the response of God to human obedience, and is thought to be the story of the beginning of the universal Christian church, the unifying of (diverse) humanity under the lordship of Jesus. The emphasis has been on the dramatic entrance of the person of the Holy Spirit, who comes to empower the global witness of Jesus as the Christ. It is only upon deeper inspection, or possibly with a different lens, that the cultural and ethnic identity implications of the event become more evident. Within both of these accounts of God's movement toward humanity, we see an active God utilizing language and ethnic identification to bring about his purpose. God seems willing to introduce the initial chaos brought about by language (Babel), but is unhindered by it in bringing about his purposes in Christ (Pentecost). Thus these two texts together may offer a theological premise for a new hermeneutic of culture.

4.1. Babel

Consistent with the genre of Genesis, we may view Babel as the beginning of the story of language and culture in the human journey. I would argue that the Babel narrative is not meant to stand alone in its interpretation, but is the backdrop and underlying theme of a divine romantic drama.[41] In this drama, the Godhead appears to be the protagonist and the human social structure, the antagonist. God seems less concerned with individual behavior than the collective system. However, it is equally feasible to

---

40. Richard J. Mouw, *When the Kings Come Marching In* (Grand Rapids: Eerdmans, 1983).

41. Romance is used as a literary form that emphasizes extraordinary events and a desired resolution at the end.

argue that God is the antagonist to human grandiosity. Either way, the narrative juxtaposes God's desire and human intention as they are played out in human structures. When we consider the whole of the biblical narrative (drama), the divine-human enmity is not unending; but we should not easily dismiss God's opposition to this sort of human unity. The authors of the text are suggesting that human unity at any cost is clearly not the intention of God. Moreover, God is willing to employ chaos and dispersion as tools to thwart human structural systems based in human impertinence and self-importance. This theme is repeated in the theological symbol of Babylon, the city/empire that is in opposition to the reign of God. "Real" human development and progress cannot be understood in terms of the human social order and its technological advantage. As offensive as this may be to modernist ideological assumptions about progress, the advancement of a unified human civilization based on technological innovation was the enemy of God's plan for human destiny.

The inclination to build a tower is a metaphorical attempt to institute a new religio-political system: a new source of power carved out of human mastery and imagination.[42] The tower is a sort of totem, a visual symbol that can reify the formation of a new civilization, an icon of human superiority. This new civilization will exemplify human proficiency and efficacy and rival the new world-order that God has intended, which is dispersion (Gen. 9:1). The threat to the Godhead is systemic and symbolic; in essence it is a threat to divine authority.

The biblical narrative would leave us struggling with the image of the Godhead responding to the threat of human ingenuity. If we allow the narrative to remain true to its more poetic form, the issue of the Godhead being threatened and potentially impotent is less relevant than the willingness of the Godhead to respond dramatically to human insubordination. It appears in this situation that human unity, or universality, is of less value to God than human dispersal. I would not argue that dispersion is indicative of God's nature; rather, I would argue that intervention was critical to the destiny that God had planned for the human family. A similar theme is repeated throughout the Old Testament with the people of Israel. God is willing to let them be displaced as a method of redemption. At Babel the result is the loss of a "universal" criterion for

42. Anthony C. Thiselton, *Interpreting God and the Postmodern Self* (Grand Rapids: Eerdmans, 1995).

interpreting meaning within the human family, and the "confusing of language" becomes the catalyst for diverse cultural forms.

God thus introduces linguistic and ethnic diversity into humanity. It would be inaccurate to treat this act of God as we would treat the fall of humanity, in which humankind reaps the harvest of its disobedience. Arguably, symbolic tools such as language and culture, meant to support human life and community, become the vehicles for rebellion and human defiance. At Babel, God acts to thwart human independence while facilitating a divine mandate. The confusing of language and the diversification of meaning systems represent God's imposition on sinful humanity to bring about his purpose. To view culture and ethnicity as simply the consequences of sin may obscure the larger purpose of God and distort the role of diversity in human relations. While we cannot view language and ethnicity outside of the context of fallen humanity, it would be inappropriate to view human diversity as antithetical to the nature and intent of God.

4.2. Pentecost (Acts 2:1-21)

In chapter two of the book of Acts, we again have the gathering of a human community, but in contrast to Babel, this gathering is done in obedience to the invitation of God. In Acts 1:4, the apostles are commanded not to disperse but to gather and wait for that which God had promised. Babel and Pentecost provide different examples of a human response to God's command. At Babel, humanity exercises its freedom and goes against God's intentions. In contrast, at Pentecost, a small remnant of believers chooses to wait in faith and in the hope that this will bring the restoration of the kingdom to Israel (Acts 1:6). This group is also ethnically concerned, but they differ in their response to God's command.

The outpouring of the Spirit at Pentecost is the dramatic entry of a new age into human history and the first installment of the promise of universal restoration and the kingdom of God. While this is not the fullness of the kingdom, it is the empowering of humanity to surrender to the design of God (Acts 1:8). Pentecost represents the empowering of God's people for a universal movement with cosmic proportions. Anthony Thiselton suggests that the "pouring out" of the Holy Spirit on all people (Acts 2:17) is a reversal of Babel, and that it fulfills the promise in Joel 2:28-29. It is the reception of the Holy Spirit that offers the hope of a social community or *koinonia* that is unified by the centrality of Christ.[43]

For this international group of Jews, the amazement of Pentecost is to hear their native tongue in the mouths of these Galileans. This cultural accommodation by God opens them to the gospel, and it becomes an arresting symbol of his transcendent and universal design. There is no need to interpret the gospel cross-culturally. God, through the Holy Spirit, overcomes the human limitations of language and meaning from within their cultural boundaries. Jews, yet ethnic aliens, hear this communication within the familiarity of their own language, within the thickness of their own "mother tongue." God chooses to work through the symbolic vehicle of language, respecting human culture but offering transcendent membership in the family of God. By so doing, God extends himself to form a new community.

These two passages, understood together, would influence the cultural notions we hold about ethnic identity and God's willingness to breathe life into human forms and "distinctives." At Babel, the human *telos* of the builders was to make a name for themselves and become strong enough to resist God. However, Pentecost reveals that God offers a universal appeal that does not erase our cultural distinctiveness. This echoes the Incarnation: Christ embodied in human clothing and in historical context, the ultimate paradox of the universal and the particular.

5. Conclusion

The central question of any interdisciplinary integration exercise is, Are we able to accommodate the epistemological differences between two disciplines and find common ground? This is the historical and/or traditional question that has been the focus of interdisciplinary and intradisciplinary integration.[44] However, rarely have we assigned culture any role in the discussion. We have typically dismissed the significance of our theology and

43. Thiselton, *Interpreting God and the Postmodern Self*, p. 130.

44. Steven Bouma-Prediger, "The Task of Integration: A Modest Proposal," *Journal of Psychology and Theology* 18 (1990): 21-31; John D. Carter and Bruce S. Narramore, *The Integration of Psychology and Theology* (Grand Rapids: Zondervan Publishing House, 1979); Jones and Johnson, "A History of Christians in Psychology."

psychology being products of a Western context.[45] Consequently, our theology and psychology are assumed to be universally applicable to "the church" with little examination of our cultural worldviews.

The present movement in Christian psychology parallels the route of mainstream American psychology in its approach to culture and ethnicity. The dialogue has been most evident in the subfields in psychology that have been concerned about application, such as therapy and counseling. The emphasis has been on the "cultural competency" of the therapist, in an attempt to avoid alienating ethnically diverse clients and, to a lesser degree, to look at the general characteristics that distinguish ethnic groups.

In mainstream American psychology, we have a critical lack of self-awareness regarding what phenomena are universal (etic) and what are specific to this cultural context (emic).[46] David Ingleby[47] and others[48] argue that the social sciences and psychology in particular are cultural products and are deeply embedded (ethnocentric) in the values and assumptions of the Western world and modernity. Ingleby states,

> The fact is . . . psychological ways of seeing and doing stand at the very centre of our culture: perhaps no other science is so quintessentially modern, in its stress on the individual, on the importance of constructively solving problems, on rationality, on gaining control over oneself and nature, and so forth. The question is, can it disentangle itself sufficiently in order to open up to us the reality of other cultures?[49]

A number of psychological theorists have begun to argue that the cosmetic changes to Western psychology ignore the deeper cultural and structural limitations that restrict the field's ability to broaden its functional paradigms.[50] For example, African psychiatrist Frantz Fanon, in

---

45. Philip Cushman, *Constructing the Self, Constructing America: A Cultural History of Psychotherapy* (Reading, Mass.: Addison-Wesley Publishing Co., 1995); Gergen et al., "Psychological Science in Cultural Context"; Schreiter, *The New Catholicity*.

46. T. Len Holdstock, *Re-Examining Psychology: Critical Perspectives and African Insights* (London: Routledge, 2000).

47. Ingleby, "Problems in the Study of the Interplay between Science and Culture."

48. E.g., Cushman, *Constructing the Self, Constructing America*.

49. Ingleby, "Problems in the Study of the Interplay between Science and Culture," p. 111.

50. E.g., Cushman, *Constructing the Self, Constructing America*; Holdstock, *Re-Examining Psychology*.

his text *Black Skin, White Masks,* argues that "the fundamental cause of mental health problems must be sought, first, in the debilitating consequence of economic and cultural domination, and secondly, in the internalization of societal inequity and violence."[51] Fanon's worldview would make the primary task of psychology and psychiatry understanding the relationship between the psyche and the social structure. This is in contrast to the most dominant voices of Euro-American psychology that emphasize the nature of the individual self (ontogenetic) and increasingly are concerned with the genetic dispositions (phylogeny) of human behavior.[52] I would argue that the ontogeny, phylogeny, and sociogeny are each necessary for us to further our understanding of the diverse human condition and thus develop a more universal psychology. To do this, we must view them as interactive aspects of the human experience that are at times indistinguishable from each other and, at their core, intrinsically spiritual.

Andrew Park suggests that there is no single Christian culture, but there are diverse Christian cultures, each created as Christ is received and expressed through a group's own culture.[53] We must make a distinction here between the church as the body of Christ and the church as a human expression of God's grace. In our desire for truth, we must avoid theological ethnocentrism. We cannot so tightly align ourselves with a high theology that we throw off our creatureliness, our limitations of time and space, and the situatedness of our perspective. We also cannot worship our cultural identities without the awareness that they are broken and must be challenged by Christ. The kingdom of God assures us that we are not ultimately confined to our localized ethnocentric worlds, but we must respect that we are context-relative in our perspectives. We serve an eternal Savior, but we are situated in a particular time, and the challenges of our faith occur in the context of cultural and sociohistorical events. What Christian psychology can offer most is some understanding of these diverse contexts of lived human experiences, but also an enduring hope in the unifying nature of the kingdom of God.

---

51. Frantz Fanon, *Black Skin, White Masks,* trans. Charles Lam Markmann (New York: Grove Press, 1967), quoted in Holdstock, *Re-Examining Psychology,* p. 142.

52. Fanon, in Holdstock, *Re-Examining Psychology,* p. 142.

53. Andrew S. Park, *Racial Conflict and Healing: An Asian-American Theological Perspective* (Maryknoll, N.Y.: Orbis Books, 1996).

THREE Alternatives to the Model

Chapter 8   *Are the Natural Science Methods of*
           Psychology Compatible with Theism?

BRENT D. SLIFE

1. Introduction

Nancey Murphy cuts a necessarily broad swath in her proposal to integrate psychology and theology. However, as encompassing and thoughtful as her proposal is, she omits many issues that are perhaps peculiar to
the social sciences. This chapter concerns one of those issues — what
might be called the *method issue*. The method issue concerns the suitability of certain methods, and thus certain ways of knowing and philosophies of science, for studying human beings. Perhaps the most visible
manifestation of this issue is the ongoing battle between quantitative
and qualitative methods in the social sciences.[1]

There are probably many reasons why Murphy does not tackle this
issue in her chapters of this volume, including space limitations and the
scope of her social-science inquiry. Still, I wonder if one reason is that
the natural sciences, where much of her work has been centered,[2] do not

1. Peter Banister, Erica Burman, Ian Parker, Maye Taylor, and Carol Tindall, *Qualitative Methods in Psychology: A Research Guide* (Philadelphia: Open University Press,
1994); Benjamin F. Crabtree and William L. Miller, *Doing Qualitative Research*
(Newbury Park, Calif.: Sage Publications, 1992); *Handbook of Qualitative Methods*, ed.
Norman K. Denzin and Yvonna S. Lincoln (Thousand Oaks, Calif.: Sage Publications,
2000); *Qualitative Methods in Family Research*, ed. James F. Gilgun, Kerry Daly, and
Gerald Handel (Newbury Park, Calif.: Sage Publications, 1992); Brent D. Slife and
Edwin Gantt, "Methodological Pluralism: A Framework for Psychotherapy Research,"
Journal of Clinical Psychology 55 (1999): 1-13.

2. Nancey Murphy and George Ellis, *On the Moral Nature of the Universe: Theology, Cosmology, and Ethics* (Minneapolis: Fortress Press, 1996); Nancey Murphy, *Theology in the Age of Scientific Reasoning* (Ithaca, N.Y.: Cornell University Press, 1990).

typically have a "method issue." As far as I know, no pitched battles are currently raging about qualitative methods or phenomenology in the natural sciences. Also, philosophy-of-science issues tend to be far less contentious and divisive in the natural sciences.

Psychology, by contrast, has been fragmented by such issues.[3] With the application of method as psychology's main claim to scientific status,[4] any debate or questioning of this method has been considered an identity crisis.[5] Moreover, method controversies in psychology are deeper than is commonly thought. Although many psychologists would like to portray these controversies as merely issues about the procedures one uses to conduct studies, trenchant analyses have shown that these disparate methods originate from radically dissimilar worldviews, including differing views of human nature, reason, knowing, and even different views about what is real.[6] Consequently, the method issue really *is* an identity crisis for psychology, because it involves the very nature of psychology itself.

The thesis of this chapter is that the method issue presents a pivotal problem for Murphy's proposal. Because she focuses almost exclusively on psychological methods that are derived from the natural sciences — what I call in this chapter *natural science methods* — she overlooks the profound differences among the qualitative and quantitative methods of psychology. Indeed, she seems to assume in her chapters that there is no method issue and thus no issue in psychology of the competing worldviews that undergird these methods.

3. Stephen Yanchar and Brent D. Slife, "Pursuing Unity in a Fragmented Psychology: Problems and Prospects," *Review of General Psychology* 1 (1997): 235-55; *Toward a Unified Psychology: Incommensurability, Hermeneutics, and Morality*, ed. Stephen Yanchar and Brent Slife (New York: Institute of Mind and Behavior, 2000).

4. Brent D. Slife and Richard N. Williams, *What's behind the Research? Discovering Hidden Assumptions in the Behavioral Sciences* (Thousand Oaks, Calif.: Sage Publications, 1995).

5. Donald E. Polkinghorne, *Methodology for the Human Sciences: Systems of Inquiry* (Albany, N.Y.: SUNY Press, 1983); Joseph F. Rychlak, *The Psychology of Rigorous Humanism* (New York: New York University Press, 1988).

6. Denzin and Lincoln, eds., *Handbook of Qualitative Methods*; Polkinghorne, *Methodology for the Human Sciences*; Frank C. Richardson, Blaine J. Fowers, and Charles B. Guignon, *Re-Envisioning Psychology: Moral Dimensions of Theory and Practice* (San Francisco: Jossey-Bass, 1999); Slife and Gantt, "Methodological Pluralism."

The first task of this chapter, then, is to describe the worldview of natural science methods. It is no secret that this worldview is naturalism itself.[7] However, the problematic status of this worldview for theism,[8] and thus many religions, is less known in psychology. Naturalism is often defined as an understanding of the world *without* God. If this understanding truly underlies the natural science methods that many psychologists use to investigate religion, then the method issue could reveal an overlooked incompatibility between psychology and the religions that understand the world *with* God.

Exploring this possibility is the second task of this chapter. Murphy's own brand of theism is compared to the naturalism of natural science methods. Indeed, her own notion of the scientific reasoning that guides natural science methods and is supposedly common to both psychology and theology is compared to her theism. Are these methods and this reasoning compatible with her theism?

7. Marcus J. Borg, *The God We Never Knew* (New York: Harper Collins, 1997); Gary R. Collins, *The Rebuilding of Psychology: An Integration of Psychology and Christianity* (Wheaton, Ill.: Tyndale House, 1977); David R. Griffin, *Religion and Scientific Naturalism: Overcoming the Conflicts* (Albany, N.Y.: SUNY Press, 2000); Phillip E. Johnson, *Reason in the Balance: The Case against Naturalism in Science, Law, and Education* (Downers Grove, Ill.: InterVarsity Press, 1995); Thomas H. Leahey, *A History of Modern Psychology* (Englewood Cliffs, N.J.: Prentice-Hall, 1992); George Marsden, *The Outrageous Idea of Christian Scholarship* (New York: Oxford University Press, 1997); P. Scott Richards and Allen E. Bergin, *A Spiritual Strategy for Counseling and Psychotherapy* (Washington, D.C.: American Psychological Association, 1997); P. Scott Richards and Allen E. Bergin, *Case Studies in Theistic Strategies for Psychotherapy* (Washington, D.C.: American Psychological Association, 2003); Brent D. Slife, "Theoretical Challenges to Therapy Practice and Research: The Constraint of Naturalism," in *Handbook of Psychotherapy and Behavior Change*, ed. M. Lambert (New York: Wiley, 2003); Huston Smith, *Why Religion Matters: The Fate of the Human Spirit in an Age of Disbelief* (San Francisco: Harper, 2001).

8. The meaning of theism here is *not* what Marcus Borg (in the book *The God We Never Knew*) calls "supernatural theism" because supernatural theism postulates a God that is "out there" and even completely passive following the world's creation. As it is used here, theism involves the ongoing activity of God in the world — closer to what Borg calls "panentheism."

2. Natural Science Methods

Historically, there seems to be no dispute that the "physics envy" of early psychologists led them to adopt natural science methods,[9] including what are now considered experimental, quasi-experimental, and even many correlational methods. Indeed, the suitability of these natural science methods was unquestioned at the time of psychology's inception, because they were considered the transparent revealers of the natural world, with no inherent biases or assumptions. To this day, many research methods texts in psychology present the positivistic logic of many natural science methods as essentially without biases or assumptions.[10] As Thomas Leahey observes, "physics envy" still leads mainstream psychologists to entertain the "fantasy" that a bias-free Newton "will arise among psychologists and propound a rigorous theory of behavior, delivering psychology unto the promised land of science."[11]

2.1. No Bias-Free Lunch

Recent scholarship in the philosophy of science has challenged the bias-free status of natural science methods. Many philosophers of science have argued that the positivistic logic of methods is underlaid with unproven and uninvestigated assumptions and values of various sorts.[12] The

9. Leahey, *A History of Modern Psychology,* p. 33.

10. E.g., Gary Heiman, *Research Methods in Psychology,* 3rd ed. (New York: Houghton Mifflin, 2002).

11. Leahey, *A History of Modern Psychology,* p. 33.

12. Sacha Bem and Huim Looren de Jong, *Theoretical Issues in Psychology: An Introduction* (London: Sage Publications, 1997); Richard J. Bernstein, *Beyond Objectivism and Relativism: Science, Hermeneutics, and Praxis* (Philadelphia: University of Pennsylvania Press, 1983); James Bohman, *New Philosophy of Social Science* (Cambridge, Mass.: MIT Press, 1993); Martin Curd and Jan A. Cover, *Philosophy of Science: The Central Issues* (New York: W. W. Norton, 1998); Patrick A. Heelan, *Space-Perception and the Philosophy of Science* (Berkeley and Los Angeles: University of California Press, 1983); Thomas S. Kuhn, *The Structure of Scientific Revolutions* (Chicago: University of Chicago Press, 1970); Richard Rorty, *Philosophy and the Mirror of Nature* (Princeton, N.J.: Princeton University Press, 1979); Charles Taylor, *Philosophy and the Human Sciences: Philosophical Papers* (Cambridge: Cambridge University Press, 1985); Stephen Toulmin, *Human Understanding* (Princeton, N.J.: Princeton University Press, 1972).

gist of their argument is that the formulation of any method must assume, before investigation, a certain type of world in which that method would make sense and be fruitful. The problem is that when these assumptions are *already* assumed to be correct (as they must be for any method to be formulated), they are not themselves the objects of test; they are parts of the test. For instance, the naturalistic assumption that methods should be based on the observable is never itself empirically tested, because this assumption is part of what it *means* to test.[13] For this reason, natural science methods may provide empirical justification for certain psychological theories, but they provide no empirical justification for themselves and the assumptions that ground them. There is no empirical justification for the epistemology of empiricism, no scientific validation for the metaphysic of naturalism.

Some traditional scientists would argue that these philosophies and assumptions of science have been successful nevertheless. There seems to be widespread agreement that these assumptions have worked well, at least for the natural sciences. Still, it must be remembered that this claim of success is merely a claim — an opinion — however widely it is held. No empirical evidence can be gathered to substantiate this claim without already assuming the validity of natural science methods in the first place.

2.2. Underlying Philosophy

What, then, is the philosophy of naturalism that underlies these natural science methods? This philosophy has been defined in various ways, depending on its context.[14] However, two common features of these definitions can serve as our core understanding of naturalism in this chapter: its godlessness and its lawfulness. First, naturalists explain and interpret the objective world as if reference to God is irrelevant or superfluous. The world is thought to operate autonomously, as a result of its own independent processes. The "lawfulness" feature of this philosophy reflects the most popular understanding of this godless operation: the

13. Slife, "Theoretical Challenges to Therapy Practice and Research."

14. Cf. E. J. Capaldi and Robert W. Proctor, *Contextualism in Psychology Research? A Critical Review* (Thousand Oaks, Calif.: Sage Publications, 1999); Griffin, *Religion and Scientific Naturalism*.

many processes of the world are all autonomously governed by natural or physical laws or principles.

Rarely are these related naturalistic features explicitly connected to psychology's natural science methods,[15] so it might help the reader to provide an obvious example of this connection (with more connections to follow in a later section): natural science methods never require that investigators pray (or generally consult God or revelation) before designing or conducting a study. This requirement is omitted because God's current activities are presumed to be irrelevant to designing and conducting an effective investigation (though God's created order might be considered relevant to the results of the investigation).

3. The Compatibility Issue

We will review other method practices in psychology and explore their relation to naturalism later in this chapter. For now, let us consider how a naturalistic philosophy might raise the compatibility issue: Is a theistic world in which God's activity *is* relevant — perhaps even required — compatible with the naturalistic world that might ground and guide the natural science methods of psychology? Is Murphy's own theism compatible with this naturalistic world? Many psychologists have attempted to formulate theistic strategies of psychotherapy, but they believed they had to overcome psychology's naturalism to do so.[16] P. Scott Richards and Allen Bergin, for instance, list a number of naturalistic assumptions of mainstream psychology, including determinism, atomism, materialism, hedonism, and positivism, which they view as incompatible with theistic assumptions such as free will, holism, spirituality, altruism, and theistic realism.[17]

15. See Richards and Bergin, *Case Studies in Theistic Strategies for Psychotherapy,* and Slife, "Theoretical Challenges to Therapy Practice and Research," for exceptions.

16. Collins, *The Rebuilding of Psychology;* Richards and Bergin, *A Spiritual Strategy for Counseling and Psychotherapy;* Richards and Bergin, *Case Studies in Theistic Strategies for Psychotherapy;* Brent D. Slife, L. Mitchell, and M. Whoolery, "A Theistic Approach to Therapeutic Community: Non-Naturalism and the Alldredge Academy," in *Casebook for a Spiritual Strategy in Counseling and Psychotherapy,* ed. S. Richards and A. Bergin (Washington, D.C.: American Psychological Association, 2003).

17. Richards and Bergin, *A Spiritual Strategy for Counseling and Psychotherapy.*

Why do they consider these naturalistic and theistic assumptions to be at odds? The primary reason is that natural laws supposedly govern all aspects of human beings, including their bodies, their minds, and even their spirits. Consequently, naturalistic psychologists have assumed that God cannot or does not govern these aspects of humanity. Natural laws essentially fill up the conceptual space where God might have been, explaining human behavior and cognition without a God (and thus without the need of prayer, revelation, and so on). Because theism *does* require an active God, by definition, naturalism and theism have been viewed as incompatible philosophies in principle.[18] As David Griffin put it in his review of naturalism, "Most philosophers, theologians, and scientists believe that scientific naturalism is incompatible with any significantly religious view of reality."[19]

3.1. Deism and Dualism

The problem is that psychology's methods are commonly assumed to be compatible with theism. As mentioned, researchers in the psychology of religion have routinely presupposed that traditional natural-science methods could illuminate (transparently) religious topics of all kinds, without any issues of incompatibility. Some of these researchers have considered naturalism to be compatible with theism through deism — God created the naturalistic order of the world, but he is not currently involved in its ongoing operation.[20] With deism, no reference to God is warranted or needed in psychology's methods because the laws or principles of psychology are currently autonomous and working essentially independently of him (except perhaps in rare "supernatural" instances). The problem is

18. Cf. Collins, *The Rebuilding of Psychology;* Griffin, *Religion and Scientific Naturalism;* Johnson, *Reason in the Balance;* Richards and Bergin, *A Spiritual Strategy for Counseling and Psychotherapy;* Richards and Bergin, *Case Studies in Theistic Strategies for Psychotherapy;* Slife, Mitchell, and Whoolery, "A Theistic Approach to Therapeutic Community"; Smith, *Why Religion Matters.*

19. Griffin, *Religion and Scientific Naturalism,* p. 11.

20. Cf. Borg, *The God We Never Knew;* Johnson, *Reason in the Balance;* Richards and Bergin, *A Spiritual Strategy for Counseling and Psychotherapy;* D. H. Wacome, "Evolutionary Psychology," in *Science and the Soul: Christian Faith and Psychological Research,* ed. S. W. Vander Stoep (Lanham, Md.: University Press of America, 2003).

that this kind of deism obviates those religions that believe in a presently active rather than a passively deistic God (e.g., Christianity).

Many types of dualism have been marshaled to attempt to make naturalism and theism compatible. Descartes perhaps framed the prototypical dualism with his claim that the mind or soul permitted God's actions and influences but that the body was mechanistically autonomous (except, again, in rare supernatural cases). D. H. Wacome exemplifies a variation of this dualism when he holds that God is involved with some entities of the world but not with others, as in this passage:

> Christians, unlike deists, believe that God miraculously intervenes in his creation, but our essential commitment is to God's intervening in human history; in human experience; and, above all, in the life, death, and resurrection of Jesus — *not to God's intervening in nature as such*. We accept a great variety of explanations of things coming about by natural processes that are what they are in the world God has created without feeling the need to postulate divine interventions.[21]

Here, Wacome distinguishes his position from deism because he believes God is currently active in the events of humans (e.g., their history, their experience). However, he then postulates a deism of nature where God created the processes of nature but they now "come about by natural processes."

Actually, such dualisms do not resolve the incompatibility of naturalism and theism. They merely assign these two philosophies to separate corners of the universe — Descartes separating the soul from the body, and Wacome separating human experience from nature. Deism, in this sense, is dualism across time, with God having been active in the past (as creator) but now passive. Indeed, this separation of the naturalistic (no divine intervention) from the theistic (active and current divine intervention) in both deism and dualism is a tacit admission of their incompatibility. The two philosophies apparently cannot co-exist in the same time and place. No dualism or deism would be necessary if they were really compatible. The important point, for the purposes of this chapter, is that natural science methods of psychology have been formu-

21. Wacome, "Evolutionary Psychology," p. 200 (emphasis added).

lated to investigate one side of this dualism — the godless side,[22] making their conceptual foundations incompatible with the God-filled, theistic side.

3.2. Reductive Naturalism

Some scholars would still view this conclusion as a bit hasty. David Griffin, for example, has argued that incompatibility depends on the *type* of naturalism. He reviews the main historic and contemporary types and finds two primary forms: reductive and nonreductive. Griffin's reductive form of naturalism is basically what we have been describing in this chapter as naturalism. After an extensive review of its history and conceptual foundations, Griffin appears to concur with our observations regarding its relation to theism. Reductive naturalism "rules out not only supernaturalistic religious belief but also any significantly religious interpretation of reality whatsoever." He believes that "since the nineteenth century . . . the scientific community [has become] increasingly committed to" this form of naturalism. "The atheism of this worldview," according to Griffin, "besides denying any transcendent source of religious experiences, combines with the reductionism to rule out the idea of a divine creation of the world and even any divine influence in the world."[23]

However, Griffin also describes a form of nonreductive naturalism that is compatible with such "divine influences," including theistic influences. Space limitations prohibit an explanation of its postmodern philosophical tenets here. Nevertheless, it should be noted that variations on these tenets have important method implications, because many qualitative researchers claim nonreductive forms of naturalism.[24] Could some sort of nonreductive naturalism also undergird the natural science (quantitative) methods of psychology? Our focus in this chapter on psychology's methods makes this question especially relevant because so

22. D. Hedges and C. Burchfield, "Depression and Its Treatment: The Assumptions and Implications of a Conceptualization," in *Developing Critical Thinking in Psychology*, ed. B. D. Slife, J. Reber, and F. Richardson (Washington, D.C.: American Psychological Association, forthcoming). See also, in the same volume, Brent D. Slife and R. H. Hopkins, "Alternative Assumptions for Neuroscience: Formulating a True Monism."

23. Griffin, *Religion and Scientific Naturalism*, p. 14.

24. Slife and Gantt, "Methodological Pluralism."

many scholars have presumed that the naturalism of these methods is essentially nonreductive,[25] and thus effectively neutral to theological claims.[26] Therefore, it is important to know whether the assumptions of psychology's methods are reductively naturalistic.

4. Specific Assumptions of Reductive Naturalism

To address this issue, I review key method practices of psychologists to examine whether their natural science methods are underlaid with the assumptions of reductive naturalism. I examine many of the assumptions that Griffin identifies as reductively naturalistic through three categories: objectivism, materialism, and reductionism. To help illuminate these assumptions and practices, I contrast them to the method assumptions and practices of qualitative methods that are widely acknowledged to be nonreductively naturalistic.[27]

4.1. Objectivism

In its most basic form, objectivism is the study of "objects" that are external to the observer's mind. Reductive naturalism requires this assumption because nature and social processes are presumed to exist and involve study external to the mind. In other words, the ultimate subject matter of natural science methods is not subjectivity — the mental world of opinion, biases, values, and feelings. Their subject matter is the objective world that presumably occurs *outside* our subjectivity — the natural world in its pristine form — and thus the world without biases and values.

What allows reductive naturalists to think they can get outside the biases and values of individual scientists? As methods texts in psychology exemplify,[28] natural science methods are considered the chief tool for accomplishing this task because they ideally provide a value-free,

25. Heiman, *Research Methods in Psychology.*

26. Cf. Brent D. Slife, Stephen Yanchar, and B. Williams, "Conceptions of Determinism in Radical Behaviorism: A Taxonomy," *Behavior and Philosophy* 27 (1999): 75-96.

27. Capaldi and Proctor, *Contextualism in Psychology Research?*

28. E.g., Heiman, *Research Methods in Psychology.*

transparent method or logic that does not affect the outcome of investigation.[29] Although investigators themselves may have biases and values, the ideal or logic of natural science methods is to work toward eliminating these biases and values, either through experimental control or precise measurement, or some combination of the two. Objectivism, in this sense, is not the claim that all scientific research is absolutely free of values,[30] but rather that scientific research should *strive* to be as free of values and biases as possible. As Griffin notes, striving to be value-free contrasts sharply with the frankly value-laden methods of theism, such as prayer and Scripture reading.

Contrast objectivism also with many nonreductive qualitative methods. Whereas biases are bad in natural science methods because they supposedly distort objective description and true knowledge, biases and assumptions are not only considered inescapable in qualitative methods but necessary to true understanding. Mainstream psychologists often view qualitative methods as pertaining to a different domain than natural science methods — subjectivity rather than objectivity. However, many qualitative researchers never separate these domains. Even the so-called objective natural world is interpretively known. In other words, qualitative methods are distinguished not by a different domain of inquiry but by a different philosophy of science, including the notion that no method can proceed without interpretive biases of one sort or another.

From this perspective, saying that natural science methods are objective is like saying that multiple-choice tests are objective. Neither are objective in the sense of being value-free, or even in striving to be as free of values as possible, because both are structured through and through with the biases, values, and assumptions of their authors (e.g., that one *should* be "objective"). Yet, method practices in psychology continually neglect to mention these structured biases, portraying the logic of these methods as transparent indicators of the natural and social world.

29. E. A. Burtt, *The Metaphysical Foundations of Modern Science* (Garden City, N.Y.: Doubleday, 1954).

30. E.g., T. D. Borkovec and L. G. Castonguay, "What Is the Scientific Meaning of Empirically Supported Therapy?" *Journal of Consulting and Clinical Psychology* 66 (1998): 136-42; D. L. Chambless and S. D. Hollon, "Defining Empirically Supported Therapies," *Journal of Consulting and Clinical Psychology* 66 (1998): 7-18.

For example, research on therapy outcome is often conducted and reported as if the logic of the methods is transparent — that is, not itself affecting the outcome of the investigation. Indeed, the mark of objectivists in this research is that they believe the logic of scientific method does not favor one type of therapy over another.[31] This belief has also been pivotal in recent moves to objectify therapy. Many eclectics now favor divorcing the techniques of therapy from their theories and then testing them objectively for their effectiveness.[32] Empirically supported treatments are a similar type of professional endorsement of objectivism.[33] In both cases, the logic of therapy research is assumed to be without any systematic biases of its own. This logic is universal for all relevant subject matter and unconstrained by culture or context. Consequently, the objectivist aspect of reductive naturalism clearly abounds in the natural science method practices of psychologists.

4.2. Materialism

Materialism is the notion that "the ultimate nature of reality is material,"[34] or, as I have put it elsewhere, "matter is all that really mat-

31. Slife, "Theoretical Challenges to Therapy Practice and Research."
32. Cf. Larry E. Beutler and John F. Clarkin, *Systematic Treatment Selection: Toward Targeted Therapeutic Interventions* (New York: Brunner/Mazel, 1990); Barbara S. Held, *Back to Reality: A Critique of Postmodern Theory in Psychotherapy* (New York: W. W. Norton, 1995); Arnold A. Lazarus, "Different Types of Eclecticism and Integration: Let's Be Aware of the Dangers," *Journal of Psychotherapy Integration* 5 (1995): 27-39; Arnold A. Lazarus, Larry E. Beutler, and John C. Norcross, "The Future of Technical Eclecticism," *Psychotherapy* 29 (1992): 11-20; Brent D. Slife and J. Reber, "Eclecticism in Psychotherapy: Is It Really the Best Substitute for Traditional Theories?" in *Critical Issues in Psychotherapy: Translating New Ideas into Practice,* ed. B. Slife, R. Williams, and S. Barlow (Thousand Oaks, Calif.: Sage Publications, 2001).
33. American Psychological Association, Division of Clinical Psychology, Task Force on Promotion and Dissemination of Psychological Procedures, "Training in and Dissemination of Empirically Validated Psychological Treatments: Report and Recommendations," *The Clinical Psychologist* 48 (1995): 3-23; Chambless and Hollon, "Defining Empirically Supported Therapies"; Peter E. Nathan, "Practice Guidelines: Not Yet Ideal," *American Psychologist* 53 (1998): 290-99; Peter E. Nathan and Jack M. Gorman, *A Guide to Treatments that Work* (New York: Oxford University Press, 1998); Martin E. P. Seligman, *What You Can Change and What You Can't* (New York: Knopf, 1994).
34. Leahey, *A History of Modern Psychology,* p. 33.

ters."[35] In other words, a reductive naturalist does not study intangible constructs or entities, such as spirits and ghosts. Rather, the important and valued things in materialistic science are tangible, visible, and substantial, making it impossible, for instance, for a theistic "Holy Spirit" to matter in this context. Materialism manifests itself in psychological method through the traditional natural-science notion that only material things are knowable. That is, materialism is typically linked to the primary epistemology of science — empiricism. Only our sensory experiences can supposedly be known (empiricism), so only tangible and observable materials can supposedly be important and thus candidates for knowledge (materialism). The widely endorsed definition of psychology as "the study of behavior" is a product of this naturalistic assumption.[36]

The problem is that psychologists investigate social as well as natural relations. Because social relations cannot be observed (only the things having the relations can be observed), much of the subject matter of the social sciences is, by its very nature, *non*-material. Consequently, the philosophies of empiricism and materialism require these nonmaterial constructs to be operationalized — made into material things or processes (e.g., behavior) — so they *can* be observed. Otherwise, the methods are useless, betraying their dependence on materialism. Indeed, materialism is so pervasive in psychology that many psychologists would be hard-pressed to know how the nonmaterial aspects of the discipline *could* be investigated, if not through operationalization.

Contrast this philosophy of method with the nonreductive philosophy underlying many qualitative methods. First, qualitative methods begin with a different epistemology. Although their province is experience, they do not narrow or reduce experience to the sensory only (e.g., observation, as in natural science methods). They consider their source of knowledge to be the entire realm of *lived* experience or meaning, which includes observations and sensory experiences, to be sure, but also can include our experiences of thoughts, feelings, and even spiritual events.

Do these qualitative researchers "operationalize" their findings?

---

35. Slife, "Theoretical Challenges to Therapy Practice and Research," p. 58.

36. Heiman, *Research Methods in Psychology;* Gregg Henriques, "Psychology Defined," *Journal of Clinical Psychology,* forthcoming.

Although it is true that all qualitative researchers attempt to specify and clarify their findings, they do not operationalize in any conventional natural-science sense because their focus is meaning rather than the material objects of the world, such as behavior (or other material manifestations). Meaning is not a sensory experience as such because it does not fall on one's retina (though it is a lived experience). For this reason, the primary interest of qualitative researchers is not the objective material world, which from a reductively naturalistic philosophy is without subjectivity.

This contrast makes the materialism of natural science methods apparent. These methods cannot study meanings in themselves because they are formulated for objective and material things, not for subjective and nonmaterial meanings. At best, they study meanings secondarily, as they are supposedly manifested in more observable characteristics, such as behaviors and surveys. For example, some natural science researchers would assume that the meaning of love can be studied through its observable (and material) manifestations, such as hugs and kisses. However, from a qualitative perspective the meaning of love itself can never be studied in this manner. Studying manifestations (e.g., hugs and kisses) is not the same as studying the thing doing the manifesting (e.g., the meaning of love). Moreover, hugs and kisses can occur without love, and love can occur without hugs and kisses. These problems expose the materialism of conventional operationalized methods as well as the difficulties in psychologists' exclusively relying on them.

4.3. Reductionism

Reductive naturalism also assumes that all change is ultimately reducible to, or governed by, unchangeable natural laws and principles. This reduction implies not only that everything is ultimately determined — with the unchanging controlling the changing — but also that unchangeable and universal natural laws and principles are the most fundamental realities.[37] As a result, natural science methods have been formulated to

37. Griffin, *Religion and Scientific Naturalism;* John Sanders, "Historical Considerations," in *The Openness of God*, ed. C. Pinnock (Downers Grove, Ill.: InterVarsity Press, 1994); Slife and Williams, *What's behind the Research?*

detect these fundamental and unchangeable universal laws. The need for replication is perhaps the most obvious manifestation of this formulation of the scientific method, because unchangeable natural laws should be detectable (under the right conditions) anywhere, anytime. However, the importance of standardization and "reliability," as Murphy terms it,[38] also follows directly from the same need. Without replication, standardization, and reliability — as the logic of reductionism goes — research findings cannot reveal the ultimate realities of the world: reductive natural laws and principles.

An interesting but often overlooked aspect of this reductionism is that natural laws are not themselves physical or material entities. Although the law of gravity, for instance, is thought to govern physical entities, such as our weight, the law itself is not a physical or material entity in the conventional sense. It does not fall on the retina, nor can we touch it or weigh it. This lack of physicality may seem to conflict with materialism. However, natural scientists learned from the ancient Greeks that ideal reductions — those reductions that are the most simple and parsimonious — are unchangeable (and thus not complex). Because all physical entities change, however slowly, the reductions that are *beyond* the physical — *meta*physical reductions — are the most fundamental and natural. They transcend time and space, and so they seem to apply to all situations universally.

Unfortunately, psychologists can boast of few, if any, natural (or social) laws, despite over a century of using natural science methods. Still, psychologists consider true knowledge to approximate this universality and unchangeability. Metaphysical reductionism has led psychologists to formulate their theories as if they were metaphysical principles (e.g., universal theories of memory), with the hope that these theories would one day be tested and found to be valid. Therefore, the aim of testing these theoretical principles has guided the practices of researchers and methodologists. Reductionism has turned these practices away from subjective, and thus changeable, lived experiences and turned them toward the replicable, standardizable, and reliable objective and material aspects of their sensory experiences.

In contrast, consider that many qualitative methods require none of these unchangeable characteristics in their findings. Rather than assum-

38. Murphy, Chapter 1, section 3, this volume.

ing that the most fundamental knowledge is universal and unchangeable across individual contexts and situations, many qualitative researchers assume that at least some fundamental knowledge is inherent in particular — and thus not all — contexts. Consider as examples the indigenous aspects of particular cultures. Although these have not been ignored in psychological research, they are frequently considered less than fundamental because they are not unchangeable and universal across time and space. Indeed, many qualitative researchers contend that pivotal aspects of individual meanings also have contextually particular characteristics. If this is true, then studying only the subject matter that has the characteristics of replicability, standardizability, and reliability would *prevent* a fundamental understanding of the meaningful and cultural aspects of the world. The significance of these reductive characteristics for natural science methods is a testament to the significance of the naturalistic reductionism that grounds them.

The bottom line here is that the assumptions that scholars have long identified with reductive naturalism are the assumptions that undergird the method practices of natural science researchers in psychology, from striving to eliminate bias and values (objectivism), to limiting investigations to the observable and operationalizable (materialism), to focusing on the replicable and reliable (reductionism). This combination of assumptions and research practices has long been known in psychology as a broadly *logical positivist* framework for method.[39] Many scholars have noted the incompatibility of these positivistic assumptions with theism.[40] However, to help make this point for the present chapter, let us compare the reductive assumptions of psychology's natural science methods to Murphy's own theological assertions.

---

39. Polkinghorne, *Methodology for the Human Sciences*; Richards and Bergin, *Case Studies in Theistic Strategies for Psychotherapy*; Slife and Williams, *What's behind the Research?*

40. Collins, *The Rebuilding of Psychology*; Johnson, *Reason in the Balance*; Richards and Bergin, *A Spiritual Strategy for Counseling and Psychotherapy*; Richards and Bergin, *Case Studies in Theistic Strategies for Psychotherapy*; Slife, "Theoretical Challenges to Therapy Practice and Research"; Brent D. Slife, C. Hope, and S. Nebeker, "Examining the Relationship between Religious Spirituality and Psychological Science," *Journal of Humanistic Psychology* 39 (1999): 51-85; Smith, *Why Religion Matters*.

5. Murphy's Theology

At the outset, Murphy's theology needs to be distinguished from what she considers the "basic logical structure"[41] or "fine structure" of scientific research[42] (which she considers to be different from the Lakatosian structure of research). In *On the Moral Nature of the Universe,* which Murphy co-authored with George Ellis, Murphy explicitly identifies this fine structure with Carl Hempel's logical positivist (or neopositivist) understanding of method and makes a bold claim about this form of scientific reasoning: "While it is philosophers of science who have described this form of reasoning, we shall claim that it is essential in most other domains of knowledge, from everyday explanations of events to theology and metaphysics."[43]

This quotation makes clear that Murphy views this form of reasoning as common to both science and theology. Yet, her identification of the logical positivist origins of this reasoning would seem to place this logic of method in the category of reductive naturalism, as our analysis here has shown. Could she be using the term "logical positivism" with a different meaning? Other passages would seem to affirm her support of positivism as it is used here (in this chapter). For instance, she declares that it is a "fact that scientific reasoning moves from an observation (fact, datum, experimental result) to a hypothesized explanation of that observation,"[44] a "fact" that is clearly at variance with the scientific reasoning of nonreductive, qualitative researchers in psychology. A paragraph later, she concludes that "hypotheses must be tested by deducing further observable consequences from them and then checking to see if these predictions are confirmed."[45] Both quotations would appear to be consistent with the method practices identified with objectivism, materialism, and reductionism above.

Even Murphy's appeal to Lakatos's[46] approach to method does not

41. Murphy, Chapter 1, section 2, this volume.
42. Murphy and Ellis, *On the Moral Nature of the Universe,* p. 8.
43. Murphy and Ellis, *On the Moral Nature of the Universe,* p. 9.
44. Murphy and Ellis, *On the Moral Nature of the Universe,* p. 8.
45. Murphy and Ellis, *On the Moral Nature of the Universe,* p. 9.
46. Imre Lakatos, "Falsification and the Methodology of Scientific Research Programs," in *Criticism and the Growth of Knowledge,* ed. I. Lakatos and A. Musgrave (New York: Cambridge University Press, 1970); Imre Lakatos, *The Methodology of Sci-*

necessarily obviate this positivistic interpretation (though she distinguishes the fine structure of our focus from the Lakatosian structure of research programs).[47] Lakatos long claimed that his methods "rehabilitate, in radically new ways, a *'positivistic'* respect for the facts."[48] Yet, as we will see in her theology, Murphy contends that her Radical-Reformation theism is "radically different" from naturalistic accounts.[49] How do we square these seemingly contrary claims, especially in light of the foregoing analysis about naturalism's central role in the positivism of psychology's natural science methods? Let us examine each of the three categories of reductive naturalism in turn.

5.1. Objectivism

Murphy clearly seems to oppose objectivism in her theology. In fact, she devotes several sections to how inherently value-laden psychology and all the sciences are. She even cites Charles Taylor as having "dealt a mortal blow to the concept of value-neutrality."[50] Still, I am not clear how or even whether she applies Taylor's lessons to "scientific reason" or her "basic logical structure of research." How, for instance, can this reason or structure move "from an observation (fact, datum, experimental result)," as she insists,[51] and be value-laden in Taylor's sense? Are all other aspects of psychology inherently value-laden, but this research structure somehow devoid of values and assumptions?

If this were true, then scientific and theological reason would not be integratable in principle, because the former would be value-free and the latter value-laden. Another way to put this is that theology cannot have anything to say to the method aspects of psychology, because the basic logic of the latter operates without theological assumptions and values.

---

entific Research Programmes: Philosophical Papers, vol. 1, ed. J. Worrall and G. Currie (Cambridge: Cambridge University Press, 1978).

47. Murphy and Ellis, *On the Moral Nature of the Universe*, p. 8.

48. Lakatos, *The Methodology of Scientific Research Programmes*, p. 180 (emphasis added).

49. Murphy, Chapter 2, section 7, this volume.

50. Charles Taylor, *Sources of the Self: The Making of the Modern Identity* (Cambridge, Mass.: Harvard University Press, 1989), p. 4.

51. Murphy and Ellis, *On the Moral Nature of the Universe*, p. 8.

This point would seem to apply to the Lakatosian aspects of Murphy's proposal as well as to the "fine structure" of scientific reasoning. Neither logic would be "theology-laden," as Murphy puts it — implicitly or explicitly.

On the other hand, if this basic structure of research is inherently value-laden, then what are these values and how do they compare to the basic values and assumptions of her theology? I do not see her addressing this issue. As mentioned, some scholars have suggested that only an epistemological (methodological) and thus not an ontological (reductive) naturalism is inherent in the scientific method. However, many influential thinkers have argued forcefully that all epistemologies require ontologies, with reductive epistemologies requiring reductive ontologies.[52]

Needless to say, the analysis of psychology's natural science methods (above), especially in contrast with the nonreductive naturalism of qualitative methods, betrays their reductive origins. In other words, the issue is not the *location* of the naturalism, with a methodological location somehow allowing a kinder and gentler naturalism. The issue is the *type* of naturalism, wherever it is implicitly or explicitly held. In this sense, Murphy's theology of the inescapability of values is incompatible with the value-free pretensions of psychology's natural science methods.

5.2. Materialism

Reductive materialism is also deeply problematic to Murphy's theology. Although Murphy favors physicalism to stave off inaccurate accusations of dualism, she surely does not mean here reductive physicalism.[53] Not only does she attempt to avoid reduction to the lower disciplines of her "hierarchy of sciences," she also adds "top-down" causation to oppose any claims of an exclusively materialist reduction. Indeed, an exclusively materialist reduction would prevent any influence from the apex of her

52. Hans-Georg Gadamer, *Truth and Method* (New York: Continuum, 1995); Griffin, *Religion and Scientific Naturalism*; Richardson, Fowers, and Guignon, *Re-Envisioning Psychology*; Slife and Williams, *What's behind the Research?*

53. *Whatever Happened to the Soul? Scientific and Theological Portraits of Human Nature*, ed. Warren S. Brown, Nancey Murphy, and H. Newton Malony (Minneapolis: Fortress Press, 1998).

hierarchy, where theology supposedly lies, because only bottom-up causation from the lower disciplines would be possible.[54] Moreover, Murphy clearly endorses some versions of free will, countering any claims of materialistic determinism.

On the other hand, her endorsement of a positivist view of the structure of research is again puzzling in this regard. As she correctly notes, neopositivists, such as Hempel, allow only bottom-up processes in the hierarchy of science.[55] Positivistic methods are also traditionally understood as data-driven in this same bottom-up mode.[56] Consonant with this, but doubly puzzling in light of her theology, is Murphy's belief in the "necessity of operational definitions" and the "empirical,"[57] as if only the material and the sensory are knowable.

Can altruism and forgiveness really be studied, as she seems to contend,[58] in their operational manifestations only? Could someone *behave* in an altruistic or a forgiving manner and not truly *be* altruistic or forgiving? If so, then a conventional materialist operationalization (e.g., behavior) would be insufficient, if not completely misleading, in the study of these topics.[59] Once again, Murphy seems inconsistent. She is far from the reductive materialist in her theology, touting, as she does, the influences of top-down causation and value-laden systems. However, she seems to exempt some levels of method from these top-down and value-laden properties. Operational definition, for example, is a "necessity" rather than a top-down value.

5.3. Reductionism

Recall that reductionists (as defined above) make two basic claims about the most real and natural entities of the world, such as physical laws: they are unchangeable, and they govern all that does change. The first claim has prompted natural science methods to be formulated in such a way as to discover and discern these unchangeable entities, such as

54. Slife and Hopkins, "Alternative Assumptions for Neuroscience."
55. Murphy, Chapter 1, section 2, this volume.
56. Slife and Williams, *What's behind the Research?*
57. Murphy, Chapter 1, section 2, this volume.
58. Murphy, Chapter 3, section 3.5, this volume.
59. Cf. Slife and Hopkins, "Alternative Assumptions for Neuroscience."

through replication or, as Murphy terms it, "reliability."[60] As she puts it in her first chapter, reliability means that a measurement process "produces similar or identical readings again and again under similar circumstances."[61] But why do results require this property of reliability or replicability? The answer is the first claim of the reductionist — the need to find unchangeable principles or laws in the natural science mold, as dictated by reductive naturalism.

This first claim, as we have seen, implies that the subjective realm, with its changeability, must be either excluded from science or operationalized to meet the demands of method. Either way, research that looks to lived religious experiences, such as Murphy's poignant story of Iulia Beausobre,[62] cannot be fundamentally significant. As qualitative researchers have shown, the full import and meaning of such lived experiences require an entirely different set of method assumptions.[63] Indeed, from a reductionist's perspective, Iulia's redemptive experiences would be epiphenomenal to the reductions that supposedly govern these experiences, such as the natural laws of her neurology.[64] This line of thinking would seem problematic to the significance of Iulia's lived experiences in Murphy's chapter and her theology.

The second claim of the reductionist is that these unchangeable and universal laws determine (and predict) all that does change. In other words, all changes of the world occur in patterns that are ultimately controlled by unchangeable and universal laws, preventing human agency and possibility. Human behavior would not be qualitatively different from a boulder rolling into a hiker.[65] We do not exclaim "Bad boulder!" in this instance because we assume the boulder is completely governed by natural laws, and thus its "behavior" is without meaning and morality. Even a complex system of boulders rolling down complex mountains, and so on, would not negate these laws.[66] However, Murphy contends that the Anabaptist tradition — far from endorsing this

---

60. Murphy, Chapter 1, section 3, this volume.
61. Murphy, Chapter 1, section 3, this volume.
62. Murphy, Chapter 3, section 3.4, this volume.
63. Denzin and Lincoln, eds., *Handbook of Qualitative Methods;* Polkinghorne, *Methodology for the Human Sciences;* Slife and Gantt, "Methodological Pluralism."
64. Cf. Slife and Hopkins, "Alternative Assumptions for Neuroscience."
65. Slife and Hopkins, "Alternative Assumptions for Neuroscience."
66. Slife and Hopkins, "Alternative Assumptions for Neuroscience."

reductive notion — "restores free will."[67] She knows that without human possibility all enterprises, including her own integrationist project, are meaningless. The problem is that it is just this type of reduction that underlies the positivist methods of natural science that she endorses.

6. Conclusion

In general, therefore, Murphy rejects the assumptions of objectivism, materialism, and reductionism in her theology. In fact, she develops lines of argument and programs of research that distinctly oppose these assumptions. However, with respect to her basic logic of research (what she calls in other contexts the "fine structure" of research),[68] she appears to do precisely what many social scientists have done — assume uncritically either that this logic is established with logical positivistic and naturalistic formulations (and thus ignore the *method issue* of psychology), or that this logic is essentially free of important assumptions and values (and thus ignore the importance of values and theology for this level of research). In either case, her method is incompatible with her theology, which illustrates the incompatibility of reductive naturalism and theism more generally.

At this juncture, the question posed in the title of this chapter must be answered in the negative. The natural science methods of psychology — underlaid as they are with the philosophy of reductive naturalism — cannot be compatible with the theism of theologians such as Murphy. This incompatibility means that Murphy's candidate for an integrative bridge between theology and psychology — scientific reasoning — must be viewed skeptically. Although there is considerable evidence that this reasoning is held in common between the methods of both psychology and the natural sciences, there is also considerable evidence that theism, including Murphy's own theism, violates the objectivity, materialism, and reductionism of this understanding of scientific reasoning.

67. Murphy, Chapter 3, section 3.1., this volume.
68. Murphy and Ellis, *On the Moral Nature of the Universe*, p. 8.

Chapter 9   *Psychology and Religion in Dialogue:*
              Hermeneutic Reflections

Frank C. Richardson

1. Introduction

Nancey Murphy's proposals concerning the "integration" of Christian theology with psychological inquiry seem to me in some respects very insightful and suggestive, in other ways possibly misleading and less than helpful. To stress the positive at the outset, I certainly endorse the general idea of somehow blending the best insights of psychology and religion in a sound and honest way. I agree with what I take to be the spirit of Murphy's approach — namely, to plumb the depths of Christian revelation and experience, not water them down to suit modern taste or convenience, but also to critically examine our religious convictions in the light of modern psychology or any other appropriate means of rational analysis or source of ethical insight. Her goal of convincing psychologists that "their work is 'theology-laden' whether they mean it to be or not"[1] seems right on target to me. Indeed, as Murphy suggests, "comprehensive psychological theories of human nature" necessarily "incorporate some assumptions about ultimate reality." These "theological or a-theological assumptions" then "delimit one's vision of the human good," which in turn crucially shapes any psychological account of what is "normal or abnormal, healthy or unhealthy, functional or dysfunctional."[2] This kind of "MacIntyrean account of psychology," as she describes it,[3] appeals greatly to me, even

1. Murphy, Chapter 3, section 4, this volume.
2. Murphy, Chapter 1, section 6, this volume.
3. Murphy, Chapter 3, section 3.1, this volume.

if I think that in some ways Murphy strays from this MacIntyrean path.

However, I have some strong concerns about the basic idea and project of "integration." At the heart of the problem, as Brent Slife discusses quite helpfully in his chapter in this book,[4] is the fact that there are no neutral external criteria for resolving differences among diverse perspectives or fields. As a result, either such perspectives seem to be utterly incommensurable and incomparable — so that in choosing our views and values we are left, as Max Weber put it, to our own private "gods and demons" — or we can try to integrate them in a way in which one system of ideas defines the basic terms in which the other will be rendered, thus robbing it of its integrity and obscuring any distinctive insights it may have to offer.

2. Philosophical Hermeneutics

I would like to express a few reservations about Murphy's approach to integration and make a suggestion or two of my own on this topic. First, I will outline a few of the key ideas of philosophical or ontological hermeneutics,[5] which I think have a great deal to offer in framing and pursuing the psychology/religion dialogue. In what follows, I suggest that Murphy's adoption of Lakatos's conception of research programs in natural science as a model for knowledge in general incurs many of the limitations and dangers of a certain kind of "objectifying" approach to understanding, and that hermeneutic thought offers a helpful alternative to this approach.

Richard Bernstein defines the kind of "objectivism" that has underpinned so much modern thought and culture as the "basic conviction that there is or must be some permanent, ahistorical matrix or framework to which we can ultimately appeal in determining the nature of rationality, knowledge, truth, reality, goodness, or rightness."[6] This

---

4. Slife, Chapter 8, this volume.

5. Martin Heidegger, *Being and Time* (New York: Harper & Row, 1962); Hans Georg Gadamer, *Truth and Method,* 2d ed. (New York: Crossroad, 1989); Charles Guignon, *Heidegger and the Problem of Knowledge* (Indianapolis: Hackett, 1983); Charles Taylor, *Sources of the Self* (Cambridge, Mass.: Harvard University Press, 1989).

6. Richard Bernstein, *Beyond Objectivism and Relativism* (Philadelphia: University of Pennsylvania Press, 1983), p. 8.

objectivist faith has been rightly criticized for encouraging insupportable and imperialistic claims of final or certain truth in both science and ethics and for assimilating all kinds of understanding and insight to a detached, analytic kind of knowledge in a way that depersonalizes human life, encourages a one-sided individualism, and inscribes a narrowly utilitarian stance toward the world — what might be termed a "control or be controlled" outlook on living.[7] Numerous Romantic, humanist, existentialist, and postmodern schools of thought over the last two hundred years have proved better at detecting flaws in objectivist philosophies than in formulating convincing alternatives to them, which has no doubt accelerated the recent rise of radical relativist perspectives, including many postmodern or social constructionist views.[8]

Contemporary hermeneutics offers a distinct and possibly attractive alternative to what Bernstein identifies as a search, found in many sectors of contemporary culture and thought, for a way "beyond objectivism and relativism."[9] (With regard to the social sciences, I and others have discussed the seemingly confused and fumbling search for a "way beyond scientism and constructionism.")[10] Hermeneutic thinkers stress the central place occupied in the natural sciences by the exercise of a special capacity for abstraction that we might call "objectification." Objectivist views tend to hold up natural science as a model of objective inquiry. But to adopt an objectifying stance toward things is to ignore or abstract away from "subject-related qualities."[11] Such qualities are concerned with our shifting desires, values, and aims, and make up most of the meanings of the things that show up within our ordinary experience, as well as the relationships between them. Thus,

---

7. Frank Richardson and Robert Bishop, "Rethinking Determinism in Social Science," in *Between Chance and Choice*, ed. Harald Atmanspacher and Robert Bishop (Thorverton, U.K.: Imprint Academic, 2002), pp. 425-46.

8. Michel Foucault, *Power/Knowledge: Selected Interviews and Other Writings* (New York: Pantheon, 1980); Kenneth Gergen, "The Social Constructionist Movement in Modern Psychology," *American Psychologist* 40 (1985): 266-75; Richard Rorty, *Consequences of Pragmatism* (Minneapolis: University of Minnesota Press, 1982).

9. Bernstein, *Beyond Objectivism and Relativism*.

10. Frank Richardson, Blaine Fowers, and Charles Guignon, *Re-Envisioning Psychology: Moral Dimensions of Theory and Practice* (San Francisco: Jossey-Bass, 1999).

11. Taylor, *Sources of the Self*, p. 31.

to take an objectifying stance means to "regard the world as it is independently of the meanings it might have for human subjects, or of how it figures in their experience."[12]

Obviously this pathway of knowing, of abstraction and objectification, has proved its mettle and merit in modern science and its applications. However, there is no good reason to deny the validity of other kinds of interpretations of our experience and events, reflecting different ways of being involved with the world — interpretations and modes of existing that indeed may turn out to play an important role in human science inquiry. It no longer seems proper to many of us to insist that reality must be only that which is formulated through the approach of abstraction and objectification. We have learned to question the detached, somewhat depersonalizing, "spectator" view of knowing[13] that this approach entails and the one-sided orientation toward mastery and control that it inscribes in practical life.[14] Where the human sciences are concerned, Brent Slife and Richard Williams point out that many critics feel that "the language of science" is a "relatively impoverished language" for characterizing human activity because "we force ourselves to study human beings at a distance."[15]

Concerning relativist viewpoints, hermeneutic thinkers join other critics in pointing out the sharp internal tensions and seeming contradictions that afflict such doctrines. There is always the difficulty, of course, of confidently making the truth claim (any irony intended) that there are no real truths! A more interesting problem, in my view, is that postmodernist writings seem to "secrete" (as Charles Taylor once put it) a certain strong value position of their own. By and large, they strongly imply that just denying all metaphysical and/or moral universals will

---

12. Taylor, *Sources of the Self*, p. 31.

13. In *The Intentional Stance* (Cambridge, Mass.: MIT Press, 1987), Daniel Dennett remarks that "the objective, third person world of physical sciences" is "the orthodox choice today in the English-speaking world" (p. 5). While Dennett adopts this outlook on the world, hermeneutics insists it is derivative, not fundamental. It seems to me that Murphy adopts it to a significant degree but that it might not suit her ultimate purposes as well as something like a hermeneutic ontology.

14. Jürgen Habermas, *Theory and Practice* (Boston: Beacon Press, 1973).

15. Brent Slife and Richard Williams, *What's behind the Research? Discovering Hidden Assumptions in the Behavioral Sciences* (Thousand Oaks, Calif.: Sage Publications, 1995).

free us from tendencies toward dogmatism and domination.[16] Thus, they presuppose a version (a rather utopian one at that) of modern emancipatory or liberationist ideals that they apparently do not take to be entirely relative and optional. Moreover, this view seems to be embroiled in the contradiction of treating all moral values as purely relative or subjective in order to promote certain moral values, such as human autonomy and opposition to arbitrary authority, to which they firmly adhere! In the long run, such an approach would seem to be self-defeating. What is to keep its strong relativism from eventually undermining its own serious value commitments?[17]

In his writings, Charles Taylor argues that a certain picture of the human self or agent as disengaged, disembodied, and atomistic shows up in many guises in modern thought and culture. These include much modern epistemology with its valorization of a "spectator" view of knowing, modern individualism as a moral credo, and even many ostensibly "postmodern" theories that try to sever the connection between an enlightened or mature outlook on life and living and any settled moral convictions. This "punctual self" is "distinguished . . . from [the] natural and social worlds, so that [its] identity is no longer to be defined in terms of what lies outside . . . in these worlds."[18] The modern self is ideally ready to freely and rationally treat both itself and the outside world instrumentally, to alter both in ways that better secure individual and social well-being, however they are conceived. Thus, this view of human agency begins to look like a central, culturally embedded strand of our way of life in modern times, one often thought to purchase valuable freedoms at the price of much alienation. Indeed, Taylor suggests that the modern notion of a punctual self confronting a natural and social world to which it has no essential ties is as much a *moral* as a scientific ideal. It "connects with . . . central moral and spiritual ideas of the modern age." Thus, the modern ideal of "freedom as self-autonomy . . . to be

16. Frank Richardson and Blaine Fowers, "Interpretive Social Science: An Overview," *American Behavioral Scientist* 41 (1998): 465-95.

17. Thus, both objectivist and relativist stances seem to inscribe and entrench a wide gulf between theory and practice, between scientific or philosophical knowing and actual living, of the sort that critics have complained about with regard to social science for many decades, both from within the field and from without.

18. Charles Taylor, *Philosophical Arguments* (Cambridge, Mass.: Harvard University Press, 1995), p. 7.

189

self-responsible, to rely on one's [own] judgment, to find one's purpose in oneself"[19] dictates that any overlap between self and world will compromise the individual's integrity and dignity.

Hermeneutic philosophy tries to outline a more plausible account of human action and social life. It offers an interpretation of what humans appear to be like, so far as we can tell, or of what we seem to presuppose about our basic make-up in everything that we do. To begin with, humans are viewed as "self-interpreting beings."[20] The *meanings* they work out in the business of living make them to a great extent what they are, in sharp contrast to the viewpoint that our behavior is determined by genetic and social influences to be described for us by a branch of natural science. Moreover, individual lives are "always 'thrown' into a familiar life-world from which they draw their possibilities of self-interpretation. Their life-stories only make sense against the backdrop of possible story-lines opened by our historical culture."[21] Instead of thinking of the self as an object of any sort, hermeneutic thought follows Heidegger in conceiving of human existence as a "happening" or a "becoming." Individual lives have a temporal and narrative structure. They are a kind of unfolding "movement" that is "stretched along between birth and death."[22]

What does it mean to participate in this kind of temporal and storied existence? We sometimes follow the path of abstraction and objectification and construct a knowledge of lawfulness or of repeated patterns in events that occur regardless of the everyday meanings these events have for us or the evaluations we make of them, including technical knowledge of reliable means to desired ends. But there is a more fundamental, ultimately *practical* kind of understanding that humans always and everywhere hammer out together, one that does not mainly involve comprehending events as "instances" of a general concept, rule, or law. In everyday life and in a more systematic way in the human sciences, people seek to understand the changeable meanings of events, texts, works of art, social reality, and the actions of others in order to

19. Taylor, *Philosophical Arguments*, p. 7.

20. Charles Taylor, *Human Agency and Language: Philosophical Papers*, vol. 1 (Cambridge: Cambridge University Press, 1985).

21. Charles Guignon, "Truth as Disclosure: Art, Language, History," *Southern Journal of Philosophy* 28 (1989): 105-21.

22. Heidegger, *Being and Time*, p. 426.

appreciate them, perhaps clarify or refine them, and relate to them appropriately along the story lines of their living.

According to a hermeneutic ontology, however, this understanding or interpretation of meaning has a distinctive character. Historical experience changes the meaning that events can have for us, not because it alters our view of an independent object, but because history is a dialectical process in which both the object (meaning of events) and our knowledge of it (interpretations) are continually transformed. Thus, for example, both the meaning of the American Revolution and my lived understanding of freedom continue to be modified in the dialogue between them. We are immersed in and deeply connected to this process rather than essentially detached from it — as so much doctrine, modern and postmodern alike, tends to suppose.

On this account, a basic fact about humans, in Heidegger's words, is that they "care" about whether their lives make sense and what they are amounting to. Therefore, they have always taken some stand on their lives by seizing on certain roles, traits, and ideals. Indeed, they "just are the stands they take in living out their lives."[23] Taylor develops this notion of care with the idea that humans do not simply desire particular outcomes or satisfactions in living. Rather, they always make "strong evaluations."[24] Even if only tacitly or unconsciously, they evaluate the quality of their desires and motivations and the worth of the ends they seek in terms of how they fit in with their overall sense of a decent or worthwhile life. Humans never simply prefer or desire certain pleasures or results. They always, in addition, are building their lives around some notion (admirable or not) of what is decent versus indecent, noble versus base, or deep versus shallow — the terms vary greatly across societies and eras.

3. Science and Understanding

In her chapter on philosophical resources for integration, Murphy posits that Imre Lakatos's conception of developing research programs in natu-

23. Charles Guignon and Derk Pereboom, "Heidegger: Introduction," in *Existentialism: Basic Writings*, ed. Charles Guignon and Derk Pereboom (Indianapolis: Hackett, 1995), pp. 175-202.

24. Taylor, *Human Agency and Language*, p. 3.

ral science is the "gold standard" for knowledge or understanding in human affairs, and that "theology is sufficiently akin to science"[25] that we might be able to integrate them in Lakatosian terms. I think it is appropriate to assume a starting point in this manner and then see how it works out in the ensuing discussion. But I don't think it works out as well as one might hope in this case.

Thinkers from numerous influential and important schools of social theory, including phenomenology, critical theory, humanistic/existential approaches, and postmodern theorists of various stripes, will have great difficulty with this starting point, one that might seem to assimilate all understanding to inquiry and knowledge in the natural sciences. Eventually, their concerns and weighty disagreements will have to be dealt with. For what it is worth, I believe that the most telling of those objections are captured by the hermeneutic tenet that the pathway of abstraction and objectification that lies (quite appropriately) at the heart of natural science inquiry is not only just one way of knowing, but itself presupposes a very different kind of engagement with the world and a quite different, indelibly practical or existential mode of coming to understanding. In line with this view, Taylor argues that in many circumstances there should be no question of "abstracting from the significance for us of what we are examining."[26] In many of life's important "situations of involvement," trying to step back from things by way of something like the method of objectification would be counterproductive and harmful. In those situations, we need to do almost the opposite. We need to get closer to our feelings, motives, attachments, or convictions, get past the defensiveness that distorts them or keeps us at a distance from them, and engage them fully in reflection and dialogue, in order to better appreciate what they are all about — something that often results in our being changed in irreversible ways.

I think that support for this hermeneutic view of things comes from the fact that after more than a century of trying, we appear to have come up with virtually nothing in the way of a genuine natural science of social life.[27] Instead, the social disciplines are greatly isolated from one an-

---

25. Murphy, Chapter 1, section 3, this volume. Editors' note: It is "scientific reasoning" and not Lakatosian theory that Murphy posits as the perceived gold standard.

26. Taylor, *Human Agency and Language*, p. 160.

27. Richard Bernstein, *The Restructuring of Social and Political Theory* (Philadel-

other and enormously fragmented within their own borders. Thousands of little islands of theory and research within each discipline are pursued independently, with no apparent prospect of their being linked up in any coherent, overall picture of human activity. And there is just as much disagreement about what methods or approaches to inquiry might remedy this situation. I feel sure that if departments of physics or the life sciences were in this condition, there would be no departments of physics or the life sciences. They more likely would be studying astrology, and/ or discussing how to augment the spiritual power of rain dances.

Risking oversimplification, I might suggest that there has been some rough common ground among the critics of mainstream social science over the years, from such diverse perspectives as phenomenology, ordinary language philosophy, and postmodern theory. These theorists tend to re-envision the context of human action as an irreducible life world in which human activities are seen mainly as channeled by shared meanings and goals rather than the product of hard causal forces. They tend to re-imagine human agency as less narrowly instrumental, less of a "control or be controlled" affair vis-à-vis others and the world. They advocate a markedly different conception of genuine knowledge of the social realm from the classical ideal of empirical theory — namely, some sort of description or interpretation of meaningful human action and experience. Also, they tend to appreciate that we must abandon or seriously qualify the traditional social-science ideal of giving "value-neutral" theories and accounts of human phenomena. They suggest that aiming for strictly "neutral" accounts of meaning-imbued human phenomena is neither possible nor desirable, and that doing so probably just masks the presence and influence of the moral preferences or political partiality of the investigator and her community.

A number of thinkers point out a related problem in drawing analogies between natural science and social inquiry. Although social scientists have often latched onto notions like Kuhnian "paradigms" to try to make sense of and enhance their efforts, it may be quite inappropriate to do so. Kuhn rarely discussed social science, and it would seem that the social disciplines, in his terms, are at best *pre*-paradigmatic and not in a condition where the dynamics of paradigms or Lakatosian research pro-

phia: University of Pennsylvania Press, 1976); Richardson and Fowers, "Interpretive Social Science"; Slife and Williams, *What's behind the Research?*

grams can shed much light on social theories or inquiry, even were it appropriate to think of them in these terms. This view certainly calls into question Murphy's desire to draw close parallels between — to give one of her examples — "a theory of instrumentation in science" and "a theory of discernment" in theology.[28] Of course, these days, when post-empiricist views of the natural sciences reign supreme, according to which the natural sciences are very much an *interpretation* of the natural world, it is quite possible to draw an analogy between, say, creative efforts to save the metaphysical core of a scientific research program, à la Lakatos, and new developments in psychoanalytic theory. But such parallels are very broad or thin, to say the least. Beyond additional testimony to the ubiquity of interpretation in human life, they don't gain us much traction. Frankly, I think that drawing close parallels between the tenets of a Lakatosian "metaphysical hard core" and basic moral or religious convictions, or between "testable empirical hypotheses"[29] and ethical or religious principles of action, is a big mistake.

Thus, the terms for integrating religion and psychology that Murphy proposes either (1) seem too slender and insubstantial to bring the parties into vital contact with one another or (2) seem to force ethics and religion into an overly analytic, science-like, objectifying mold of thought that cannot do them justice. As a result, the problem of having to choose between incommensurability among viewpoints or domination of one of them by the other appears still to be very much with us.

4. Disguised Ideology

Should the problematic social disciplines, then, take up astrology and/or rain-dance enhancement? Or — who knows — become departments of Radical-Reformation theology? That might be a lot more interesting, and in the later case much more satisfying, than the standard fare in my department! But, of course, that is neither possible nor desirable. What we have in both the quantitative and the qualitative areas of the field are thousands of clusters of correlational findings, some of which seem like they might illuminate something, many of which seem trivial or mere

28. Murphy, Chapter 1, section 3, this volume.
29. Murphy, Chapter 3, section 3, this volume.

"wordy elaborations of the obvious,"[30] none of which add up to the kind of science they aspire to. Moreover, in the view of some critics, many of these findings, along with many personality and psychotherapy theories and reports of qualitative research, are colored by questionable modern ideologies. They more or less subtly celebrate self-actualization at the expense of wider or deeper purposes in living, and/or promote a narrow technicism which, according to critical theorists like Jürgen Habermas, is at the root of many of the distinctive pathologies of modern life.[31] Unless we diagnose this anomalous situation adequately, and explain our lengthy persistence in an enterprise that has borne so little fruit of the sort it promises, we will just keep on reproducing the problem, even in the new solutions we propose.

We can take a giant stride toward such diagnosis and explanation, I believe, with the notion that what drives a great deal of modern social inquiry is not so much a straightforward will-to-science as it is disguised ideology. Indeed, I would contend that the tacit ethical underpinnings of much modern social theory and research are different versions of a pervasive modern moral outlook that has been termed "liberal instrumentalism" or "liberal individualism."[32] The core ideals of this outlook are individual autonomy, dignity, and rights. Somewhat paradoxically, this ethic stresses *both* that human action is radically self-interested, such that no one can define the good life for anyone else, *and* that we should stringently respect the right of others to pursue their own, self-chosen aims and ideals. The paradox is that these ideals of respect for individual dignity and autonomy entail at least a partial vision of the good or the good life which, according to this view, is itself ultimately subjective or merely preferential and should be left to purely individual design! Therefore, this approach tends to undermine the authority and convincingness of its own best values,[33] unraveling in both theory and practice

30. Taylor, *Human Agency and Language*, p. 1.

31. Habermas, *Theory and Practice*.

32. Robert Bellah, "The Ethical Aims of Social Inquiry," in N. Haan, R. Bellah, P. Rabinow, and W. Sullivan, eds., *Social Science as Moral Inquiry* (New York: Columbia University Press, 1983), pp. 300-381; Richardson et al., *Re-Envisioning Psychology;* William Sullivan, *Reconstructing Public Philosophy* (Berkeley and Los Angeles: University of California Press, 1986).

33. Michael Sandel, *Democracy's Discontent: America in Search of a Public Philosophy* (Cambridge, Mass.: Belknap/Harvard University Press, 1996).

in ways that may help explain much of the fraying of individual character and meaningful social ties in contemporary life.[34]

Perhaps, then, we persist in relying so heavily on conventional methods of inquiry in the social sciences and so firmly reiterating the ideal of value-neutrality because they resonate so well with the disciplines' tacit liberal individualist values.[35] Thus, even the most meager of findings seem of some worth to us because they echo familiar moral sentiments. And disappointments, failures, and doubts we encounter along the way, which may be numerous, prompt us to redouble our efforts rather than rethink our assumptions, because to do the latter would be morally chal-

---

34. A key feature of the liberal individualist or liberal instrumentalist view is a fairly sharp divide between individual and society or self and world. We try to take moral direction exclusively from *inward* sources rather than culture or tradition, in order to fend off arbitrary authority and dogmatic intrusion at all costs — even the cost of throwing out the baby with the bathwater, so to speak. However, besides distorting the origin of moral insight and inspiration, this view breeds emotional isolation and great moral confusion. Elsewhere (Richardson et al., *Re-Envisioning Psychology*), I and others have argued that this same basic kind of self/society split lies at the heart of what superficially appear to be quite different kinds of modern psychologies, with their tacit but often egregious ideological coloring. Whether our preferred theory or therapy focuses on fostering "effective behavior," getting in touch with an authentic self, or cultivating the capacity for radical existential choice of one's idiosyncratic life projects, it still acquires much of its legitimacy from its broad liberal individualist credentials. It still encourages us profoundly to chart our own course while deeply respecting the right of others, even feeling obligated to encourage and enable them to do the same.

35. I have mainly used the example of quantitative or correlational methods in this discussion because of the emphasis Murphy gives them in exploring the possibilities of a Christian research program in psychology. There is not time to discuss it here, but I do want to mention that simulacra of traditional value-freedom or value-neutrality in the social sciences can be found at the heart of other, even antagonistic approaches. Thus, phenomenological viewpoints and qualitative researchers usually advocate a fairly stringent kind of objectivity or impartiality in their descriptions of human activities, and postmodern or social constructionist theorists advocate an austere detachment from seriously held moral or spiritual beliefs that rivals the modern "view from nowhere" they often excoriate. In the hermeneutic view, the elimination of bias — which really means or includes all our heartfelt moral and religious convictions — is neither possible nor desirable. In this view, to continue to engage in open and searching dialogue with other points of view, communities of insight, or traditions of meaning, and doing so in search of deeper moral insight or keener religious discernment, is an exacting but more fruitful pathway to greater understanding.

lenging and uncomfortably politically incorrect (to say nothing of interfering with career advancement).

Much of the resonance between liberal individualism and most psychological theory derives from the fact that both assume a heavily *instrumental* view of human action. In both, human behavior or action is characterized mainly in terms of how effective or efficient it is in realizing inwardly or privately determined values and aims. It appears that many social scientists find there to be a wonderful pre-established harmony among (1) the naturalistic conception of the human realm as a flow of efficient causes and their effects, (2) experimental and correlational methods of inquiry that map these cause-effect relationships, and (3) the conception of human action and agency as essentially instrumental and primarily oriented toward manipulating these causes to produce desired results. Unfortunately, this deterministic view of the human world strongly undermines the idea of free and responsible agency, even of the narrowly instrumental sort, and mainstream social science has had negligible success in uncovering context-free laws of human behavior. Thus it would seem high time to reconsider these premises along with the liberal instrumentalist moral outlook that allows them to cohere to the extent that they do.

There are rich philosophical resources for rethinking the instrumental conception of human action. For example, Alasdair MacIntyre in *After Virtue* draws a fundamental distinction between "social practices" and "technical activities."[36] Social practices are holistic, cooperative human activities that realize shared, "internal" goods or excellences that comprise the substance of the unfolding life stories of individuals and communities. Virtues such as courage or compassion are essential to engaging in such practices and are exercised only as part of carrying them out. Technical activities, by contrast, realize "external" goods of a ruder sort — payoffs, pleasures, rewards, advantages, and the like — and are only external and contingently attached to such activities. The absence of a virtuous disposition and conduct destroys social practices, while any sort of action or means will do in the case of technical activities, so long as the desired result is brought about.

In a similar manner, in order to explicate the Heideggerian notion of "authenticity," Charles Guignon distinguishes between "constituent/

36. Alasdair MacIntyre, *After Virtue* (Notre Dame: University of Notre Dame Press, 1981), p. 176.

whole" and "means/ends" styles of living. The former, more authentic approach involves acting *"for the sake of being* a person of a particular sort, and you experience your actions as constituents of a complete life that you are realizing in all you do." The latter centers on acting "in order to achieve social approval or to attain the awards that come from having acted [effectively or] properly." Guignon comments that although "both the 'means/ends' and 'constituent/whole' styles of life may consist in the same or at least very similar actions, there is an important qualitative difference" between them, such as "between helping others in order to feel good, and helping others for the sake of being a caring, decent person." Or "between telling people the truth in order to gain their trust, and telling the truth as part of being a truthful person."[37]

I might add that I find rich resources for rethinking liberal instrumentalism in the ideas of contemporary "communitarian" social theorists.[38] Amitai Etzioni, for example, contends that there can be "excessive liberty" and that without limits on choice, provided first and foremost by some "shared moral convictions," neither a coherent sense of personal identity nor social peace are really possible. He recommends that in the "next historical phase" we find a way to "blend the virtues of tradition with the liberation of modernity."[39] In this view, the good life, in Ronald Beiner's words, is conceived of not primarily in terms of the "maximization of autonomy" but as the "cultivation of . . . a variety of excellences, intellectual and moral."[40] Beiner adds that it is "not that liberal autonomy is a bad thing, but that without the 'thick' attachments provided by the kind of ethos that builds meaningful character, free choice . . . hardly seems worth the bother."[41] Social inquiry conducted within a broad communitarian framework of this sort often would look very different from what we have today. This updated civic republican

---

37. Charles Guignon, "Hermeneutics, Authenticity, and the Aims of Psychology," *Journal of Theoretical and Philosophical Psychology* 22 (2002): 83-102.

38. Sandel, *Democracy's Discontent;* Amitai Etzioni, *The New Golden Rule: Community and Morality in a Democratic Society* (New York: Basic Books, 1996); Philip Selznick, *The Moral Commonwealth* (Berkeley and Los Angeles: University of California Press, 1992).

39. Etzioni, *The New Golden Rule,* p. xvii.

40. Ronald Beiner, *What's the Matter with Liberalism?* (Berkeley and Los Angeles: University of California Press, 1992), pp. 51-52.

41. Beiner, *What's the Matter with Liberalism?* p. 37.

moral outlook is not tantamount to a kenotic ethic of the profound theological sort that Murphy recommends, but it opens the door to it, and is more consonant with it than liberal instrumentalism.

5. A Christian Research Program in Psychology

In the light of these considerations, I feel that there are severe tensions or even contradictions in Murphy's proposal for a Christian research program in psychology. On the one hand, she asserts (1) that psychology theories always *presuppose* some already-arrived-at conclusions about "ultimate reality" and the "highest human good" or the *telos* of human life. On the other hand, in places she claims (2) that as an "empirical discipline" psychology can "*describe* human nature as it is, but has no resources in itself to answer the question whether humans *ought* to be as they are."[42]

If we go with the first claim, as I would, then the wise course, it seems, would be to tease out psychology's assumed metaphysical and moral biases and put the whole package in full-blooded dialogue, drawing on all our rational and intuitive resources, with other sets of convictions, such as communitarian social thought and Radical-Reformation theology, and see what transpires down such a fearsome and unpredictable path. If we go with the second claim, we are taking a few rapid strides backward toward an implausibly "value-neutral" social science that blindly and uncritically *assumes* the answers to the really important questions and tries to insinuate them into our thinking and living in the name of an authoritative "science." This second approach forces us to study human life at a distance and imposes a resolutely calculative-instrumental stance toward life that obscures the presumably important distinction between doing things because they are good in themselves and doing them — even ethical or religious things — because of their practical or hedonistic payoffs. Iulia de Beausobre and other saints may have more readily survived prison and torture than many less profoundly religious souls, but they lived the way they did to glorify God, not procure longevity.[43]

---

42. Murphy, Chapter 3, section 1, this volume.
43. See the story related by Murphy in Chapter 3, section 3.4, this volume.

Thus, it makes me very uncomfortable when Murphy talks about defining moral and religious notions "operationally" and "confirming" them with correlational and experimental research studies. To be sure, she wisely qualifies this idea by saying that empirical studies of forgiveness and the like can do this only "to some small extent."[44] But I respectfully submit that this approach is wishy-washy as well as wise. As Brent Slife and Richard Williams argue, research methods in psychology cannot evaluate their own philosophical and moral underpinnings.[45] It is not a black or white world, as Murphy and the Radical-Reformation tradition well appreciate. But in the case of modern psychology, we are dealing with an ideologically slanted program of inquiry that forces black or white choices on us. It tends to insist that *either* "hypotheses" are confirmed *or* they are not, and if they are not yet confirmed, we have no business believing in them. And it tends to insist that *either* we adopt the liberal individualist moral outlook and make self-interest and respect for individual rights primary *or* we will be deemed ethically immature or unsound. It is not black or white thinking to reject black or white thinking and insist on a subtler approach. So, I think we have to choose between Murphy (1) and Murphy (2).

The tension between what we might refer to as a dialogical and an instrumental approach shows up in Murphy's chapters, I think, between her notion of influencing people by "luring" them through the "prophetic example of the church at its best" and, in the ensuing pages, references to "bodies of knowledge" concerning how to move toward desired ideals and even "techniques" for doing so.[46]

These considerations lead me to take a partly different view of research like C. Daniel Batson's on altruism, which Murphy discusses at some length.[47] First of all, I think it is a little misleading to attribute an unqualified "hypothesis of universal egoism" to the Western tradition and social sciences like economics and psychology that characterize human behavior as thoroughly "self-interested." There is reason to think that these social thinkers are more Kantian than nakedly Hobbesian in their views. There is evidence that they stress self-interest partly *in order*

44. Murphy, Chapter 3, section 3.5, this volume.

45. Slife and Williams, *What's behind the Research?* p. 4.

46. Murphy, Chapter 3, section 1, this volume.

47. Murphy, Chapter 3, section 3.5, this volume. See also Kevin Reimer's discussion in Chapter 6.

to advance ideals of human freedom, equality, and well-being, even if they don't always articulate these ideals. In others words, at bottom they may endorse some version of liberal individualism, with all of its internal tensions and putative shortcomings. It seems important to me to appreciate that the modern liberal outlook is a profoundly moral one, even if it may be entirely too "thin" or ethically (and religiously) insufficient.

So, it may be the case that Batson's research on altruism, his findings, tend to undermine or render less plausible a radical egoism or extreme libertarian viewpoint. However, I doubt that anyone's motives or beliefs really fit that mold, and I am not sure we need such studies to put this idea to rest. They may confuse as much as they clarify, but I am not sure about that. In the end, either a radical egoism or a more decent and credible liberal instrumentalism must be assessed through such things as moral insight, interpretation, and the test of experience — in a different sense of "test" than weighing their ability to foster desired "external goods." Thus, I think that Murphy greatly overestimates the extent to which Batson's experiments capture or "operationalize" kenotic motives or actions. I suspect they tell us only a tiny bit about even garden-variety altruism.

6. Integration or Dialogue?

In the end, I am wondering if Murphy's approach and perhaps some other "integrationist" approaches, at least in part, do not integrate religion and psychology so much as they integrate, or try to integrate, certain religious *viewpoints* and familiar psychological *methods*. However, rather than creatively merging in some fashion, in this approach theology and psychology seem to take turns dominating the scene. A theological vision is abruptly introduced and appears to define the content that psychology can explore. Then, in turn, psychology through its methods gets to confirm or disconfirm the worth of ethical and religious claims, which is a pretty commanding or authoritative role to play. Of course, most integrationist thinkers would never be that arbitrary or that deferential in actual practice. But the logic of the approach seems to point in that direction, and a less disjointed and problematic logic of inquiry seems to be needed. It really isn't integration or balance of a credible sort to have in turn first one authority and then the other rule the roost.

Just ask yourself, What would we do if these authorities disagree? We would probably go with the most compelling religious insights available to us. So much for integration.

If psychological studies claimed to show that more effectively self-interested human agents lead happier and/or healthier lives, we would not simply accept these findings and proceed to adopt a more individualistic outlook on life. Instead, we might criticize them as failing to appreciate fully what human fulfillment is all about, either in a qualitative sense, over the long run, or both. If studies showed that religious belief or practice leads to greater stress or interpersonal conflict in our kind of society, we would not reject or modify our religious orientation but re-evaluate the place of stress in the good life or reconsider the cost of discipleship. Now, perhaps such findings would heighten our awareness of certain dimensions or costs of authentic religious belief or practice. This awareness might even lead us to refine or deepen our understanding of what that belief and practice are all about. But this comes about through a process that seems described better as reinterpretation than integration, a creative blending and transformation of insights that is unpredictable in its exact outcome and not entirely under our control.

It seems to me that the strongly pragmatic or quasi-utilitarian dimension of the integrationist program, at least as I have described it, troubles many thoughtful theologians today. For example, concerns about the influence of narrowly psychological and "therapeutic" views and values in our culture have led thinkers like L. Gregory Jones to worry about the quality of some of the phenomenal interest these days in "spiritual" beliefs and practices of all sorts.[48] Jones wonders if they reflect a "thirst for God" (in the language of Bernard of Clairvaux) in the best sense, or a kind of "consumer spirituality" that reflects a search for a "new commodity" that can somehow "satisfy the desires other commodities have failed to quench."[49] He concludes that they have "if anything, little to do with morality, social institutions, or political power," and imply that "what really matters are the inner experiences of

48. Jones, "A Thirst for God or Consumer Spirituality? Cultivating Disciplined Practices of Being Engaged by God," in *Spirituality and Social Embodiment,* ed. L. Gregory Jones and J. Buckley (London: Blackwell, 1997), pp. 3-28.
49. Jones, "A Thirst for God or Consumer Spirituality?" pp. 3-4.

isolated individuals, cultivated and evaluated largely by those individuals."[50] It is going to take a lot more than conventional psychological research on religious "variables" to counter these trends.

To my mind, a compelling alternative to this kind of integration is hermeneutic dialogue. Modern psychology represents a complex of more or less disguised ideology, social practices, research methods, and applied technical activities. Religion comprises not just values or visions of what life is all about but ingrained institutions and practices that minister to many human needs. They may appear to clash or to be so different as to be "incommensurable" at times. But, as Brent Slife argues, that does not mean that they are "incomparable."[51] Dialogue and mutual influence between seemingly incommensurable viewpoints, leading to deepened insight and greater understanding, happen every day in marriage, friendship, communities, and across cultures. There are resources in hermeneutics and elsewhere for clarifying what such dialogue is all about.[52] The philosopher Georgia Warnke explicates Hans-Georg Gadamer's notion of hermeneutic dialogue as a kind of interplay between self-defining convictions and sometimes painful openness, neither of which can maintain their integrity without the other.[53] Charles Taylor has recently described this as a dialectic between "identity investment" and "identity cost," something he suggests comprises the basic movement or pulse beat of our existence.[54] Rowan Williams characterizes this process in terms of "conversation and negotiation" that are "of their nature unpredictable, 'unscripted'"; their "outcome is not determined." Williams says that when he is in such dialogue, the "other speaker/agent" often seems "obscure" to him, as if the two of them were "speaking in a different language." However, the "difficulty of mutual understanding" is

50. Jones, "A Thirst for God or Consumer Spirituality?" p. 21.

51. Slife, Chapter 8, this volume.

52. There is no time here to explore this matter in any detail. Let me just say that it might be wise to stop being bewitched by philosophies that say what does happen can't happen (scientism and postmodernism alike), and turn "phenomenologically," in the best sense, to what really seems to take place. That, of course, is just what a hermeneutic ontology tries to do.

53. Georgia Warnke, *Gadamer: Hermeneutics, Tradition, and Reason* (Stanford: Stanford University Press, 1987).

54. Charles Taylor, "Gadamer and the Human Sciences," in *The Cambridge Companion to Gadamer,* ed. R. Dostal (Cambridge: Cambridge University Press, 2002), p. 141.

"inherent" in such exchanges and "could not be removed by a more adaptable or familiar medium."[55]

This not to deny that there is a kind of supple structure or living logic to this process. Alasdair MacIntyre outlines this logic in a remarkable little paper.[56] In his view, every major moral culture or standpoint presupposes some view of human nature, activity, and morality that it claims or assumes is by and large true. Thus, some of us have argued, both scientistic and social constructionist viewpoints in psychology may try to hold moral values at arm's length and treat them as purely subjective or relative, but these viewpoints actually *presuppose* defining ethical commitments without which they would not make the sense or have the appeal they do. Therefore, according to MacIntyre, when we encounter others with whom we differ in some significant way, within one of our communities or traditions or from other communities or traditions, we implicitly present our judgments and way of life as deserving assent by these others. As a result, at least tacitly, "we invite those others to radical self-criticism."[57] But this invitation, if we are honest about it, presupposes "that truth is a good." MacIntyre has in mind not truth as an abstract ideal that swings free from particular moral standpoints, but truth as a "good that is already implicitly acknowledged"[58] within the warp and woof of the actual practice of any standpoint that claims to be worthy of the allegiance of rational, reflective people.[59]

Furthermore, this recognition of truth as a good obligates us to "undertake the tasks of radical self-criticism to which [we] have invited others."[60] It commits us to what might be termed an "ethics of enquiry" that has as its main goal the "achievement of truth through a dialectical development of critical objections to our initial shared beliefs."[61] We have to start from our own beliefs, but anyone is a potential partner in this inquiry. In the nature of the case, our interaction and conversation

55. Williams, "Interiority and Epiphany: A Reading in New Testament Ethics," in Jones and Buckley, eds., *Spirituality and Social Embodiment*, p. 30.
56. Alasdair MacIntyre, "Moral Pluralism without Moral Relativism," paper delivered at the Twentieth World Congress of Philosophy, August 1998.
57. MacIntyre, "Moral Pluralism without Moral Relativism," p. 5.
58. MacIntyre, "Moral Pluralism without Moral Relativism," p. 5.
59. MacIntyre, "Moral Pluralism without Moral Relativism," p. 6.
60. MacIntyre, "Moral Pluralism without Moral Relativism," p. 6.
61. MacIntyre, "Moral Pluralism without Moral Relativism," p. 5.

with others will have to be governed by "certain rules" and "exhibit certain virtues," including such principles as that each person should be able "to speak in turn and at appropriate length," and that attention should be directed to the "substance of the arguments and not to who utters them," both of which are forms of the virtue of "justice in conversation."[62]

I worry that an integrationist approach — as least as I have characterized it, perhaps not always fairly — is inadequate to many of the challenges we face. We need to clarify and explain the sources of religious authority and values more fully in a modern context, not just adopt a point of view that appeals to us, which courts both fuzziness and arbitrariness. We need to sharply criticize modern ideologies of autonomy, technicism, and the like, not make our peace with them too hastily in order to be part of the current scene, or to gain membership in the "Church of What's Happening Now," as the comedian Flip Wilson used to put it. In others words, I worry that an integrationist project courts inauthenticity on both fronts. I have tried to indicate some of the reasons I think hermeneutic dialogue and ideas like those of MacIntyre concerning the dialectical development of deeper understanding may offer a more ample and adequate account of progressive inquiry in spiritual matters.

I don't think we know how, in a really satisfactory way, to harmonize freedom and responsibility, or to harmonize legitimate autonomy and compelling authority, in a better vision of our quest for good and God in these late modern times. I certainly find myself drawn to Murphy's idea of finding a "median position" between the "ordering of loves" tradition that stresses the goodness of basic human affinities and affections and the one that calls for "totally self-disinterested love" as our chief moral obligation. I just think we have a lot more work to do in crafting such a median position. It seems to me that integrationist thinking in general and Murphy's approach in particular concede too much to the instrumentalist strain in our culture and therefore to the very individualism that they rightly wish to curb. To give another example, I have no doubt that there is much to learn from Iulia de Beausobre's profound experience of redemptive suffering. But it seems to me that we are a lot clearer about the goodness and power of her testimony in a prison con-

62. MacIntyre, "Moral Pluralism without Moral Relativism," p. 7.

text than we are about how to put it into action in the hurly-burly of everyday life, in the egalitarian even though strained and morally confused context of our kind of society. However, we need to work that out, urgently, it seems to me, if we are effectively to counter the psychological gospels of happiness and success in a consumer society. I suggest that we turn to issues like these in a more frankly and fully dialogical way. To be sure, psychology (the whole package) should be one voice in the conversation. But let's be very sharp-eyed and critical-minded about how much familiar brands of quantitative or qualitative social science research have to contribute. As one step toward this end, I suggest we put integration and dialogue in dialogue.